ALSO BY JILL JOHNSTON

Marmalade Me

Lesbian Nation

Gullibles Travels

Autobiography in Search of a Father, Volume I:
Mother Bound

Paper Daughter

Autobiography in Search of a Father
Volume II

PAPER DAUGHTER

Jill Johnston

ALFRED A. KNOPF   New York   1985

THIS IS A BORZOI BOOK
PUBLISHED BY ALFRED A. KNOPF, INC.

Copyright © 1985 by Jill Johnston.

Library of Congress Cataloging in Publication Data

Johnston, Jill.   Paper daughter.

(Autobiography in search of a father ; 2)
1. Johnston, Jill—Biography.   2. Authors, American—
20th century—Biography.   I. Title.   II. Series:
Johnston, Jill.   Autobiography in search of a father ; 2.
PS3560.03894Z46   1983   vol. 2   818'.5409 s [B]   84–25028
ISBN 0–394–53939–7   [818'.5409] [B]

Manufactured in the United States of America

FIRST EDITION

After all, it is no more surprising to be
born twice than it is to be born once.
Voltaire

Pater semper incertus est.
Freud

Paper Daughter

1

Smoke

In August 1965 I went on a big trip to a place nobody I knew had ever been before. I had never been there myself. Nor did I know where I was going, or afterwards, where I had been exactly. It was a place without any name or specific location. Upon returning, I was debriefed and quarantined like an astronaut, but I wasn't congratulated or decorated or anything like that. On the contrary, I could have returned from a leper colony. Nobody was interested in hearing about my trip. Only the authorities in the "quarantine center" were interested in it. Wherever I had been—and the question remained where indeed, since my trip had not been planned or authorized—it was never considered a desirable place to go. In fact, it appeared that the only place I had actually been was the debriefing and quarantine center, the last place in the world anybody would ever want to go to. As a result, far from being welcomed home like an astronaut, I became an exile in my own community.

Three months earlier, in June, I had moved to a loft building on Liberty Street that would be torn down to make way for the World Trade Center. With my dancer friend I occupied a floor one hundred feet long and twenty-five feet wide. The rent was seventy-five dollars a month. The only other occupants of the building were a couple I knew from Toronto, the Irish artist Les Levine and his Japanese-Canadian friend, Atsuko. Two nice features of the building were its deeply recessed windows lining the exposed eastern side and an old-fashioned hand-operated elevator that we could use ourselves. My friend made her studio at the back, separated by a plasterboard wall from the kitchen area and the rest of the loft. I had my desk and books up front where three windows faced the southern exposure, and the bed was more or less in the middle. We painted the walls white, sanded the whole floor, and applied three coats of urethane—a backbreaking job which ended in a small catastrophe. I had just finished applying the third coat and was standing at the end of this wet surface, barely over the line on the linoleum of the kitchen area, holding the broom-handle stick with the roller at the other end sitting in the pan of urethane, and my friend was standing a few yards away near the stove. Either I asked her if we had any coffee or she asked me, I can't remember which; but as soon as she turned on the gas I was rocketed off my feet, and out of my life, I thought, by a great explosion all around me.

Unaware of the precautions necessary when using a highly combustible substance like urethane, we had failed to turn off the pilot lights before using the stuff. A sheet of fire had erupted at my feet, sizzling and scooting instantly across the length of the floor toward the front windows, like flaming oil sweeping across water, diminishing in height as it went. I didn't wait to see it, though; I shot off like gunpowder toward the back of the loft through the dance studio to the fire escape, screaming over my shoulder at my friend to follow me. I thought the building was going. Out on the fire escape I paused, and not hearing anything or seeing my friend, I waited a moment, then fearfully returned to the scene to find her halfway down on the floor beating out the fire. I joined the fray, stamping and throwing water, and soon all we had was a ruined floor surmounted by billowing clouds of black smoke.

I also had a bad case of nerves. The way I handled this was to buy a quart of vodka, get drunk, and go out with my friend to find anybody we could to tell what had happened. This became the story of the Great Fire. When I told it that first day, I would suddenly find it enormously funny, doubling over in spasms of laughter, no doubt a hysterical reaction to the fright I had experienced. Later, in August, the Great Fire played a role in the trip I made to the place where nobody I knew had ever been before, a trip that altered my life so dramatically that I would begin referring to everything in terms of "before Christ" and "after death."

It seemed I had died in the fire somehow. I clung to the fire to explain the supernatural events of August. But other things happened that summer that could be seen in retrospect like preparations for this arduous voyage of mine to nowhere. The most obvious was that I had stopped smoking cigarettes in June, the month I moved to Liberty Street. The way I did it was to run out of cigarettes one night and decide not to buy another pack in the morning. I was thirty-six years old and had smoked fiend-ishly since the age of fifteen. At that moment I believe a great fog began to lift out of my head and lungs, a wonderful thing for a healthier future but a dangerous sudden exposure to the clear light of day. In the beginning all I felt was the deprivation I had brought upon myself. But later, during July, I felt increasingly light and happy, though I did not connect this feeling with stop-ping smoking. Nor was I particularly aware of how light and happy I was. I had often felt this way during my life; there was nothing unusual about it. Still, it lasted too long and it got out of hand. My tolerance level for a rebuff or a disappointment be-came severely reduced; and, at the other extreme, my response to nice things happening—and nice things were happening increasingly—was to become lighter and happier, until I was so attenuated and transparent that I lacked the density to keep my feet on the ground. The nicer things were, the better I felt; and the better I felt, the nicer things got—an upward spiral in which I was being incorporeally wafted. The discrepancy between my life situation as it really was and this paradisiac turn of events became an ever-widening gap; I had pushed off from my life as if I were an astronaut leaving a doomed earth to enter a celestial atmosphere of everlasting peace and relief. Unlike an astronaut, though, I had no Houston control center. I was drifting along on my own; there was no plan for return—and I didn't even know I was out there.

Even more significant, since I had not in actuality left earth, I began colliding with earth's objects along the way, and as soon as that happened I was in a lot of trouble. But that point wasn't approached until the end of August. The first "symptom" I noticed that I later associated with my flight was a sensation of heat in my left big toe. Sometime in July I had gone out to Long Island with my dancer friend to see Merce Cunningham dance in a huge tent. I remember sitting near the back of the tent with my legs crossed when I felt this heat in my toe, and I uncrossed my legs, and recrossed them, and so on, to relieve the pressure I thought was causing the sensation. The sensation then went away, and there was no more to it than that. The reason I later incorporated it into the morphology of my flight was that sensations of heat in my legs accompanied a more florid set of symptoms in late August. If I tried to identify the moment of takeoff, I would have to pinpoint the Merce Cunningham concert in July on Long Island. It's true I took off (like the bromidic bat out of hell) in our Great Loft Fire in June, but that was merely circumstantial, whereas the sensation in my big toe was apparently without cause and to no effect. Also, it occurred during those light and halcyon days when fortune appeared to be smiling on me.

It sounds as if I had become a rock star or a bank president or something; actually I was still quite poor, and I was nothing more than a dance critic for the *Village Voice* and a reviewer for *Art News*. My feeling of good fortune was not attached to my status or economy; it had more to do with the sun shining and people smiling and ordinary things like the garbage collection suddenly looking splendid. This was 1965, after all. I was hardly alone in my revery. But most Americans at this time who were getting that far out were doing so on drugs. I knew about drugs, but I had no inclination to take them. Alcohol and coffee were my drugs. At any rate, I had slipped into a condition typical of the sixties: bliss and contentment for no apparent reason. The "flower power" side of the sixties challenge to Establishment values was the insidious aspect of revolution. Nothing may be so challenging to a progressive capitalist economy as the spectacle of hordes of middle-class dropouts. The belief that how you feel and act is more important than what you are and do and how much money you make or things you own was the centerpiece of this revolution. Getting high meant rising above the American indices of success. For myself, it meant floating involuntarily away from my life; I never entertained doctrinaire ideas about anything except art. Certainly my career was too important to me to be considered disposable. I was a little old in any case to be a dropout; it was not careers so much as schools that people were dropping out of. It was not my conscious intention to jettison my career at that point. I had been writing for only seven years; I enjoyed writing, and I was appreciated as a critic. Moreover, I was in step with the times: the art I championed was the new and the shocking. But there was an underside to my life that I knew nothing about. My position as a critic was compromised and confused by personal involvements with the artists or by personal needs that I had been acting out in the arena of my work.

In August 1964, one year before I went into orbit, I had become romantically involved with the dancer who now shared the loft with me on Liberty Street. This dancer, though only twenty-four, was a standout in a small group of choreographers whose work had been gaining both prestige and notoriety since 1961. I was the only critic at that time serving the interests of this particular renegade group. As such, I was naturally feared, loathed, and valued, in various mixed, constantly shifting proportions and distillations. I, however, was not aware of the power I wielded or how much I meant to these people—at least consciously. Since the wages of power were never discussed, any acknowledgment of them depended on some private educated understanding, which in turn might have suggested methods of dealing with them. Ambition and power were never acknowledged in this milieu. Only politicians and businessmen were thought to be so crude. The kind of power I had was similar to that of a mother unaware of the towering effect she has on her children. A mother like this may destroy her children if she is too strong, or be frightened by them if she is weak; that is, unaware of her own effect, she can fail to associate her power with the ways in which the children respond and behave. She then perceives them as acting autonomously; the *children* are the ones with the power. That accurately describes the way I perceived the artists whose work I reviewed. My position was authoritative, but I had no inner authority. I had strong aesthetic convictions, and I didn't shrink from expressing them, but I couldn't accept or understand the consequences of my job. Critics perform a parental function in society, and artists represent the play of children in adult design. My motives for being a critic were more those of the artists than any normally associated with critics. I was really more child than parent.

I acted out my critic/child role in the domain of real parenthood as well as in the art world. In 1964 my two children, a boy and a girl, were six and five years old. The power they had over me was of course even greater than the power I gave the artists. With my real children I tried to deny my authority completely. As a result, I was always coming from behind. I let them do more or less what they wanted until the point of destruction became obvious; and then I had to act with *great* authority at the last minute, thus enraging the child in me. My son tried to keep me in line by frequent cliffhanging—walking out to the edge of something with a wild, mischievous look in his eye, taunting me to get my attention, testing the limits of my control. In the summer of '65 he and my daughter, who was under her brother's protection in a strange sort of way, were both staying in the country in Connecticut with my mother. The life I floated away from that summer was one in which I had power over children and artists that I didn't comprehend. After death, as I called my life subsequent to the events of August, my power in both realms was greatly reduced and curtailed. With the onus of parenthood gone, I became freer to live like the child I still was.

Beginning with the Great Fire and the heat in my left big toe, the things I experienced or the way I began to experience things in July and August of 1965 was without precedent in my life. Yet I didn't recognize this until I was very far outside the sphere of my normal experience. The reason for that, I believe, was that I left earth, so to speak, very gradually, like a slow glider leaving the ground at an imperceptible increase in altitude. Changes were so gradual that I didn't notice them. I experienced them, certainly, but I never monitored them. I had never monitored my experiences before, so there was no reason to begin doing it then. Only when events in my life coagulated into a crisis did I notice them, and then all I could do was react to the emergency at hand, the time for contemplation having passed.

Something very much like that happened at this juncture. I was gliding along enjoying the novelty of my airborne state when one day I looked down and saw suddenly that earth was very far away and that there were no controls in front of me. At that point I identified heavily with *Gemini* V, which went into orbit August 22 and was plagued with a power loss—a breakdown of its electrical system—and which also had trouble landing after power was restored, because of a tropical storm in the designated recovery zone. Typically, the only news I ever seriously read was disaster news—not the daily stories of rape, murder, theft, accidents, etc., but the rarer and splashier stuff: the airliner collision over the Grand Canyon, the My Lai massacre, the Kennedy assassinations of course, the three astronauts who burned to death in their capsule, and so on. I would not normally have bothered with something like the problems of *Gemini* V, and in fact I didn't actually read about it. I just tuned in to the fact that it was up there and that its fate was in doubt; I don't believe I even knew exactly what the problem was. At any rate, by one of those personal/cosmic coincidences I found myself superimposed on a national event. *Gemini* V was in orbit eight days, which corresponded closely to the final epiphanic stages of my own flight. When astronauts Cooper and Conrad splashed down on August 29, I did too. I even had a kind of reentry burn. And I had plenty of frogmen surrounding my ship.

But I made all the analogies much later on. At the time, *Gemini* was simply one of my obsessions, and the only concrete association I made with it was astrological: I decided one day that I must be a Gemini, the sign of the twins, though in reality I was born in Taurus, a few days short of Gemini (I had never known I was Taurus). Other newsworthy events in August never caught my attention. A man from Ohio crossed the Atlantic in a thirteen-foot sailboat. The government declared a four-state drought disaster. The London *Times* took exception to calling a woman judge "Mister." Mayor Daley met with Chicago leaders to try and prevent riots. The Richard III Society in New Jersey offered eight tributes to try and clear his name of the murder of two princes. Bobby Fischer played a championship chess game by cable. Le Corbusier died. President Johnson's fifty-seventh birthday was celebrated the day *Gemini* V splashed down.

One item, however, on the same day of the *Gemini* launching, August 22, was impossible to ignore, because I found myself featured in it. In the Arts and Leisure section of the Sunday *New York Times* that August 22, Allen Hughes had written a piece called "Living Dolls and Literature" in which I was commended and quoted, along with three others, as a critic of the new wave of dance. Hughes wrote that I had said Gertrude Stein's question about prose and poetry might be applied to the dance. "What is dancing, and if you know what dancing is, what is nondancing? The trained dancer is an exceptional creature who can do many things a nondancer can't do. But if a performer walks across a stage and calls it a dance, who is to say it is not a dance?" That was certainly a good question, and I can't say I wasn't pleased to see myself quoted.

But I was also quite shaken up by it. It was a great surprise really, for I saw things one way only, which was that critics wrote about artists. Much as I subverted my role, resented the artists for valuing the attention I gave them more than my writing, wished subconsciously that I was an artist myself, and thought in grandiloquent terms of my function as critic, I was not prepared to take success seriously. I was only secretly ambitious, and I projected success onto others. I had none of the goals normally associated with success. Recognition, for instance, meant expressions of gratitude on the part of the artists, not any mark or sign of official status. Money meant having enough to survive every week and continue participating in the art world, not security or savings or investments or the wherewithal to travel or improve my circumstances or impress people. The article in the Sunday *Times* hardly signified any great success, but it stirred my inner opposition to the role of power that was being ascribed to me. These are retrospective remarks; at the time I was simply flustered by that kind of attention. It seemed much more significant than it really was. Yet it was one of the last things I remember happening at that time that remained connected to my real life. Possibly it was the "booster" that sent me out of earth's atmosphere into actual orbit. In the week or two before losing contact completely, I was confounded by everything I ordinarily took for granted and was disproportionately affected by things that upset my equilibrium in any way. A high-powered magnifying glass had installed itself somewhere inside my reception centers. If the *Times* article blew up into something insupportably good, at the other extreme an incident in the country one Sunday struck me as unaccountably bad.

2

Orbit

On that Sunday in late July or early August I drove up alone to see my children. Soon after I got there I drove them over to Marilyn and Bob's place a few miles away, a summer encampment on the side of a mountain. Marilyn and Bob were friends of mine from the city who had twin girls a little older than my son. Our relationship had become strained since my separation from my husband, but we still remained friends. I never tried to change anything. I assumed the passive position completely in all my affairs. Only intellectually did I take any initiative, and then only to argue opinions or analyze art and people, never my own life. Actually, I was quite a bull intellectually, and the discrepancy between this feature of my personality and an extreme emotional passivity was a contrariety in my makeup that could be viewed as a structural basis for the separation from myself that occurred during this month of August 1965. The incident in the country involving my friend Marilyn and her husband, Bob (the more accurate description of our relationship), dramatized my emotional predicament as a kind of bystander to my life.

The approach to the side of the mountain where they camped out all summer was a long, narrow dirt road through the forest which turned sharply to the left in a wide sweep about fifty yards from their site. On this particular Sunday the road was muddy and slimy from several days of rain. Driving there in my Oldsmobile heap, I got stuck in the wide-angle turn in such a way as to block traffic. When I walked to the site with my kids and told Bob what had happened, he stormed down to the scene of the impasse in a towering rage. He yelled and fumed and eventually freed my heap from its muddy berth. I don't remember what he yelled exactly, but I'm sure the gist of it was that I was an inconsiderate wretch to have blocked the traffic on his road and caused him so much trouble. I felt completely obliterated. Of course I was an idiot to get stuck like that. It was all my fault. What could I ever do to redeem myself? How would I get away? Were these people my friends or what? These must have been some of my unarticulated thoughts. Gradually it would sink in, long after the opportunity to act and defend myself had passed, that my abuser had acted irrationally and unjustly. Then I would behave as indirectly as my tormentor (who, I assume, had used the incident to express feelings he already had about his life or mine), saying something mean and contemptible out of context and unrelated to the exacerbating event. This way I would remain stuck with my central and static emotional position: that I somehow deserved any inequitable treatment I received. Later on that Sunday, having made my escape from the side of the mountain, trying to salvage my feelings at the lake where we often took our children to swim, I had my chance to spit out some childish vitriol when I passed Marilyn and Bob and their twin daughters as they were walking into the lake area and I was leaving. I never saw them again. Returning to New York that night, I babbled obsessively to my friend about the incident. She said afterwards that I couldn't stop talking about it. As I talked, I described the scene over and over, never reflecting on my attacker's motives or my own vulnerabilities. I didn't really know that he disapproved of me as a single mother. I did know that he was jealous of his wife's friends—that had been mentioned by her and by mutual friends; but in itself this wouldn't seem enough to explain his outburst. I knew also that his wife was having a crisis over her priorities, between her obligations as wife and mother and her career as a dancer. This was perhaps the main clue to his behavior. But it was far beyond my grasp to put everything together and perceive the threat that a single mother like myself might constitute for a man like my friend's husband. Had I even suspected such a threat existed, I might have stayed away or at least armed myself with sympathy for his fears. But I was incapable of excusing people on grounds that they had problems that had nothing to do with me. I couldn't separate their use of me from their problems. If they acted out on me, I was sure the problem was me. The perception that people used each other to play parts in their life designs was not apparent to me.

For all these reasons, the incident in the country that Sunday struck me as unaccountably terrible. It violently disturbed the euphoric state I was in and threw the draconic quality that certain men had for me into high relief. The rupture of an important friendship—one that involved my children and mother too —helped sever me, I'm sure, from a reality from which I had already been set loose.

Sometime between then and August 22, the beginning of my last week at large in orbit, I retreated within my loft to enjoy the visions I had begun producing. I had fallen into a kind of trance. I'd like to say coma, because I had a portentous dream preceding my retreat in which I fell into a coma; but of course I was not unconscious except in the social sense. Napping lightly one afternoon, I dreamt I was flying around the ceiling of a huge vault when suddenly, like Icarus, I plunged earthward—but into a coma, from which I awoke gazing at my left hand resting to my left in a relaxed fist. I had often had flying dreams, but this one was unusual in two respects: instead of flying as if I had wings and was a bird (customarily I flapped my arms violently in order to rise), I was flying in the breaststroke; also, I had never before fallen from such a dream. I should say *in* such a dream, but I did fall *from* it in the sense that when I fell the dream was over. If a coma is a kind of dream state, then I had dreamt about falling into a dream, which rather accurately describes my "real" waking condition. But I fell out of the dream as well, and that also describes the denouement of my flight. I took off in a glider and returned like a pilot kamikaze. The astronauts seemed to return in a kamikaze-Icarus style, which I thought (much later, when I integrated the dream with my flight plan) might account for the unusual breaststroke I had used to fly around the ceiling of the vault. Dreams can be more logical than life. If I knew by some prescience that I was going to plummet out of my dream flight, I would naturally want to be swimming while I was flying in order to land in the proper element. (I don't remember if I had begun identifying with the *Gemini* mission just then or not.) In every astronaut mission the rocket-phallus (dreamer) penetrates the sky (ceiling vault), explores the universe (flies around), descends to earth (falls into coma womb water sleep), and emerges from a capsule (awakens to new life). Birth means entering the womb as well as leaving it. An equation of life and death is typical of the waking dream that the specialists call schizophrenia.

I was now dreaming awake and sleeping dreamlessly. The properties of sleep and wakefulness had become inverted. A dangerous loss of sleep is a characteristic prelude to such a state; another is loss of appetite for food. A loss of sleep in this case is not an ordinary sort of insomnia, in which sleeplessness is an ordeal to be remedied by the use of drugs or other means. Nor is the loss of appetite here due to such normal disturbances as depression or anxiety or problems of self-image. There is a disturbance, to be sure, but a disturbance that transcends the merely neurotic, which implies a certain grasp of reality. I had never been particularly neurotic; I was too oblivious to my social (-political) context to be anxious about my position or relationships within it, and I had many cultural diversions and intellectual preoccupations. I might except the distress of my marriage from this appraisal, but even in marriage my tendency was to abstract myself from my immediate environment by reverie or ideation and by plunging forward to the scenes of art, looking neither to the left nor to the right, then every so often crashing into something and having a big crisis. I lived essentially in a state of oblivion punctuated by crises. After picking up the pieces from one crisis or another, I would never be the wiser, and I would then go right on pursuing my distractions under the happy illusion that my progress would never again be impeded. In the summer of '65 I became simply overextended in my illusions and absentmindedness. Attributes of these states took on a kind of life of their own, generating ever more rarefied editions of detachment. The way I assume this started was by my sudden withdrawal from nicotine in June, after years of heavy smoking. Then, as I became gradually lighter and happier and more immaterial and disengaged, I lost interest by degrees in food and sleep—two of the things that bring the body down. Then, as that happened, naturally I became even more attenuated, until I was inhabiting an ethereal atmosphere of my own making in which I might create an autonomous world. By then the streets and the world outside had become too disturbing, and I retreated within my loft to invent the specters of my dreams. I was now on automatic pilot.

At first my specters were nothing more than images—but very grand images they were indeed. Sitting at my desk, I became transfixed by an ordinary light bulb, which assumed a luminosity of ultraviolet phosphorescence. I sat there a long time absorbed in this light. It didn't occur to me (yet) that I had never before found a light bulb worthy of this sort of attention. Sitting at the kitchen table, I became magnetized by a simple green-and-red drawing tacked on the wall, the gift of an artist friend, which had begun generating and reflecting afterimages all around itself on the wall as if the ensemble were a lumia machine. Lying on the bed, I watched some red-white-and-black striped curtains on the windows, which had become similarly pregnant with designs of their own making. The curtains, the drawing, the light bulb: these three objects exhausted my interest aroused just then by strange visual phenomena.

I had other things to do and experience that last week beginning August 22, before I was discovered, as it were, to be missing. And, I should add, before I discovered myself to be missing—the two events, not surprisingly, overlapping and coinciding. Like any astronaut operation or business trip, this one was charged with certain tasks and purposes; it was not a vacation, no matter how much the primary intention of such trips is thought to be to get away from it all. Even so, the first leg of my journey was like a vacation, and I can imagine that some people go away like this and never come back.

In reality of course I was not charged with any particular responsibility at all. I had not received orders or instructions or anything of that nature, not even from my own center of consciousness. It was, in fact, the very lack of such directives in my life in general that had something to do with my departure at that time, which was so eminently pointless from any traditional social perspective. The way I had conducted my life and gotten from one place to another or made up my mind to do this as opposed to that was purely by convention or accident or inertia, or by imitation and peer pressure and osmosis, or by reaction to events around me, or simply by invitation. Now, suddenly, by a great ironic twist, I began generating very strong directives within myself that were completely disconnected from the world. Everything that had been outside was unexpectedly lodged inside, except that the outside (now inside) had metamorphosed in the form typical of dreams: autonomy, self-generation, make-believe.

The day I noticed this flip-flop I tried to put the brakes on as if I'd been doing ninety on a turnpike and went into a skidding screeching spin to avoid the oncoming traffic. This event transpired in several stages. First I just recognized that I'd slipped into a different reality. This frightened me a lot, as much because I didn't know where I was as because I suddenly became aware that I had been in this place where I didn't know where I was for some time by then. The obvious thing to do at that point was to make some contact with the world I knew. With that in mind I put in two desperate calls to friends I thought might have a clue as to where I was. I tried to sound cool, but I know I told them, with bated breath, that I was having visions, and asked them what they thought I should do, as if I'd lost control of my life. "Visions" was the word I used.

Very cleverly I confided nothing in the friend and lover who shared my loft, and I don't even remember where she was during this time when I was flying around so happy-go-luckily. I do remember her sleeping the night I was sitting at the kitchen table engrossed in the red-and-green drawing on the wall. Most of the time, I can imagine, she was busy rehearsing in a studio someplace for one performance or another. I also remember that I had lost interest in where she was. There was no question certainly of a social life that last week in August. The only people we socialized with that summer, in any case, were Robert Whitman and his wife, Simone Forti, who were hardly close friends. During the year we had been living together, we really didn't have any friends. Friends who had been mine before we got together had evaporated, and so had hers. One close friend I had, Charlotte, was now just a confidante when I was troubled by my relationship. And I had been deeply troubled all year by a serious challenge to the relationship on the part of a successful young painter, who had pursued my girl friend as if he were a knight in quest of a princess tied up in a tower. That summer, however, he was not in town, and there was no serious challenge from any other quarter. The reason we socialized with Robert Whitman and Simone Forti was that Bob had used my friend as a performer in a couple of his Happenings that year; also, he liked me as a critic. Simone had chucked her career as performer/choreographer to immerse herself in her marriage to Bob. They both lived in a loft on Mulberry Street, in the heart of Little Italy. Lofts at that time were not elegant and finished looking, but theirs was pretty nice.

Simone recently recalled the four of us walking along the street somewhere, I with Bob, she with my friend, and thinking that she and my friend were the "wives" and Bob and I were the "husbands." Nobody ever articulated things like that at that time. I would have been shocked myself to hear such notions. I never thought about genders, and if I had, I would never have cast myself as husband. But I wouldn't have cast myself as wife either. I had been a wife for four years and had failed badly at it. At any rate, as the sixties progressed, clearly a number of people saw me as a man or a husband, and they got that idea perhaps by drawing certain inferences from the way this relationship of mine looked to them. I was the tall one, and my friend, though not short, was shorter. I was the critic, and my friend was the dancer. I was funny looking, and my friend was beautiful. I was older and had banged around sexually, and she could have been a virgin. I was socially aggressive, at least when drunk, and my friend was always aloof and controlled. The fact that I was a mother somehow didn't count, probably because my children were rarely visible in that world of parties and art events, and my ex-husband had never been seen by the artists at all. Had I been thinking about things like this, I might have observed that in social settings the main conversation was often between me and the man, or husband. With Bob and Simone the main conversation was between me and him. With George and Helen Segal, whom I visited frequently in New Jersey, I talked mainly to George. In each case, where the man was an artist and his wife his wife, the part I played was the artist's intellectual buddy. George even concretized this state of affairs by plaster-casting me as "one of the boys" in a dinner-table sculpture scene that he made in 1963; he had me seated at a round table with himself and Lucas Samaras and Allan Kaprow—and with George's wife, Helen, and Alan's wife, Vaughan Rachel, standing nearby in domestic-supportive postures. In the case of Marilyn and Bob, Marilyn was the artist (dancer) and friend; but we talked more like two women together, about our children and mothers and idle stuff about Merce Cunningham's company, in which she danced. Her status as artist and mine as critic were secondary to our roles as wives and mothers. I was not her critic because she wasn't doing choreography at that point, and certainly she meant more to me as a mother than as a dancer.

I knew plenty of dancers, but mothers were a rare species to me. During 1964–65 except for Charlotte, I lost my friends who were mothers on the Lower East Side. As for the women who were ambitious choreographers—those who made up this avant-garde pack of exciting new dance—excepting one, I never had any serious conversations with them, either personal or intellectual; and I think that was because by the time I knew them well enough to talk to (1964), I seemed to have a threatening (i.e., different) life-style. To Marilyn and all the others, it must have become apparent during that year that I had failed to follow up my divorce with the search for another man, or at least with the proper appearance of a single lady-in-waiting. But I was also their critic, a condition that never scared the men but set me apart from the women.

These conversations of mine did not signify real friendship. I had many acquaintances and professional connections and one confidante, and I went to all the parties, but I had no real friends. It wasn't difficult to decide whom to call when I became frantic about my location late that August.

The two people I instantly thought of were socially somewhat neutral. One was Laura de Freitas, who was neither mother nor wife, nor even an artist. She usually had a boyfriend, but she appeared more independent than attached. She was a dancer, but not a serious one (or she had been and was no longer). I thought of her mostly as a sort of wise lady. She wasn't more than thirty-two at the time, but she seemed very experienced and sounded very authoritative. What she was actually doing at the time was going to school and making her living as a dance or movement therapist; eventually she became a shrink. I liked her warmth and directness and wanted to be her friend, but to her I seemed too crazy or different. Yet I knew she liked me. The reason I called her that day in August was that I assumed subconsciously that she was socially benign and that I thought of her as one of those people who know everything. If your hair was falling out or you had a mole in the wrong place or you needed the name of a doctor for something, Laura was the person to call. Now I was calling her about these "visions"— and expected, naturally, some excellent advice.

The advice she gave me was practically the same I got from the other person I called, John Giorno. John was a homosexual and a loner and quite an attractive, mysterious guy. I never found out what he was really thinking because he spoke mono-syllabically if at all and was always sweetly and dumbly agree-able. I met him around 1961 and saw him metamorphose from a preppie living on the Upper East Side who worked on Wall Street to an offbeat poet under the influence of Andy Warhol and William Burroughs, living in a small, shabby loft on the Bowery. John was the subject of Warhol's *Sleep* movie, which lasted eight hours and showed close-ups of John sleeping. I knew he had had about eight acid trips, which impressed me tremen-dously. That very year *Life* magazine featured an article about this explosive new drug that was driving America crazy. The fact that John had had eight acid adventures and survived made him seem to me like some sort of frontier hero. The one thing about acid that stuck in my brain was that it had been used as a cure for schizophrenia. That was outrageous, of course; I must have confused this notion with the experimental, therapeutically guided "trip." Certainly I had no idea what schizophrenia was. But by the time I called John, I must have believed I had it. Actually, I made two calls to him; when I made the first, all I thought I had was visions. Possibly one or two days separated the calls. The space between them was critical. Everything that happened in between represented a colossal but vain effort to reverse my course, to integrate the outer and inner worlds which had separated so drastically, to "put my house in order" before drifting away definitively.

3

Speed

Both Laura and John told me I should relax and enjoy my visions. That was the advice they gave me. John in particular thought that whatever I was having sounded great. I told him there was a Fluxus concert uptown that I wanted to go to (Fluxus artists did strange Happenings), but I was afraid to go out, and I thought the concert would overwhelm me. On the contrary, he said, I should have a wonderful time; so I decided to go—a decision that was a little like resolving to leave my spacecraft for an exotic descent to the moon. The concert was at Carnegie Recital Hall on Fifty-seventh Street, and the ride up there in my Oldsmobile heap set a record for slow-motion trips on the West Side Highway. I may have been doing twenty-five but it seemed like ten or less. The gear I was driving in was not on the box. Vehicles in space may be traveling close to the speed of light, but they also appear to be frozen out there. Great speed and great stillness—the two states were characteristic of my mental and physical conditions at that moment. While I had been speeding away from earth in my flights of fancy or what you will, I had been slowing down in my body to a weightless sort of standstill. I had ceased walking purposefully from one place to another; instead I glided evenly and slowly, as if sleepwalking or in some weightless element where movements are performed with an uninflected distribution of energy, giving the appearance of a smooth, effortless surface. I had not, however, lost any sense of purpose—not at all. But my sphere of purpose had altered; the emphasis had changed. Where we ordinarily move quickly and purposefully from one activity to another—say, from kitchen to desk to address, seal, and stamp some envelopes —I was now moving as if I were *only* in transition, as if every activity or focus were equally meaningful. That also meant that my plans were different. I wasn't addressing, sealing, and stamping envelopes anymore. To do just one envelope would have been a momentous feat, requiring an enormous period of time to accomplish. I had already tried writing, which had turned into a meditation not unlike staring at the light bulb or the curtains. Sitting at a card table in my friend's studio behind the partition (I can't remember why I wasn't at my desk), I set out to write an article about dance that Richard Schechner had asked me to do for the *Tulane Drama Review*. My handwriting, usually scratchy and jumbled looking in rough draft, began writing itself in a lovely, even, clear script, as if my pen were held by an electrocardiograph machine that was recording a very regular, unbroken series of wavy lines. Words and sentences ran together without punctuation or paragraphs. The content of the article ran together too; slipping away from the main subject, it became a circular display of digression from which a new subject emerged, a romantic diatribe on the pathos of the actor/spectator dilemma—i.e., the split between the two, a popular ideology in the theatre of the sixties. In the mood I was in, apparently my own dissatisfaction as a spectator had surfaced. The tone of the article was absurdly declamatory, including such blasphemous phrases as "I am the resurrection and the life." The writing was writing (by) itself. And after perhaps an hour or two of this, I remember stopping and thinking I could go on doing this forever, so I might as well not do it anymore. It seemed as if I had been sitting there writing forever already. That was the way everything I did or saw seemed then. The drive uptown to the Fluxus concert was interminable; and it must have been freighted with anxiety, because I had momentarily left the security of my loft and ventured into zones of manifold stimuli. I don't remember where or how I parked the car or how I maneuvered from the car to the concert hall, and all I remember about the concert is seeing Billy Kluver and Nam June Paik there.

Billy was a scientist at Bell Labs in New Jersey who had offered his services, and the facilities of Bell Labs, to a number of artists interested in technology. Ultimately he developed a corporation called Experiments in Art and Technology. Just two weeks earlier a piece I had written about him and his work with the artists had appeared in the *Village Voice*. I think I identified with Billy as an insider's outsider. He was Swedish, for one thing, having emigrated to America in the fifties; and, like myself, he was a medium between artists and others, and he worked as hard as I did at being an acceptable member of the artists' community. But he was still a scientist, he always wore a business suit, and he lived in the 'burbs in New Jersey. At this concert at Carnegie Recital Hall, I told him I'd been reading Norman O. Brown's *Life Against Death*, conveying, no doubt, my feeling that this was an apocalyptic book; he smiled indulgently, and collusively, I thought. He was quite tall and blond and he smiled a lot. By contrast, Nam June Paik, the video artist, the other person I remember seeing there, was short and dark and Korean, and his face was always contorted with tics and twitches. Nam June was cutting off somebody's tie in the audience. This was one of the events for which he was famous. He used a large pair of shears to sever the tie a few inches below the knot. That evening one tie was enough for me, and I returned home to Liberty Street, having stayed no more than ten minutes, I'm sure. At home I found my friend lying prone on the bed, dead asleep in all her clothes. Earlier that day, a crisis had developed when she left the loft with a suitcase, saying good-bye as if she were going away for a while but not telling me where or why.

Had I been responding normally, I would have asked her where she was going and why and would no doubt have tried to stop her. I knew she had no performance scheduled out of town, and she never stayed overnight at her parents' apartment uptown or at any other place. But I said good-bye to her at the door quite matter-of-factly, kissing her lightly on the cheek, as if we both knew beforehand she had somewhere to go that warranted taking a suitcase. She was cold and arcane looking, but she frequently appeared that way; any anguish she felt in this instance made no impression on me. I saw that she was going away and I didn't care; I would've been just as happy to have her stay. The fact is that her presence or absence had become immaterial to me for the past week or more. No doubt that was why she was leaving. This leave-taking at the door could have been a mysterious, dreamlike scene in an Antonioni film. As she left with her suitcase, she seemed like a stranger whose name I hardly knew. A fog had enveloped my emotional life. Yet my behavior indicated that I was still reacting in the gamelike manner of any unresolved intimacy. It was either that day or the day before that I awoke to the shock of being far away from home, even while clearly I had not really gone anywhere, and I called two people for help. And it was after she left the loft that I prepared to go uptown to the Fluxus concert, suggesting that my effort to wake up and re-enter the atmosphere was at least in part a reaction to my friend's distress, even though I was unaware of it. When my friend left, I felt nothing whatever, but I sensed I would be hearing from her soon. In fact she called me within the hour, and I remember answering as if the whole event, beginning with her departure, had been programmed by a computer, and I already knew my part, which I had only to enact on given signals. I listened as she told me in a low monotone that she was in a phone booth somewhere and she felt like jumping off a bridge. I asked her what her number was and wrote it down and told her to wait in the booth while I called Laura. I hung up, called Laura, who happened to be at home, and asked her to call my friend in this phone booth because she was very upset. Then Laura called me back to say she had made contact, that my friend was going over to her apartment to see her, and I put it out of my mind, mission accomplished.

On August 22, Sunday, the article about critics of the new

dance appeared in the *Times*. The day before, the *Gemini* flight had been launched. August 24, Tuesday, the astronauts broke a space endurance record, entering their forty-first orbit, and successfully conducted a major operational task of the mission: a rendezvous with an imaginary rocket. August 27, Friday, the astronauts began flying in a "rolling tumbling" fashion to conserve electrical power. August 28, Colonel Cooper was asked if he thought we could "sell that thing" as a ride at a carnival; he said, "I don't think you can sell this day-to-day drifting flight as a ride anywhere." August 29, *Gemini* V splashed down in a secondary recovery zone because the designated area was threatened by a tropical storm. On the 28th, Saturday, I attempted to alight in a "secondary" zone of my own by fleeing the city because I had come under suspicion in my loft, the alarm having been sounded for my whereabouts. But my own splashdown didn't take place until Monday the 30th, when I was corraled by friends, brought back to the city, and deposited at the debriefing and quarantine center. Between the 28th and 30th I carried out the main tasks of my own (solo) flight: various rendezvous with imaginary rockets! The 27th was the day my friend left with a suitcase and returned that evening. The 28th was my zero hour. While my friend was out dancing or rehearsing, I mobilized a scenario to ritualize a death and a new life: the rosette, cross, and mandala of this convergence of the two great opposites. I had no outline for the drama; it unfolded out of its own making from one step to the next, like any logical series of parts in a design or mechanism or piece of music. This "creation" of mine developed from a single idea, a kind of idée fixe, which came to me sometime that week, if not the morning of the 28th. The idea was perhaps carried by a voice, in the sense that it emanated from a source outside myself; yet I didn't actually hear it. I was compelled to think it, it took possession of me; but it wasn't hallucinated as a "voice" exactly. The thought was equal to a command, which does form the traditional clinical picture of a voice. I had to do what it said.

What it said was to give up criticism. I wasn't surprised or affronted. I offered no resistance at all. Every day we have thoughts like this about our jobs or homes or relationships that we don't take seriously. Normally such thoughts are implemented only after prolonged periods of conscious dissatisfaction, having been allowed to mature and gather evidence to support a change and to generate alternate plans for survival. There was nothing in my recent history to suggest such a change. On the contrary, the signs of encouragement that were forthcoming that summer might have renewed and confirmed my calling as a critic. Besides the small but noteworthy attention in the *Times* that Sunday, a long essay I had written about the new dance had appeared in July in a book called *The New American Arts* edited by Richard Kostelanetz. Even my mother, who had remained opaque to my career, demonstrated her knowledge (if not understanding) of it by telling me she was going to order the book and have me sign it; she said Marilyn had told her I was doing good work in New York and that she ought to be proud of me. But having "heard" a voice ordering me to stop writing criticism, a delegation from the President could not have persuaded me to continue. Some people hear voices that tell them to walk into the ocean and drown themselves, or cut off one of their ears, or lead an army to help crown some king, or lead their people from one place to another across a great desert, or locate Atlantis or the Lost Continent of Mu. The stories of voices and how far they succeeded are legion. Mental hospitals are full of people who were "saved" from their voices. But the world is equally full of stories of people who had a crack at implementing some of these commands and either died in the attempt or lived to tell the tale. History, certainly, is in no small measure an accounting of events that were authorized by voices —in particular that history designated "ancient."

My own individual history began, in a sense, with this voice commanding me to give up criticism. Until then my life had been essentially my mother's: i.e., all my directives had been social and external to myself. A hallucinated voice, heard exteriorly, is actually a projection of an inner thought, a thought seeking an audience or forcing itself to be heard. I had never heard my thoughts before, except those I committed to conversation or writing reflecting my intellectual interests. The thoughts of my daydreams, for instance, like the images and events of my nighttime dreams, were autonomous and disconnected from consciousness. In a life so repressed, the eruption of a thought in the form of a "voice" may be classically expected. The problem with such commands is that they tend to be taken literally rather than symbolically. They might well be worth following; but in the spirit of dream interpretation, what do they mean? Do we want to follow them, or are they merely telling us something about ourselves? Did I really want to give up criticism, or was this a message about my life that I could accept only in a metaphor? Neither, actually—or both, perhaps. Since I was dreaming, yet fully awake, I acted on the message in the form appropriate to that combined state: by creating a ritual. When people enact rituals, traditionally they enter a trance or a trancelike state. "Trance" derives from *transire*, to go across, pass over. Literally it means a passage (from life to death). In a trance, people lose their individuality, enabling them to enter the communal spirit of ritual, in which ceremonies of passage are enacted, forecast, or remembered. Giving up criticism simply meant giving up my life as I had known it. The solo nature of rituals performed in a so-called psychosis may represent the bizarre effort of individuals adrift in society to establish lost connections. Everything in my own case pointed to this. At first, "as though in a dream," I went through the motions of giving up my work. Having conceived the project, I called Steve Paxton to come over to the loft and play a leading part in it. I had selected Steve to be my successor. Though Steve had never expressed an interest in writing criticism, I'd divined that he was the right person to replace me: he was smart and articulate; he was at the center of the movement I championed; he didn't care for my criticism, and I found his choreography dry and boring.

As a critic, it was rarely my practice to put down things I didn't like; instead I ignored them or at best described them. I had good training at this in my reviewing for *Art News*, which sent me out once a month to cover a number of painters and sculptors, many of whom did pathetic, derivative work. It was the magazine's practice to collect these artists in catch-all paragraphs, a single sentence allotted to each one. These were called "junk reviews." At one vanity gallery I might be assigned shows by five artists. This was easy work, because I got three dollars per review whether I wrote one sentence or ten. Anyway, it was clearly pointless to damn an artist in one sentence, and I considered it a challenge to try and convey some essence of the work in a thumbnail description. In general, whether writing about art or dance, I could more readily say why I liked something than why I didn't. Since my criticism for the *Voice* was not by assignment, I had carte blanche to ignore whatever I pleased and talk only about the things I liked. Later on, when the paper became solvent and depended on advertisements, they needed a dance critic to cover the field. For me the field was limited basically to the territory carved out by Judson choreographers, so called after the Judson Memorial Church on Washington Square, where most of the collaborative concerts took place between 1961 and 1966. I had a fair grasp of the history of American modern dance, and I was certain I was witness to an innovative period comparable in depth and dimension to the great Graham and Humphrey eras of the late twenties and early thirties. Analogously, I saw Merce Cunningham, lone innovator of the fifties, as progenitor to the new movement, the way Denishawn had been earlier. A number of choreographers in the Judson concerts had either studied with Cunningham or danced in his company.

Steve Paxton was one of them; he joined the company in '61 and left it in '64, his career with Cunningham occurring in tandem with his activities as organizer and choreographer at Judson. Dancing with Cunningham meant doing real dancerly stuff: suave, technical, near-balletic entertainment. Steve's own work during this period was resolutely and programmatically tedious; he was at the forefront of work committed to pedestrian, antitheatrical forms of movement. It's hard to imagine work like his presented outside the supportive context of a group like Judson. Others found his work more interesting than I did, but they were his friends in the group. He was much more the insider's choreographer just then, hermetic and insulated, not with appeal to the commoners. I was an insider's critic, but I liked being entertained too.

In 1964–65 our opinions of each other were a noteworthy component in the seething nexus of Judson politics. The virulence of these opinions was a measure of their implicitness. Behind Steve's distrust of my criticism and my imperviousness to his choreography lay the unknown and undefined struggle of sexual politics. Steve thought that because I liked women I didn't value men's work as much as women's. I thought that since he was living with a man, he naturally had no use for women. Actually I didn't think that at all, nor was it necessarily or altogether or more than partially true. But the stereotypes with their attitudes cast long shadows everywhere. Of the two of us, Steve conformed more pleasantly to some fixed idea of his sex than I did to mine. He was a good-looking, athletic, well-built, straight-shooting sort of guy, no camp or swish or extravagance in his manner at all. I, on the other hand, was a good-looking, athletic, well-built, straight-shooting sort of girl, no camp or swish etc. I still had a couple of dresses in my closet, however, and I still wore lipstick when I got "dressed up," and, unlike Steve, I had a retiring, awkward, self-conscious personality except when drunk. Between '62 and '64 I went through an aberrant phase, dressing up in high ladies' drag, looking more like a parody of some fixed idea of my sex than anything closely resembling it. No matter what we both were, we shared the culture's main ideas about our respective sexes: men like men, women like men, and men and women like only beautiful women—or so things still basically were at that time. Add to that that for myself I also liked powerful women (provided they remained in striking range of beautiful), and you have some idea of what it was that disturbed Steve about me as a dance critic.

It wasn't that I preferred the work of women to men (I had championed Cunningham, upheld Paul Taylor and Jimmy Waring, once venerated José Limón, and admired the whole Balanchine oeuvre, to mention a few); I just happened to be involved in a medium that was historically dominated by women. Of every field in the world, from politics and business through art and ballet, modern dance was the only one that claimed founding mothers rather than fathers. It wasn't surprising to find, in the early sixties, a woman, Yvonne Rainer, once again at the forefront of this indigenous American art form, which actually arose at the turn of the century in reaction to the constraints and ethereality imposed on women in ballet. I had no political (feminist) point of view in 1965, but I wonder how it would be possible to participate in a medium like modern dance without some predisposition to serve its matriarchal tradition. Cunningham was actually the first independent male to make an original dent in the tradition. The three prominent males who preceded him (Limón, Weidman, Shawn) were attached to two of the great female pioneers. My enthusiasm for Rainer, whom I called the greatest thing since Isadora or heralded as receiving the mantle of Martha Graham, set me up against three powerful males whose work I greatly esteemed and who had seniority and position and whom I wished wholeheartedly not to offend. For two of them, Cunningham and composer John Cage, my defection couldn't have mattered much, for by then Cunningham had the support of mainline critics; and while Cage always enjoyed my support, he had been well established himself for some time. It was I who needed *their* support and approval, even while the thrust of my criticism had begun to revolve around the younger Judson group. Cage, in any event, remained very important to me, for like many people in the art world in the early sixties I had fallen under his tireless influence—the intellectual fountainhead, it seemed, for everything exciting and worthwhile that was happening in New York then.

But it was Robert Rauschenberg—American heavyweight painting champ, Cunningham's set designer and stage manager since 1956—whose opinion of me now mattered the most, since he was living with Steve and performing with him in Judson concerts. Rauschenberg's personality and position were pretty overwhelming. By December '64, when he and Steve returned from a Cunningham/Cage tour abroad (Rauschenberg triumphant as the winner of the Venice Biennale that summer), having just severed their relationship with the company, and throughout '65, when all their energies (or whatever Rauschenberg had left over from painting, which seemed considerable) could be devoted to Judson events, I felt their presence and discrimination everywhere. A new "art family" seemed to be in the making: Paxton and Rauschenberg, like Cage and Cunningham, as the parents of a company, though never identified as such. Steve's feeling about me as a critic had cogency through his powerful alliance with Rauschenberg. And it wasn't just my criticism (never the medium to endear one to artists) but also my occasional forays into production that vexed them, for Steve, using Rauschenberg's name, was producing concerts too, and engaging the same choreographers: the small band of the Judson elite which could almost have been called a company, and to which they themselves belonged. Then, combined with these irritants, I was the wrong kind of girl. Steve and Rauschenberg, despite their relationship, were regular guys who liked hanging out with the prom queens and cheerleaders; and I had the gall to be living with one of them, which meant she was now excluded from their intimate social circle. In a way, by "appointing" Steve to succeed me, I seemed to be saying, "Here, if you guys don't like me, take it yourselves and see what you can do with it." Faced with such extraordinary competition, my lack of confidence or inner authority had collapsed the thin veneer of my position. And since I wasn't conscious of any of this, in my altered state I dumped it all into the dream process. By thus confusing realities I was about to become a captive of the State.

4

Miracle

When Steve arrived, he sat down at the long table in the kitchen area, and I floated back and forth across the expanse of loft from my desk and files near the front windows, a good seventy feet away, bearing photos and clippings, announcements and letters —the paraphernalia of my job—to Steve at the kitchen table. I suppose he just thought I was showing him all this stuff for the hell of it, while I assumed he knew exactly why I was pulling it out and bringing it over. He didn't give anything away. His demeanor was passive, attentive, and receptive, as if he understood that this was a transaction and he was willing to go along with it. Very possibly he'd been informed before he arrived that I'd slipped my gears or gone strange or something. After unloading my criticism, so to speak, I floated over to the bed and lay down on my back as if to rest, having discharged a major assignment after all. Now I was as light as I could be. The burden of criticism was gone, and I seemed to have liquidated my relationship as well. What was left, besides my body? Apparently only motherhood, which I had conveniently forgotten, since my children were staying with my mother in the country.

The most amazing thing now happened. Lying on the bed there, I had a kind of pseudocyesis, or hysterical pregnancy, consisting of an entire minute or two of full-term labor pains, or sensations that were distinct enough to be identified as labor but not real enough to cause actual pain. What they caused mainly was great astonishment. A miracle had transpired. Slowly I rose to my feet and escorted myself across the loft desert to the table where Steve was still sitting, evidently lost in thought. As I got closer, Steve stood up and approached me, and as we met, a few feet from a corner of the table, I swayed and swooned as if I were going to faint, and indeed I blacked out momentarily (something I had never done before) but without going down. Recovering equilibrium, I peered deeply into Steve's intense electric-blue eyes and asked him to go over and lie down on the bed with me. He had no objection, and we both lay on our backs there staring at the ceiling for a minute or two, during which time it was possible for me to imagine, by some dream logic, that Steve was the agent of my conception. Such great labor pains as I had had required some agency. The miraculous conception had its angel after all. That accomplished, I rose to my feet again, and Steve followed toward the kitchen area. Near the table I stopped and peered once more into his intense electric-blue eyes, this time engaging him in a bizarre conversation about keeping secrets. Since I believed he knew exactly what had happened and had acted somehow in collusion with me, I thought it was necessary to extract an agreement from him not to tell the world about this. I knew nobody would believe it. It seemed incredibly portentous, possibly something of relevance to the entire universe. But Steve of course had no idea what was going on, and at this point he balked, not by trying to tell me that nothing had happened or that I had imagined whatever had happened (nothing had been conveyed verbally), but ideologically, by questioning the necessity or wisdom of secrets. I recalled this later as a "black Zen" dialogue: a study in riddles and contradictions, a debate on the head of a leaning pin. I don't remember the words, only the essence.

The next part of this "dream" that I remember was the arrival of Rauschenberg, followed by my friend, who had been visiting our friends upstairs, Les Levine and Atsuko. Rauschenberg brought a big bag of sodas and potato chips which we sat down to eat by the front windows. I was overcome by his back, which I had never consciously noticed before. He seemed to have an extra back all up around his shoulders and neck. I had the strange impression that his whole personality was in his back. I felt vaguely threatened or menaced by it, a feeling that gathered momentum as the minutes passed. If I had not taken stock previously of the antagonism that existed between us, I now saw it all in his back. After five minutes I wanted to get away from him. I wasn't fooled by the "party" of potato chips and soda; I knew now that both he and Steve were there to see what was wrong with me and what they could do, especially when my friend appeared looking stricken and bearing a tranquilizer that she had obtained from Les upstairs. At this point I started "rolling and tumbling" the way Colonel Cooper described *Gemini*'s flight August 27 in its effort to conserve electrical power. Compared to the style in which I had been moving, liquid and even, I began casting about in a manner perhaps more nearly resembling that of somebody in a normal state who feels anxious and exposed. The next stage of my "flight" was earthbound and realistic, a stop en route: there were specific people to get away from, a definite place to go to, and a practical justification for the move. I even had a "re-entry burn," tearing through that layer of atmosphere separating our own from outer space. The heat that I had felt earlier in my left big toe, the "symptom" I later identified as the first one associated with this outrageous trip, had traveled up through my legs and body to my head. As a result, perhaps, of my demanding and defensive dialogue with Steve, the energy previously diffused or directed to simple tasks or consumed in "meditations" now collected in my head, which started burning up. The feeling was that a red-hot fusion was taking place in my skull. My entire history, separate, identifiable features (dates, names, ideas, places, spaces, and the sense of chronology), melted and blended into one burning ball. What had been everything in the sense of many discrete parts became nothing in the center of a fiery vortex. I was overwhelmed by nothing. Biochemically, it could be said that my brain had flooded with certain substances that normally act as neurotransmitters (of electrical impulses from one cell to another), or that these substances had become wild and toxic, causing the various parts of my brain to (con)fuse their functions. While it's generally agreed that chemical transformations occur in these experiences, which may cause them and/or be caused by them, nobody knows exactly what they are. I had already decided myself that my system had created acid, which by some illogically deduced vaccine principle would therefore be the proper antidote for my condition. This provided the excuse I needed to get away from my visitors.

When my "burn" was over (and it lasted only moments), I translated my way out of it by observing that I was unable to separate things; I wasn't exercising the usual judgments: this was good, that was bad. Differentials had vanished, opposites merged, contrarieties coalesced. There was no place to go, nothing to do, no reason to think one thing as opposed to any other. I remember standing near the front windows there listing to one side, lost in this vacuum. It seems I had collapsed in on myself like one of those black holes in quantum physics. I was wearing a purply blue print madras dress which hung around my body like an aerated drape. I count this as an axial moment in my life. The confusion that was my normal modus operandi had culminated in something real. I mean I was now utterly confused (confusion was an actual feeling or assessment), whereas before, never recognizing my confusion, I was in the habit of simply expressing it. Now I was too detached from reality to benefit from any experience that might have some bearing on it. I was like a balloon growing, expanding, and crowding out the space of some room, the real world displaced inside me. The immediate purpose of my confusion was apparently to make me reach desperately for some controls. (After their "burn" the astronauts take over from Houston and guide their ship to its landing.) I had to get away from my visitors and I had to obtain the antidote for my condition. The thought had actually occurred to me that I was probably crazy. I was "rolling and tumbling" again. My fear of Rauschenberg, with Steve swept along in it, came back into focus. I was certain they were there to entrap me.

Where would they take me? To some crazy house, I thought. I had the normal prejudice and limited understanding of insanity. Some unfortunate families had people who were locked away for life, and nobody was ever supposed to say anything about it. In the movie *The Snake Pit* I had seen what kind of eternal damnation these people lived in. As I hovered near my front windows on Liberty Street in a great panic about my situation, the word Bellevue crossed my mind. My first effort to escape involved feinting jumping out the windows. I thought, "What do they want me to do, jump out the windows?" and made a sort of mock rush for them; then, since nobody tried to stop me or respond one way or another (no doubt it went unnoticed, though for me the thought alone was tantamount to a broadcast), I abandoned the pretense and headed for the elevator, telling them that my friend and I had to go to the country. In a flash I had conceived an escape plan. We could head for Stony Point, where I might find Gerd Stern, who knew Timothy Leary. The four of us got in the elevator, nobody opposed the plan (I mentioned only the country, not acid), and out on the street Steve and Rauschenberg kissed us good-bye next to my car parked at the curb. I remember feeling as if my dress were rising over my head, and pressing it down from my hips, trying to keep it and/or myself on the ground. I remember Rauschenberg's kiss—big lips puckered up and pushed forward, thrust hard against my mouth.

In the car I went right for the West Side Highway and across the George Washington Bridge and up the Palisades Parkway, heading for Stony Point. This was no slow-motion ride. I broke the speedometer trying to get there. My friend was silently frantic. She had a performance scheduled in the city that night, and she was racing into the unknown with a mad person at the wheel. At the Land in Stony Point (the artists' colony where John Cage and David Tudor lived) we obtained directions to Gerd Stern's place. Gerd was a poet turned Intermedia artist who was running something called USCO, an Intermedia psychedelic art group, with Steve Durkee at Durkee's remodeled

Church in Garnersville. Durkee was the man who later went to New Mexico and developed the Lama Foundation, which sponsored men like Richard Alpert, who came back from India as Baba Ram Dass in 1968. I never met Durkee, but Alpert a.k.a. Ram Dass captured my attention in the late sixties when I was looking for religion.

That August 29 in '65, the Church in Garnersville was a wildly appropriate place for somebody in my state. Years later Gerd told me my visit was not unusual, because plenty of people dropped by there in drugged-out conditions. And though I was not really "drugged out," I might as well have been. The Church functioned as sanctuary as well as art center for communal psychedelic apparatuses. Art compromised by religion never interested me as a critic, and by the time religion interested me I felt alienated from art. That afternoon when I walked into the Garnersville Church, the first thing I saw was a big, optical sort of painting of Durkee's in golden yellow colors of the Shiva Shakti, the god with lots of arms. The painting was vibrating, and it made me dizzy; I was already inside that kind of space. The only people there were Jim Kennedy, a tall, handsome youth, and his wife, Judy. Jim said he expected Gerd soon.

I told him I wanted to lie down, so he led me upstairs to a big room with a bed in it. Momentarily I had forgotten that the purpose of my visit was to obtain some acid. I was now obsessed with one idea, and that was to generate hate. I thought I had fallen in love with the world and that that had made me dysfunctional. I had to separate things out again and begin thinking in opposites. I told Jim I had to generate hate. He had slid down against a wall in this big room and was asking me what had happened. He wanted to help, but without meaning to he made matters worse. However, he did liberate me from this vise or deadlock in which my brain had been foundering since earlier in the afternoon. With one remark he turned the key that unlocked my thoughts, but the thoughts thus liberated were commandeered by a fiction. The most interesting phase of these experiences—the dream proper, or delusions, as they're commonly called—was about to ensue. I told Jim I had had labor pains in New York, which he summed up with glib conviction, saying it sounded as if I had had a "holy experience."

Forthwith I rose from the bed and walked downstairs to prepare for the "second coming" by taking a bath. The bathroom had no door, and the tub was an unusual structure of copper and wood. There were lots of hanging plants, and the windows were covered with glass negatives of starlets from the twenties cut into strips of transparencies. Stepping out of the tub, I put on a white terry-cloth robe that was hanging on a hook on the wall. In the robe and my white sneakers I believe I felt properly dressed for my new role. I never decided who I was or what my part was exactly, but I assigned parts to others left and right, and I made up the story and decided how it would turn out, so I guess I was the writer, director, manager, and producer.

The plot, of course, was to save the world. Christ had tried once and failed, and now it was up to me. Or maybe Christ had done his part but the project needed to be updated. Christian delusions are as common as winter colds in experiences like this. Christians and non-Christians alike hew to the story of Christ to explain supernatural events such as labor pains that have no issue. The issue had to be made up. In Norman O. Brown's *Life Against Death*, the phrase I had lingered over was *"causa sui,"* meaning to cause oneself. I was a very good candidate for a virgin birth because my mother had been a virgin before me. The essence of my (life) story concerned a father who was not real. My mother always said I had a father, but I never met him or saw him, and the same was true (for me) of her own father. Moreover, she brought me up as if fathers in general did not exist. She never married a man or introduced me to a single man who meant anything to her. I was born quite anachronistically, really. My mother simply disregarded twenty-five centuries or so during which fathers established their paternity by right of law. I could have been born in a time when it was not even known that fathers played a part in birth at all (if indeed such was ever the case); my mother could have been one of those birds, like the vulture or the scarab beetle, that according to myth were all females, and sacred, and reproduced themselves by just stopping in the midst of flight, opening their vaginas and becoming impregnated by the wind. As I hastily reconstructed a world, I cast it naturally in the divine mold, corresponding to some archaic understanding of how something was created out of nothing, e.g., oneself. I had enormous energy after all. I felt unbelievably powerful. Thus all this energy and power that I had withdrawn from the world was available to reinvest in a creation story, a myth about how I had arrived here. This would be my ticket back to reality. In some cases, evidently, this "ticket" carries the traveler beyond reality forever. A story or delusion becomes the only endurable substitute for a deficient reality. Or the delusion may evaporate but the deluded one is locked up and shut off from reality anyway. The collapse of personality represented by the whole arsenal of symptoms called schizophrenia, of which delusions are the centerpiece, has generally been considered fatal. In the 1890s schizophrenia was called dementia praecox, a diagnosis according to which a patient progressively decayed until reaching a state of idiocy. This is an immense subject, to which I add my own story.

At that moment on August 29, 1965, the story of Christ became a kind of bridge back to my ongoing personal story. The function of myth, in fact, has always been to bridge the two realities, the other world and the here-and-now. I had died, and a metaphysical birth was in order. The story of Christ in our culture provides the best-known array of images symbolizing the birth of self. The virgin birth is a theological proposition, not a statement of fact. Prior to this moment, I had never entertained thoughts about the birth of Jesus or any other such birth. I didn't know, for example, that virgin births are common to all cultures, primitive and civilized. The six years I had spent in a High Episcopalian boarding school operated by nuns had never made me religious. In this I simply imitated my mother, who always made a point of saying she was a heathen ("heathen" was the

word she used, not "atheist") and who had sent me to a religious
school purely because it was convenient. After I graduated I
never went to church, and I lived among people who were
heathens like my mother or who believed God was dead. By the
time I graduated, however, I had a good background in Christian imagery. For six years I was saturated in Christian symbolism. I basked in the rituals too; I actually enjoyed all the
singing and chanting and marching around and genuflecting and
vestments and incense and wafers and wine and so on. Even
when I was bored, I amused myself by singing too lustily, or
cutting up with a friend, or caricaturing the nuns, or watching
them keenly like an amateur anthropologist. When the question
of my faith came up, over some inappropriate behavior, perhaps
in chapel or church or Scripture class, I simply told them I didn't
believe in God.

Two decades later I heard from God. When it was all over, I
was agog to think that a veteran heathen like myself had succumbed to a Christian experience. Yet I knew the background
was there, and I would also remember the impact of a movie
called *He Who Must Die*, based on a Kazantzakis novel about a
Passion play performed annually in Greece.

The "play" I put together in the Garnersville Church was
quite a primitive little affair, and some of the people to whom I
assigned parts never appeared. Nor was there any rehearsal or
actual performance or for that matter announcement of intention; the play unfolded strictly in my head and in imagined
fragments. For instance, at one point I was sitting on the floor
with Jim and my friend and I had a piece of bread in hand which
I broke and offered to each of them, imagining that this was a
legitimate, however truncated, version of the Last Supper. It
was very peaceful and quiet there, and the late afternoon sun
was bathing us in a chiaroscuro light. Jim was one of the Apostles, maybe Peter, and my friend was the Virgin, despite the fact
that I was the one who was going to give birth. Nine months
hence, I said (to myself), on my own birthday (May 17), I
would deliver twins, a boy and a girl. The Gemini association

here was perhaps the connection I made with twins. But there were other twin motifs in my life at that time. My friend Marilyn had twin daughters whose closeness and differences fascinated me; and every Sunday in the country at the lake where my mother took my children swimming I gawked at two good-looking redheaded identical twin boys, aged about eighteen, who shadowed each other into the water and all around the beach. One Sunday on my drive up there I saw Siamese bananas at a fruit stand and bought them to give to the twin boys, hoping, I suppose, to stupefy and amuse them, which might reflect the way I felt about them myself. When I gave them the bananas, they registered no emotion whatever; I guess they thought I was an idiot. Even when sane, I often behaved symbolically and unsuitably. This aspect of my behavior now absorbed and filled up the husk of my personality. Everything was symbolic and nothing was suitable.

In the course of my day and two nights at the Church, symbols gave way to symptoms as my attempts at restitution were exhausted or dissolved in the bodily signs of chemical disturbances or pathologies. I had hardly eaten or slept in days. My friend told the others at the Church that she thought I would be all right if I could just get some sleep. Gerd's wife, another Judy, tried forcing me to lie down and sleep by punishing me in the bathtub. She got me into a cold tub and threatened to strangle me in it by gripping my neck and shaking it with her bare hands. Judy Kennedy, like her husband, Jim, was by contrast altogether benign. Gerd on the other hand was like neither Jim and Judy nor Judy his wife. Despite his neutrality and apparent acceptance of my presence there, I could sense his discomfort. Gerd was practically my age, but like the men I knew in New York who were successful and close to my age, I perceived him to be a lot older. He was the patriarch of the Church there in Garnersville, and in my Christian seizure I assigned him the role of Judas, ostensibly, I suppose, because he refused to produce any acid or guide me to Leary's outpost in Millbrook. I had no role for his wife, or for Jim's wife, either; the only women I cast were my friend as the Virgin and Laura, who was in New York, as the midwife. As for the men, I had only Judas and the rest of the Apostles, whom I numbered fourteen rather than the traditional twelve, and of whom I recall naming just Steve and Jim. I didn't even cast Christ, but I can only assume that I was this august victim myself and that my inability to name myself implied some residual contact with the real world as well as a wish to spare myself the ultimate fate associated with him. Also, I never fancied myself a man. If anything, as shown by the delusions I cooked up the following year, in 1966, I wished to be a *daughter* of a (great) man.

5

Falling

The story of Christ was quite inconclusive for me; Christ had no daughter, and Christ as a father figure was of no consequence to my friends in the art world. But the purpose of my Christian delusion at that point was apparently just to explain a miraculous birth; i.e., separation from mother. The issue of twins, a boy and a girl, was symbolically reparational. Emerging alone in the world, we make continual efforts to (re)locate our parents inside ourselves. I had had a boy and a girl (they were born twenty-one months apart); but they were real, they were mere children, and they appeared to be leaving me. With some prescience (as a captive of the State I would become an "unfit mother") I enacted a ritual in the Garnersville Church of letting my children go, even intoning that particular biblical phrase to give my case cogency. I was very emotional about this. I remember walking and crying and wringing my hands as I gave up possession, imagining I had to let them go in order to answer some special calling. The twins I planned to deliver nine months hence were no doubt my new children, the parts of myself I hoped to interiorize. My "special calling," as I've said, was to save the world. By grand coincidence Christ's birth has been calculated to have taken place in Gemini, the double sign of the twins. But Christ is most widely associated with Pisces, the sign of two fishes, because his birth corresponds to the inception of the Piscean age, which is linked to the fish symbolism in Christ's story. I say "by coincidence" because I had no knowledge of this sort (or the sort of knowledge I had was unconscious), and the image or symbol I produced in connection with it was of the class of things (archetypal) that delight Jungians. Ten years later I found my way to Zurich, where I consulted one of Jung's daughters and in general delighted Jungians with my story. In 1965, I had read only one book by Jung himself, a slim volume called *Psychology and Religion*, which had impressed me a great deal without meaning much to me.

As I died that week in August, I lived only in these symbols, the components of a myth, the link between the two realities: the life I had lived as a dead person (alive to ideas) and the life I had yet to live (alive to myself). A psychotic experience is an involuntary reaction against an unnegotiable identity theme. I had been living like a man without a man's privilege without knowing it. Or I had been living like a girl without the protection of a man without realizing I needed it. Obviously the world that needed saving was whatever world had made my position in it untenable. The grandiosity of my project just at that moment could be attributed to the extremity or gravity of my immediate predicament. If I had always lived dangerously, unconvinced of my own control over things, thus essentially abdicating management of my life to others, I had now reaped the full consequence of that kind of insecurity. To the people around me it looked as if I needed to be saved in a very big way. As a result, I could see for the first time that I needed to be saved from those who would save me—that is, I'd better save myself. I wasn't an astronaut, after all. Astronauts aren't afraid of the people in Houston who bring them back to earth. They know exactly what will happen when they get back and what's expected of them. They haven't left in order to get away from anybody. In an important sense, they haven't really gone anywhere. And if they should happen to get lost on the far side of the moon— sayonara, as is said—they could have a religious experience with impunity. It's quite a different kind of trip. However, if they were to get lost, and then have a religious experience, and contact with Houston were somehow re-established, they could be in the sort of trouble I was having lost on earth. Then they might *really* be someplace else, not just physically transported. Their strangeness would be a condition for mutual paranoia. Should an astronaut return in a visionary state, he wouldn't likely view those who had failed him, so to speak, with much trust or confidence; he might even be terrified of them, especially if he managed to get back without their help. This is the heart of the paranoid aspect of the so-called schizophrenic plight. The classic "delusions of grandeur" are like the dream of a lost child rescued by an extraordinary prince. Incapable of saving myself, having abandoned or been abandoned by my friends, I invented a savior, or rather invoked one—the one best known to the Western world. The appeal was to the highest authority, the one we imagine in lieu of any mortal one. I was a perfect candidate for an experience like this. The father I never knew had rushed into the void created by his absence to save me from myself. Until then the void had been filled up with cigarette smoke, as it were. But while I was busy being omnipotent, walking around in a white terry-cloth robe making up the world, deciding matters of grave import and so forth, my friend and my hosts were trying to resolve how to take over for me; clearly I had usurped some power that didn't belong to me.

Gerd noticed the power in my eyes—he said they were very intense, "boring into"—but my friend perceived my power in social terms. I was behaving like a child who takes up all the attention space. She remembered that I kept everybody awake, an indefensible way to act, even for a child. Jim remembered that I walked around all the time and talked incessantly and that my friend was very concerned and worried. I remember her sitting immobilized on a chair in a rumpled black raincoat, her hands in her pockets, staring awesomely at me. I remember trying to get away by saying I was taking a walk and getting as far as a lamppost on a corner about thirty yards down the road, then racing back (in my mind; very slowly on foot), terrified that I would be locked out. Outside, I felt locked out, and inside, locked in. The dreamer's body is an unwelcome ghost when it isn't safely sleeping.

The dreamer's body in this case was also inexcusably strung out. Late the second night that we were there, I jackknifed on my stomach over a stool in a fit of convulsions. After Gerd's wife, Judy, tried to bring me to my senses by "strangling" me in the bathtub, I let Jim "tuck me in" on a pallet against the far wall of the immense room of the Church, the room that must have been the nave. It was probably about 4 a.m. on Monday the 30th, the day of reckoning in this particular journey. I think I slept briefly, as much as an hour or two perhaps, before rising again, with renewed, enormous energy, to resume my dream. Advanced dreamers can become aware that they're dreaming within the frame of their dream. By then, I had not left any part of myself outside my dream to see myself in it, but Jim performed this service admirably as he put me to sleep by answering a couple of my questions realistically. This was a moment of reprieve. I asked Jim what was happening, and he told me I had been "hallucinating" and was in a "state of shock." Those were his exact words as I remember them now. Then I told him I was afraid that my friend was dead, and he assured me she was sleeping in a room nearby. Then I said she must have died in the Great Fire in New York, and again he assured me she was sleeping nearby. Then I said she must have died in the car trip from New York up to Stony Point (I imagined she had fallen out of the car, an image conceivably based on a real incident the day before, when we had pulled over on the highway to debate the merits of going on or returning to the city), and again he explained patiently that this was not the case. Here was the first intimation of my friend as a primary intro-projected part of myself.

My friend was as close to me as my mother was, a closeness of intense identification without much sympathy, a symbiosis of antagonism and mutual distrust. The circumstances that had originally thrown us together had of late been driving us apart. If a certain absence of men had facilitated our union (the departure of her friends, led by Rauschenberg, for Europe in the summer of '64; the hiatus in my own life following the separation from my husband), it was the same absence—aggravated by a sense of social isolation and the suspicion that our intimacy was doomed because it was fugitive, and by the avid pursuit of my friend by a man—that drove a wedge between us. The same could be said of my relationship with my mother, who had had me and become alienated from me under similar conditions of absence. And if my friend had become vulnerable to a male advance, I had one-upped her by forsaking her for God, as it were. Now I had even imagined her dead. Any similarity between my mother and my friend was inconceivable to me at the time. My friend was eleven years younger than me, and her manner and bearing never reminded me of my mother. Yet she was personally aloof like my mother, and she regarded me increasingly with disdain as my own bad feelings about myself emerged in the wake of our romance. Our union was belied by mutual idealization (always the basis for disappointment) and the assumption of difference or complementariness. I liked to imagine I was different from my mother; but our liabilities and assets were ever interchangeable: either she was better and she was right about me, or I was better and she was wrong about me, and vice versa. (The illusion of difference was sustained by style, making it ever possible to overlook substance.) In the case of my friend, I took the ancillary position; but clearly I had undertaken to overthrow her, and by proxy of course my mother. The fire in our loft that June was one clue to the fury that lay anterior to our alliance.

Later I vividly recalled my friend standing by the stove, just before she turned on the gas that caused the combustion that sent me rocketing off my feet and flying toward the fire escape, smiling at me complicitly, as though she already knew what was in store for me (and us) before she turned it on, and that I was a willing party to it. After all, it was with my knowledge that she turned it on, and we both knew as soon as the accident occurred that neither of us had understood the precautions necessary when using inflammable substances. But since she actually made the move that caused the damage and I was the one in the midst of it (it happened at my feet), I decided she had probably meant to kill me. This was a useful psychological perception for me. It gave me an excuse for trying to get away, a reason I never had when I was simply dying over the threat to our relationship from a young man or as I wallowed in my abject feelings of worthlessness and justified betrayal. But it was only *after* I got away that I registered consciously this fearful image of my friend smiling at the stove. The whole incident, as remembered in a psychological sense, was temporally inverted; that is, I made up a motivation for it after the fact. If at the time it happened I read an unconscious design in it, in my own unconsciousness I acted (to escape) by slowly going crazy, an event already prefigured by my withdrawal from nicotine, and by everything else that led up to that particular agency of change. The life can be seen to stretch behind one with a certain inexorable causality. At stake in my life at that moment were issues of consciousness and control. I had been living, evidently, just at the tip of a large burial mound. Now the contents underneath me had begun to move as a result of some emotional/chemical changes and had overwhelmed and sucked under what small consciousness I possessed. This trip was a dive as well as a flight—a flying sort of dive. Professional divers, like astronauts, go under to retrieve things and explore the past: *reculer pour mieux sauter*. Step back, the better to jump ahead. The past was to loom up ever larger and larger as my future. The mistaken idea that my friend had died was evidently a twisted rationale for leaving her. I simply equated her absence with death. When she woke up and reappeared to join me, the *truly* dead one, she seemed once again, like myself, extremely lively. Absence and death here were also equated with great life. This was an insurrectionary state of affairs, and I wasn't going to get away with it much longer. The last thing I remember in the Church the morning of the 30th was my friend standing at a counter in the kitchen in her rumpled black raincoat, talking on the telephone.

A decision had been made to get back to the city. My friend had called Robert Whitman, who said he would locate a shrink for us to talk to. I didn't know what the plan was, but instinctively I sensed treachery. On the ride back to New York in the car I hurled a clock out the window. The clock was on the dash; I don't know if Jim, who was driving us back, brought it along for the time, or if I had insisted on taking it to represent the system I was missing and would obviously need wherever they were taking me. Within twenty-four hours, certainly, the time would once again mean a lot to me. The other thing I did was nearly black out close to the city somewhere. I had the feeling I was falling out of the car and blacking out or that I was just about to.

Parking on Liberty Street, the three of us ascended the elevator to our loft. We had left the place only forty-eight hours before, but as we re-entered and I looked around, I felt that this was an abandoned ruin. An astronomical period of time seemed to have elapsed since our departure. Two mostly eaten halves of pink grapefruit sat on the kitchen table like relics of Pompeii. I was still wearing my purply blue print madras dress. Who knows what I would have cooked up next, in this new millennium back on Liberty Street, had I been on my own. I had already said good-bye; before we left, the afternoon of the 28th, I had called up a few artists (LaMonte Young, the composer, I remember specifically) to tell them how beautiful I thought their work was—something I never did in my real waking life; I saved my encomiums for my criticism. And I had called up Judson Memorial Church to reserve space and time there for a "midnight lecture"—a lecture I imagined beginning at midnight and continuing indefinitely, perhaps endlessly, into the future. And of course I had given up criticism. Now I was back again, but not in any condition to say hello. At any rate, there was nothing for me to do or think about. Robert Whitman arrived; Jim left to return to Garnersville; and we were soon out the door and back in the car to go to the shrink. Before we left, I imagined that Whitman's wife, Simone, was dead, apparently just because Whitman was there without her. He said she was at the beach, but I thought he was lying and just wanted to save me from the truth. As in the case of my friend, I must have thought that if someone close to me was dead, it meant that I wasn't. Or that if she was dead the way I was, at least I had company. Clearly, Simone was also a kind of double for my friend. A few hours later, when I was dumped at the quarantine and debriefing center, I imagined they were both there somewhere on the premises and even went looking for them—notwithstanding the fact that when I had entered the place, I had left one of them (my friend) downstairs at the reception desk or admissions office. The time was hugely present. The past meant nothing in the usual sense in which we logically infer events of the moment from events just seen or experienced. I didn't make the connections. I was inventing everything to suit my hopes and fears. The terror of my new surroundings would obviously be ameliorated if I found somebody I knew there. That I expected to see one of the people who had just deceived me should indicate how impaired my judgment was.

The way Whitman and my friend got me there, incidentally, was, of course, via the shrink. The shrink we saw was a woman in Greenwich Village somewhere, whom I remember as being larger than average and in her young middle age and having auburn-red hair swept away from her face and perhaps on top of her head. I remember nothing of what was said. I only remember trying to appear normal. I did know I was on trial. But perhaps what I said or did had no bearing on the outcome, which had already been decided by the nature of the visit. It was an emergency appointment after all, and my friends had expressed their concern and perhaps even conveyed an impression of my bizarre behavior. I doubt that we talked longer than ten minutes. After we talked, she conferred briefly with my friends, advising them to remove me to Bellevue. Looking back, I behaved like a lamb being led to slaughter. I offered no resistance at all. I must have been apprehensive, but I had become so preoccupied trying to save myself by making up worlds in my head that I was allowing my body to be moved around. I had left my body behind somewhere. By now things were just happening

Above: Members of the younger generation— Robert Rauschenberg, Alex Hay, Deborah Hay, Lucinda Childs, Robert Morris, Yvonne Rainer, Jill Johnston. *Photo © Al Giese.*

Left: Two "parents" of the sixties avant-garde, John Cage and Merce Cunningham. *Photo © A. Roveri.*

Robert Rauschenberg

Steve Paxton

Robert Morris

Yvonne Rainer

Deborah Hay

Alex Hay. *Photo © Al Giese.*

to it. The huge energy I had was a disembodied force. The separation from my body had occurred at least a week earlier. It's been said by people wise in these matters that the best thing to do upon leaving your body is to make sure you stash it in a safe place. That's good common sense, but it presupposes some control over the process. I had left my body accidentally and was unaware that I had done so. The only model we have for this separation is sleeping and dreaming. In 1965 I was not yet informed about Eastern or yogic disciplines in which people leave their bodies by meditation. Not that such knowledge, should I have had it, would have done me any good. Even yogis sometimes leave their bodies, or fall off the world, by mistake. In 1976 I read an autobiography all about this by an Indian yogi. But not long after my experience of 1965, I read *Black Elk Speaks*, the story of the Native American (born 1863) who left his body in yet a different way: neither by accident, in the psychotic tradition, nor by meditation, in the Eastern tradition, but rather by illness, in a culture which awaits the fruits (dreams) of such occurrences. In Black Elk's case, his body was safe because he was lying in a coma. His state of dreaming (he was only nine years old at the time) was as good as sleeping. And when he recovered, he had the sense to keep his big dream, or "Great Vision," as it was called, to himself, until he came of age and he knew he could tell everybody about it. During 1966 I clung to the story of Black Elk to justify an experience that my own culture condemned. In this, of course, I was quite loose with my analogy, but I was prepared to seize anything to support my case, which had been settled against me the moment I walked into Bellevue. Ironically, the aspect of Black Elk's story that best reflected my own was not apparent to me for years, though I could have read about it in the very first paragraph of the preface to the edition I had.

During the 1880s, when Black Elk was growing up, there was a "Messiah craze" among the desperate Plains Indians. Black Elk clearly identified his Great Vision with the problems of his people. One of the grandfathers, for instance, who appeared to him in his vision said, "My boy, have courage, for my power shall be yours, and you shall need it, for your nation on the earth will have great troubles." Nations and individuals alike create saviors when they're in trouble. Before his illness, Black Elk even heard voices. He said, "I was out playing alone when I heard them. It was like somebody calling me, and I thought it was my mother, but there was nobody there." The displacement endured by Native Americans in the 1800s was enough no doubt to drive them mad, and perhaps Black Elk went mad by certain Western diagnostic criteria; but in the context of his tribe, closer to bicameral civilizations, in which the ego was relatively undeveloped and voices (directives from "above") were considered a sacred trust, his experience was the basis for becoming a medicine man.

The schizophrenic personality is a modern individual thrown back on a tribal (egoless) mentality without a tribe to support it. Delusions are "tribal" entities that modern nations have either relegated to history or reinvested in outstanding individuals. The class aspect of schizophrenia is fascinating and unexplored. If in my own case I belonged to a certain class (adult, white, female, Protestant, artist, middle), the moment I entered Bellevue I was classless, or *sine iuribus civilibus*—without civil rights. My class attributes already included a significant non-status—that is, my legal condition as a fatherless daughter, a condition identified on birth certificates in parts of Europe not so long ago as *non noto*, meaning father unknown. At this moment, as a result of entering a classless state of mind, so to speak, my mother's cover-up for my bastardy came unglued. The State laid hold of me just as surely as if I had been abandoned at birth. For me, the mental hospital became a halfway house between my mother and the world (I had been part of the world in a nominal sense only). Of course mental hospitals are essentially containment, not processing, centers; thus the survival of Bellevue and its reputation became as critical as the necessity of getting away from my mother. The immediate effect of my incarceration was a certain forcible return to my body. Bellevue is not exactly the first place you might think of to stash a body in safety, but there could be no question of its whereabouts once delivered behind locked doors. Anyway, secured in a threatening place, I quickly reflected on my predicament.

6

Captivity

The moment I was admitted to this incredible institution, my body was under assault. The admittance procedure itself promised nothing of the arsenal that lay behind the front office. I talked briefly to a mild-mannered young doctor who asked me how old I was and where I lived and things like that. I had to wait a long time, or what seemed a long time, sitting on a bench with Whitman and my friend in a corridor outside the doctor's office. There I engaged them both in an obsessive, repetitive dialogue about trust. I kept asking each of them in turn if they trusted me and if they thought I trusted them and if they trusted each other. My affect was inappropriately flat, under conditions of fear. The need to believe I would be all right had occluded my ability to perceive the reality in front of me. That belief is of the essence in the delusory phase of a so-called psychotic break. The delusions themselves, of whatever nature, are mobilized to make things appear to be all right once the personality has collapsed. The dialogue I had with my friends was unreal, but not so unreal as the delusions that preceded it. I was trying to say something in code, an SOS to my friends from a ship in distress. I wondered if Bellevue was the best splashdown area. Was this the only "secondary recovery zone" they could locate? Obviously it was. This was the end of the line. I resisted my fears with hopes and trust. I made just one misguided effort to withstand the pressure to land there. I tried to tell the doctor that it was really my friend, sitting outside the office on the bench, who was disturbed. Otherwise I don't know what I said or didn't say to give myself away. Once more I tried to appear normal.

But soon the papers were signed, my friends left, and I was ushered into a sort of decontamination area. The room thus designated contained a couple of big vintage bathtubs and a large black woman in a starched blue uniform. This lady presided over my transition from citizen to inmate. After a bath and a change of clothes to hospital gear, I was officially a paper daughter, one who exists only on paper, a name and a diagnosis —in this case, "chronic undifferentiated schizophrenia."

Bellevue is a charnel house for the living dead. The ghosts that are set to dancing in any full-blown psychosis are here laid to rest. The inmates are ghosts whose dreams have been murdered. I saw a whole family of these apparitions when my attendant unlocked the double doors to the sixth-floor ward and ushered me in. They were women of various ages and backgrounds, but they all looked the same: huddled over themselves sitting at plastic card tables, eyes vacant, hair in wisps and strands or sticking out like matted straw, a deep pallor, the hands visibly doing nothing, imitations of palsy, a Stone Age crew petrified and encapsulated in a time warp, fossils of an unidentified Pleistocene era, refugees who had stumbled somehow into "modern" civilization and lost their way in it. The atmosphere was a haze of gray and yellow gloom. The walls might have been painted back in 1930 when the building was erected but were now an indeterminate color of diluted pee. I had walked into a set from *The Snake Pit*. I felt immediately like a tourist at a freak show; I had never been in a place like this before. Within twelve hours I was assimilated. My trip was over and my ship had plunged into purgatory. I was like a white girl in one of those New England captivity stories of the 1600s. All the attendants were very black and fierce looking; if I ever got out alive, I would never be (considered) the same when I got back home. I wandered down the hall in this sixth-floor ward with one of my captors and started asking for Simone and my friend. I was sure they were there, though I had just left my friend downstairs and had been certain a little earlier that Simone was dead. My captor was perhaps alarmed that I was looking for two people who were not there, and for that or some other reason I was whisked from this floor and transferred to the seventh, the "violent ward" at the top of the building.

Bellevue, the psychiatric building, is an interesting piece of architecture. Situated on the East River between Twenty-eighth and Twenty-ninth Streets, the heavy dark-brick seven-storey structure, seen aerially, has a rectangular belly or center with right-angled U-shaped legs at either end, like a lobster with claws front and back, the male wards in the eastern claws, facing the river, the female wards in the western extremities, facing First Avenue. Until the advent of the neuroleptic drugs in the 1950s, these wards would accommodate ninety-nine patients; now they hold twenty-nine. When I was there in 1965, patients still slept in the corridors. The violent women's ward on the seventh floor consisted of just one-half of the U shape of a floor, so that the entrance faced south into the corridor that ran parallel to the belly of the building and then west as it angled into the leg. It was two sections of corridor, in other words, running at right angles. I remember being sort of rushed through its double doors as if they couldn't get me in there soon enough. Evidently they thought I was capable of anything once they knew that I thought I could find two people on the premises who were concretely not there.

A classic encounter was about to take place: the violent containment of a disoriented but harmless person. The violent ward is a place where violence is done to patients before patients have a chance to do violence themselves, on the grounds that anybody admitted to a place like this is dangerous to himself or herself or to others. But it is also the ward where violence is done to patients who have been made violent by violent containments. For some patients, this means just being locked up. I saw people enter the wards who got scared as soon as the doors locked behind them, then behave as if they were trapped in a burning elevator. The attendants would then punish them for reacting to their environment. For myself, I was scared as soon as I entered the violent ward, where several oversized black attendants in starched white, one of them a man, appeared to be awaiting me. Straight ahead of me down the corridor, possibly thirty feet away and outside the door of the dining room that formed the corner of the two right-angulated corridors comprising the ward, I saw another "family" of female ghosts sitting on benches in faded, rumpled hospital gowns. Like the others, they were staring, their hair hung in wisps and strands or like matted straw, their hands visibly doing nothing, imitations of palsy, et cetera. As I approached them, a huge black attendant right at my elbow, I was rushed suddenly against the wall, pinioned, and shot with a needle full of something I later found out was called paraldehyde. I was very astonished, and even more frightened, and I reacted by letting out a yell that was part fake and part real, the part that was fake being calculated to give my assailants what I thought perhaps they wanted. "What do they want?" flashed through my brain the instant they shot me in the backside with this stuff. "They must want me to yell," thought I, and did forthwith; but momentarily I swooned, and felt faint and gargantuanly thirsty, and fell across the corridor into a water cooler to assuage myself. I was now walking slowly down the leg of the ward, closely accompanied by an attendant, once more looking for Simone and my friend. We stopped outside a thick-looking door with a small, horizontal, rectangular window cut into it at eye level. A pair of eyes peered at me very intensely from behind the glass. My attendant asked me if I wanted to go in there. I said nothing, but instantly the attendant's key was in the lock, the door was opened, and the body that belonged to the eyes that had been peering at me was pulled out and I was thrust inside and the door was slammed and locked behind me.

It was a small room, furnished simply with a dirty, pee-stained mattress. There was a barred window. The walls were grayer, more colorless, and more streaked and smeared and cracked than the walls of the corridors. There were places where the walls had caved in like a plate smashed into wet cement. But

I didn't notice anything except the mattress and the size of the room. Immediately I started hollering my head off. I don't know how long I screamed like that. I was dreadfully thirsty and I screamed for water when I wasn't just screaming. At length an attendant opened the door and threw a paper cup of water at me.

Possibly an hour elapsed, how long I have no idea, when two of these hefty attendants came to fetch me. By then, obviously, they knew they had a mad person on their hands. They gripped my arms on either side of me, hoisted me off the floor, propelled me through the door and down the corridor to the dining room, where I was tied to a bed. At night the dining room doubled as torture chamber; during the day, at visiting hours, it accommodated friends and family members. I was now too petrified to scream. Nor was I so foolish as to try to resist them as they tied me on my back to the bed. However, I did regale them with an obsessive monologue about names; I wanted to know what their names were, and I told them my own name over and over again. I hardly think they felt regaled; one of them never looked at me, and the other glanced at me occasionally with dark contempt, as they roughly and swiftly dispatched the business at hand.

This was the night of August 30, a Monday. My "labor pains" of three days earlier, and my plans for twins in nine months, terminated in a kind of hospital abortion. The issue was a large amount of waste from my kidneys. Having been tied too hastily and insecurely with strips of cloth or bandages, I got loose of my bonds soon after my captors left the room, at which very moment they returned with a straitjacket to finish the job. Now I was so tightly bound, my movement so completely restricted, that I began yelling again at top lung volume, the way I had in the solitary confinement space. I yelled my name over and over and I yelled for water and I simply yelled. I don't know how long I did that, but I know I yelled myself into unconsciousness, from which state I awoke in the early morning hours, at hospital rising time, like a baby, in sheets saturated with urine. I was swaddled in wet warmth inside a straitjacket in a bed next to a black woman who was at least eight months pregnant. She had been there before they brought me in. I remember how black and pregnant she was and how pitifully she moaned. I remember feeling worse for her than for myself. I felt nothing actually about myself, because I was simply reacting like a desperate, trapped animal, trying to free myself by yelling bloody murder. The long night of perhaps two hours was over when I woke up and my captors released me from the jacket and the bed. It was daylight, August 31, and I believe the first thing I did when I walked into the ward was to notice the names of the attendants pinned to their uniforms.

I became obsessed with learning as many names as possible. I learned dozens of names during the three weeks I stayed there: attendants, nurses, doctors, patients, social workers, visitors. The namelessness of my situation was not lost on me. My instinct was that I would do better if I called my captors by name when I wanted anything. I often wanted a match (I had begun smoking again at the Church in Garnersville), which patients were not allowed to have, so I always addressed an attendant by name preceding my requests—an unnecessary formality, no doubt, and even inappropriate, but without it I felt I would be ignored, if not directly punished.

I was in fact punished twice after my brutal initiation to the place; the second punishment arose immediately from the first. I was back on the sixth floor and wandering the corridors as usual, and particularly distraught that there was nothing comfortable on which to lie down to rest (the beds were hauled into the corridors at night, locked in a room during the day), and I made a sort of demonstration by the main office near the double-door entrance by noisily throwing two plastic chairs together for a mock bed, which I showily displayed as unfit by lying down on them in dismembered postures. Instantly I was removed for the second, and last, time to the violent ward on the seventh floor, where I remained for four or five days. On one of these days I wanted to see a doctor, I think because I had not seen one and I associated seeing one with my release from this ward. A doctor, however, was not like a match or a telephone call. A patient could ask for a doctor, but she was not likely to get one, and the request for one was considered out of line even (or especially) if a doctor was clearly on the floor. I might have gotten away with a single request, possibly two—but I was more adamant than that. I was desperate to get out of the ward. So the attendant who appeared to be standing between me and the doctor and who felt harassed by my entreaties just grabbed me under one armpit and propelled me down the corridor to the isolation room and impounded me. I spent about an hour in there; but this time I knew where I was and was reasonably certain I wouldn't be there forever, so I sat still on the edge of the mattress and played with a couple of pennies I had in my pocket until they released me. My heart was in my mouth, to be sure, but there was nothing to do except to wait or pass out. I did finally see a doctor—in fact, several of them at once, when I was called before a sort of review board in a small room in the violent ward and asked some questions, among which I remember only being asked if I knew why I was there. I assumed they meant in the violent ward, not at Bellevue itself, and I responded hesitantly (one hoped at all costs to give a correct answer) that it must have been because of my hapless attempt to create a bed out of two plastic chairs on the sixth floor several days earlier. This satisfied them evidently, and I was remanded to the sixth floor. Certainly I knew by then not to ask for anything except a light or a laxative or to make a phone call. Anything else would be construed as a complaint against the institution—the one exception being an appeal directed against a disorderly fellow patient, an appeal likely to be disregarded or held in contempt. My obsessive use of proper names to ease the way, as I thought, for any request or communication (sometimes I tried to make conversation) was useful no doubt only in reassuring myself—not a minor consideration in a place like this.

One reassurance in naming people was its function as a reality-testing exercise. The moment I got out of the straitjacket

and walked into the ward, I initiated the arduous task of reclaiming my ego. At its simplest, this meant just noticing the
time and relocating myself in space. I found out what streets and
avenues bounded the building and which direction I was facing.
More confounding and demanding was the issue of my identity.
When I saw the middle-aged woman doctor that morning, I tried
to tell her who I was, obviously hoping to impress her enough
to release me. But what was really impressive was how quickly I
remembered I was a critic in these dire conditions. Now that it
didn't matter who I was, I was hard pressed to be *somebody*. By
the time I left Bellevue, in fact, I had vowed to be somebody a
lot more important than I was. I had no idea what that would be
exactly, but at the time I could conceive of nothing better than
fame to save me from my present fate. For this idea I was in-
debted, I believe, to Norman Mailer, whose brief impoundment
at Bellevue in 1960 for stabbing his wife had made a strong
impression on me. The incident was headline news in all the
sleaze rags and the subject of intense gossip among my East
Broadway friends, several of whom had known him and his wife
in New York or Provincetown. The message Mailer got across
was that his artistry and imagination put him above the law. His
wife, though seriously injured, refused to sign a complaint. A
year after the stabbing, he received a suspended sentence, the
headlines reading NORMAN MAILER GOES FREE IN KNIFING CASE.
Since I had not hurt anybody myself and yet was incarcerated a
lot longer, and since I was nobody next to the author of *The
Naked and the Dead*, I naturally concluded that I would do
better to be more famous. Six years later, in 1971, I was seated
next to Mailer himself on the stage at Town Hall for the scandalous public forum on feminism that he moderated. The way I
got there was by exploiting the discoveries I had made about
myself while crazy, becoming, in a sense, what "crime had made
of me," as Sartre said of Genet. Though I never liked Mailer or
his writing, his outrageousness was an example that entered my
own gestalt during the sixties. Moreover, the very vehicle of my
fame, the *Village Voice*, was partially owned by Mailer, who

had founded the paper in 1955 along with Dan Wolf and Ed Fancher. During 1956 Mailer briefly wrote a column of outrage in the paper, in opposition to his more conservative co-owners. At Town Hall in 1971, Mailer, who I could only suppose abhorred me personally (if not because of his attack on feminism, then because he was rude to me whenever I saw him), introduced me as "the master of free association of the *Village Voice*." This was a certain moment for me. It telescoped six years and signified an accomplishment that perhaps only I could appreciate. Between '65 and '69 I lost my mind three times, furthering my resolve after each episode to strengthen my ego. While it gradually dawned on me that my best protection was not necessarily fame or fortune but a sense of my own worth, in August 1965 the small worth I felt I had depended utterly on my position as a critic—on how I viewed myself through others' views of me through that position. Thus when I woke up in Bellevue without civil rights, having myself already abrogated any claim to position, I quickly reverted and tried to tell the doctor that I was somebody after all. I remember how meekly and hesitantly I made my testimonial. I knew that if I was really somebody I wouldn't be there—and that it didn't matter what I said anyway, since I was now just a common prisoner. But it did mean that I saw no choice but to re-enter the world, which knew me as a critic.

In reality there was hardly a break in my career at all. The break occurred mainly in my head that last week in August. There were perhaps two issues in which no column appeared, the weeks of September 2 and September 9. I was in Bellevue from August 30 until September 23, and on September 16 a column appeared that I wrote in the wards. It may seem extraordinary that a newspaper would print a column directly out of a mental slammer, but at that time the *Voice* was still an "underground" rag; it thrived on countercultural material, it was barely solvent, it paid ten dollars per column, and I was a regular contributor long before it paid anybody. Even so, within a few weeks of my incarceration the paper expressed concern over my ability to continue as a critic. My editor actually asked me on the phone if I might recommend a dance critic; it was not their intention to fire me necessarily, though they hoped perhaps that I would stop on my own. Anyway, I in turn expressed so much anxiety that the appearance of my column September 16 was followed up with a kind of bonus check for one hundred dollars.

The column I wrote was called "Critics' Critics," a very curious little complaint, as the title implies, about the lot of critics. It was the first thing I had ever made up that was not a review of a concert, art show, book, or Happening. I said, in effect, that I resented my authority, that criticism wore me out, that I intended in the future to criticize anything ("the constellations if that's what I happen to be looking at") and to be an artist, a writer ("if that's what I'm doing when I get to the typewriter and decide that I like something well enough to say what I think it's all about"), and that I thought dancers should write more about their own work, the way painters and sculptors did. Also I hailed an infamous piece of criticism by Louis Horst, a blank column in the *Dance Observer* about a Paul Taylor concert in '57 or '58, as "a model for the criticism of the future." This may have been what gave my editor the idea that they should look for another dance critic. It did read something like a manifesto. And in fact it forecast the future rather accurately. In the end, I heeded the "voice" that had ordered me to give up criticism, though I went through several modifications of my job to get there. (Or, instead of giving up criticism per se, I turned it into something else.) The column I wrote at Bellevue was remarkable more for its presence of mind than for anything it said. I don't know how I managed to write so syntactically so quickly after blowing a main fuse. I was certainly unable to read; one word on a page captured my full attention, its capacity for association by itself superseding its dependent function in a sentence. But by September 10 or 11, presumably about the time I wrote the piece, though still deluded and autochthonous, I had laid claim to reality again.

For a while I occupied both worlds, the one I had left and the one I had made up, the latter becoming increasingly circumstantial. For example, instead of casting people in a creation play, as I did at the Church in Garnersville, I simply confused the identities of the people around me in the roles they already had. I thought patients were doctors or nurses, and doctors or nurses were patients, and visitors were patients or doctors or nurses in various permutations. Confusing patients with non-patients served the purpose, I assume, of persuading myself that I was perhaps there by some misunderstanding and could be sprung at any moment by an infiltrator and/or impostor. I never thought I was anything but a patient myself, but of course I was incredulous over my position.

Appropriately, the patient I came to know best there said she was a grandniece of Albert Schweitzer. Her name, she said, was Susan Elaine Schweitzer. She was the one who had peered so intensely at me from behind the small rectangular piece of glass in the door of the isolation room the night I was hauled up to the violent ward. She may well have been Albert Schweitzer's grandniece (not the most common sort of identity to delude), but she was also crazy in a way similar to myself, a similarity I sensed strongly but never tried to corroborate. In any case, the Schweitzer connection seems significant in retrospect. I too was in a jungle, which I survived by "saving" the people who lived in it. I did a lot of saving the three weeks I spent there. Again, the grand idea I had conceived at the Church of "saving the world" had become circumstantial. Here was my first chance to put it into practice. I listened to people, and sympathized with them, and collected their drawings, and tried to keep or help them out of trouble. I had a "savior" mannerism peculiar to my hospital sojourn. Walking the corridors in my Thorazine trance, holding my belongings in a bag in my right hand, I let my left hand, held waist-high, dangle at the wrist like a broken wing. Saving people was simply a way of relating to them and thus of re-entering the world of mutuality. But it also set me apart from the institution, which I viewed without qualification as a place to get away from. By perceiving myself as a savior or helper, I distanced myself from the place to some extent. In this way, perhaps, I even imagined I was the "true" doctor, in lieu of any who were there to really help—a conclusion that would be foregone from the observation that it was clearly the institution itself, of which the doctors were an integral part, that put these people in the position of requiring help in the first place. I sought in vain while I was there to discover any good reason why these people happened to be locked up. This is not to say that any or most or indeed all of them didn't need help, if only to learn how to stay out of places like this. Obviously help would be very hard to find in a place devoid of life's basic amenities. Nobody would expect to find help where problems are actually created. One generally associates help with being freed from something, not with being imprisoned. Such prisons may "free" people from the stresses of life, but the cost of this relief can be much greater than any problems that were thought to necessitate it.

This is a well-known conundrum, and one that plagues all penal institutions, including many types of schools and most nursing homes, or at least casts great doubt over their necessity and effectiveness in the public mind. As soon as an institution is established, it requires a certain quota of inmates to sustain its existence. Many inmates of mental hospitals oblige this requirement by accepting the definition of them made by those in charge. The percentage of recidivists, and of those who never emerge after a first admission, is always high. A very small element, like myself, refuses to believe the sentence imposed on them. Possibly in my own case I was too old, too rebellious, and too established in a profession. Even so, I was back the following year; my career for a period of time seemed very much in question; my social status for a long while afterwards approached zero; and since then a number of my life moves have been motivated by nothing more than a fear of entrapment by this particular type of institution.

I often wondered what happened to Susan Elaine Schweitzer —and to a woman called Pam, who was about twenty-three and was admitted one day because she confessed to having yelled in a restaurant. Pam thought Bellevue was a clinic where a sympathetic doctor might advise her. Due to a misunderstanding, a naive citizen had become part of the rations that feed one of our institutional monsters. The rations I saw at Bellevue were a cross section of the least privileged variety of this "food." Poor black women, old abandoned women, and middle-class white women of disadvantaged circumstances, retarded or deprived or outcast for various reasons, made up the quota the three weeks I belonged to it.

At Mt. Sinai, where I spent the next thirty-three days, the demographics were significantly upgraded. A good portion of the Bellevue feed goes on to state hospitals, which are the intestines to the mouths and stomachs of the admittance depots, city hospitals such as Bellevue. The Bellevue staff take it for granted that their patients will be digested by the state hospital system. My medical record abstract from Bellevue included the statement that I "improved somewhat but [was] still in need of state hospital care." It went on to note that I was "discharged in the custody of friend to go to Mt. Sinai Hospital." The lore of Bellevue is steeped in threats of the state hospital as its natural terminus, along with the more immediate threats of shock treatment, violent containment, increased drug dosage, and even lobotomy (which had been waning in recent years). For myself, I felt threatened by the possibility of fire and by being at the mercy of attendants with fistfuls of keys. I felt continually threatened also by most of the other patients, who no doubt felt similarly threatened. The weekends were especially bad, because the doctors and nurses were off duty and their lackeys, the attendants, had full rein.

The threat of other patients was both general and specific: in general, the others were as threatened as I was by the machinery of the hospital, thus equally prone to unpredictable acts or reactions; and they were mostly not the kind of people to whom I had ever lived in any proximity. In fact, quite a few of them reminded me of the black women in Harlem hanging out of their

windows whom I had regarded as *National Geographic* Zulus
when I watched them flash by from train windows twenty years
earlier en route to boarding school or Grand Central Station,
pressing my face to the dirty glass, transfixed by their difference.
Now I was sharing a "bedroom" with them in the corridors of
Bellevue. More specifically, the threat of other patients was due
to their bizarre behavior, which was not necessarily more bizarre
than the behavior of my art-world friends but which, unfortunately for them, was not called art or excused on grounds that
they were different from society to begin with because they were
artists or assimilated and understood by other strange people such
as fellow artists. Some of this bizarre behavior in the hospital
was quite inventive indeed. One woman busied herself setting
and unsetting the top of a card table in the "recreation room"
with a few pieces of silverware she carried around with her.
(This room contained a couple of card tables, a few benches, a
TV set, and a Ping-Pong table.) Another woman, who happened to be quite old, utilized the mattresses, when they were
out, and other hiding places, to stash little packages of junk or
waste that she found—string, paper, hairpins, Kotex, cigarette
butts. She tied them up and hid them, then "found" them and
untied them and possibly redistributed the contents and collected them again to tie them up and hide them . . . and so forth.
I believe she was the woman who thought Bellevue was a
country or a territory squashed somehow between Poland and
Russia. If so, I suppose she was "packing" to go there and "un-
packing" when she arrived, going back and forth between here
and there, as it were. She might also have been hiding "valu-
ables" in preparation for exile. This is not a bad idea when you
go to a place like Bellevue; since you are civilly dead, friends,
strangers, or relatives often feel free to plunder belongings left
behind and intestate. At the hospital itself, belongings had to be
carried around on one's person at all times. Clothes, jewelry,
and wallets were kept by the hospital somewhere in safe deposit.

The threat of other patients was heightened by the total absence of privacy. Even the bathroom and the toilets were with-

out doors, and the shower rooms were communal and supervised by attendants. Exposure is structural in the penal institution, as well as thematic in madness. Vestiges of a time when mad people were held like animals, naked and in chains, were much in evidence at Bellevue. Confinement itself suggests the freedom to exist in the raw. I'm not saying that any of the patients were running around naked; if they had done so, in fact, they would have been swiftly contained. But I did observe two or three patients exposing themselves in the manner associated with "perverts"—and I did see some naked action involving patients and staff that looked alarmingly zoographic and infernal. These were fast clips, and my mind sees them now like flares in the dark, vividly etched and as quickly extinguished, cut off from the penumbra linking them to the environment, perceived completely out of context. It was impossible to tell how they got the way I saw them. I surmised, however, that one of them had disrobed in the isolation room where she had been impounded, because the image she cut in her altogether was framed by the door of that infamous room: held or dragged on either arm by an attendant, sitting in a twisted half-fetal position, both knees swerved to her left, her head and torso turning away to the right and dropped toward her heels. I also saw through the door of a big bathroom of tubs (tubs so recently used for the infamous ice-pack treatments) a large young woman lying belly-up like a floating dead whale, being "bathed" and taunted by the expected pair of black attendants.

No other image from Bellevue was so threatening and disconcerting—unless it was the woeful sight of a thin, dark-haired, middle-aged woman who drooled and was partially paralyzed and was barely able to move. I had, and still have, no idea why she couldn't move—or why she was in custody in the psychiatric ward at Bellevue at all, when her condition was so clearly physical, no matter its assumed emotional origins. Perhaps the most threatening aspect of this lady was that I couldn't do anything for her. She was in any case, I realized later, a reminder that the psychiatric hospital is still, after several centuries, a catch-all for various sorts of misfits: the dispossessed, the unemployed, the ill or hungry, the self-abused, the suicidal or depressed, the immoral, the criminal, the homosexual, the eccentric and the foolish—as well as the genuinely demented, if there is such a thing. For all I knew, this woman who was drooling and half-paralyzed had walked in as physically fit as I was and had since had an adverse reaction to drugs or shock treatment, if not simply to the fact of being there. I know I must have looked dramatically different from the way I looked before I got there—a difference that in my case was perhaps for the better.

After a few days of Thorazine, the king of the phenothiazine group of drugs, which belongs to the great family of so-called antipsychotic, or neuroleptic, or psychotropic, drugs developed in the 1950s (of which there are at present writing perhaps twenty), I would have looked decidedly duller than I did before taking them. If I say I looked "better," I mean I was no longer so dangerously intense. I was on four hundred milligrams of Thorazine daily, a medium-high dosage. The neuroleptics have sedative properties but are not sleep inducing and not to be confused with the tranquilizers such as Valium, Librium, or Miltown. The way they are said to work is by blocking a particular neurochemical called dopamine which has been most implicated in schizophrenia. Within days, if not hours, the speed of my chemistry was arrested. At the time, while I chafed under imprisonment and vowed to get back at the world, I was led to believe that Thorazine probably saved my life. Later I became even more convinced that a life saved by Thorazine in a mental hospital was not particularly worth living. The following year, still believing in Thorazine, I tried to pre-empt the hospital by acquiring the drug and taking it in self-prescribed doses while I remained at large. Finally, I wondered if it wasn't possible to get through one of these experiences alive and intact without the intercession of drugs, and I had the opportunity to find out in 1969. Drugs as potent as Thorazine (I called it a "thunderous metal," imagining the word was derived from "zinc" and "Thor"), which are linked with "psychosis," are not the sort of drugs readily dispensed outside the hospitals. If you are thought to need antipsychotic drugs, you are thought to need the hospitals.

A number of patients, unlike myself, resisted the drugs prescribed them, either pretending to take them while hiding them in a cheek or under the tongue, or flat-out refusing them, thus inviting reprisals, most immediately the forced hypodermic injection. Most patients were inordinately, if understandably, preoccupied with the kind and amount of drugs they were taking. I may have been one of the very few for whom the neuroleptic drug, used so indiscriminately in the mental hospital, made any sense, given the fact that it was developed to stop precisely the sort of runaway chemistry that had afflicted me but which claims just a small percentage of mental patients. Lots of "mental patients" covet the hospital, their sole refuge in a hostile world, and the drugs serve only to disorient and incapacitate them. But drugs have become a fixture of the mental hospital, as intrinsic to them as, say, gas and oil are to a car. A mental patient can actually be defined as somebody who needs drugs to stay alive and get from one place to another. I knew one young woman at St. Vincent's Hospital, in 1966, who had been in and out of these places since she was eighteen (she was twenty-six when I met her), who warred continually with the hospital authorities over the drugs they gave her and had quite a few ugly-looking scars from wrist to elbow from suicide attempts. Once she had slashed herself and drawn blood, a special nurse or attendant was assigned to watch her constantly, the drugs were enforced without question, shock treatments were initiated, her weight increased dramatically (a side effect of the neuroleptics), and she turned into a vegetable and at length was shipped off to Rockland County State Hospital. I assume this cycle had been repeated a number of times since she was eighteen. About seven years after I knew her, I saw her in Washington Square Park; she told me she had not been in the hospital system for several years and that she lived in a walk-up in the Village and was teaching karate. I bumped into her several times, but I haven't seen her since 1978. After spending two and a half months in St. Vincent's in 1966, I could understand myself the institutional security and protection that drew people back into the hospital fold, despite the abuse and threats and destruction of self that went with it—something I had forgotten about after leaving boarding school and college, those more benign buffer zones between childhood and the real world. But in 1965, I managed to escape the hospitals before I had that chance to feel comfortably institutionalized.

7

Sleep

On September 22, three weeks and two days after my admittance to Bellevue, the two friends who brought me there came to take me uptown to Mt. Sinai, a voluntary hospital with several psychiatric wards on Ninety-first Street and Lexington Avenue. This was arranged through a doctor associated with Mt. Sinai, Hank Edelheit. Hank's wife, Marty, was an artist and a friend of Bob Whitman's and the Segals and a number of other artists I knew.

It would not have been my mother's choice to send me to a private hospital, but under pressure from my intimate friend she contributed some money toward the bills there. Later she balked when my friend asked her to pay the bills for a private psychiatrist in whose care I was released from Mt. Sinai, saying that she had not "authorized" such treatment and therefore would not pay for it. She wrote to my friend: "Although I appreciate your efforts for Jill, you should understand that my income is limited and that any care you arrange for Jill without my prior approval is your own responsibility." Among my mother's effects after she died I found three canceled checks made out to my friend, dated September, November, and December '65 and totaling $1130, along with one hostile exchange of letters between them.

My mother was sixty-four at the time, and she lived in the country in Millerton, New York, where she worked as a relief nurse on private duty and in hospitals. She made one trip to Bellevue to see me, of which I remember nothing except for her passivity and apparent lack of interest in the situation, and her showing me some snapshots of my children that she had taken that summer in the country. The attitude toward my mother that I picked up from friends was that my current disaster was all her fault, and I think she shared that view, though she was willing to let me go, and she had long passed an age or a time when she might have felt there was anything she could do about it. My new family of artists, for the moment at least, seemed to indicate that I was a lot more valuable to them than to her. Indeed, I had been serving their interests for six or seven years, while all I had done for my mother was to give her a couple of grandchildren, a gift she found it convenient to consider a burden, in light of the fact that she judged me to be unfit and irresponsible. She certainly loved having them, and she tried to get them whenever she could from me or my ex-husband and his new wife, but she thought of herself more as a rescuer (in a plot with villains and victims and such) than as a family participant.

Sometime in the early sixties I had passed up the one opportunity I had to offer my mother a gift with the potential to move our relationship positively. Knowing that I was an art critic, and being a serious Sunday watercolorist herself, one afternoon in the country she trotted out her watercolors for my inspection. I found them beneath my consideration. Alas, I had no appreciation at that time for the work of amateurs, much less an amateur who was my mother. But my mother, for her part, had made no effort to dissolve my resistance by any sign that she appreciated me as an art critic. Her belated and expansive gesture of approval that July of '65, after my friend Marilyn told her she should be proud of me, was immediately followed, as I've described, by a revulsion on my part against being a critic. If my revulsion had anything to do with her sudden approval, it surely illustrates the resourcefulness of a powerful adversary. Or should I say ally? For perhaps she instinctively computed Marilyn's assessment of my career as a threat to my stability. Her demonstration—surprising me when I visited her by an exhibition of framed photos of me as a baby and as a child—was sufficiently contrived, excessive, inappropriate, and unparalleled to raise suspicions over her motives, had I been suspicious. At face value, I was being encouraged, yet her encouragement exceeded the limits of my actual accomplishment, and it looked backward instead of ahead, as though to say that I was great all right, but only as she remembered me—i.e., as a baby.

After August 1965 I saw her as a menace to my well-being and put more and more distance between us, until by '67 I ceased seeing her for eight full years, excepting one brief visit that lasted five minutes. We had been alienated for a long time; the difference now was that I knew it and acknowledged it and made her responsible for it. Even so, I continued feeling responsible myself, however unconsciously, for her refusal to accept me. In my new life, I resumed acting out this position, incurring a full share of the wages of guilt and remorse; but I added an externalized enemy in the form of society (eventually becoming political) and treacherous friends or opponents in the art world. So once again I let my mother off the hook, in the sense that I buried our conflict by not seeing her or dealing with it. Yet in its updated version, in which I could imagine that I had disposed of it simply by making it even more invisible than it had been and by taking on the world in her stead, I was able to bypass the role (of critic) that my mother had unwittingly helped me to overthrow and to advance to an even more dangerously independent position. I had, after all, failed as *her* critic, both socially and artistically, and she was the measure of all my undertakings. By negating my mother's paintings, which represented her expression of independence apart from the life she had forged independent of a man (a life that had not freed her creativity), I supported her primary feeling that my own work was at the expense of my family, thus justifying *her* failure to be better at painting or to take it more seriously. But since I had lost my family anyway, or what remained of it, I became free to do more childish, i.e., independent, work. I also lost my art family, which made me feel like not being their critic anymore, in turn leading to the same outcome. Criticism for me had been nearly synonymous with support, a stance that crumbled in the wake of my imprisonment. But the artists who interned me also liberated me, and for a while it seemed as if they had called me in good faith back to my former life.

That feeling collapsed the moment my friend left me by walking out of our Liberty Street loft only three weeks after my release from Mt. Sinai. This time she left "for good," and I cared very much. Emerging from the hospital, I had tremendous illusions about the future. I had no particular projections; I was no longer deluded, and not yet acquainted with the idea of making plans, but the future just seemed very bright. Regardless of official opinion, well documented in the medical abstracts and persuasively conveyed to my friends, I clung to the belief that my experience had been extraordinary and apocalyptic. A clue to my intransigence lay in several sentences of the Mt. Sinai abstract, or "final summary," under the seventh and last section of the report:

The patient became grandiose, demanding many extra privileges. Her behavior on the ward was somewhat seclusive; she did not make friends with any of the patients, rather kept to herself, and in group mimicked the group leader, posing enigmatic questions to the other patients. She refused medication and threatened to sign out against medical advice on many occasions. This behavior arose whenever it was attempted on the part of the therapist to point out to her that she might possibly have an emotional illness. She employed the mechanisms of denial and of association to an extreme degree and felt threatened by any attempt to point this out to her. It was attempted to have the chief resident state the rules of the hospital to her so that she might feel less threatened by me as her therapist, but she remained essentially unapproachable, and we had to consider whether or not her provocative behavior was really a plea for stringent control, and if so, consider the overwhelming threat which such controls posed to her masculine identification.

The report concluded:

> The patient gradually became less provocative and anxious and it was felt that she might do well outside the hospital in private psychotherapy. She was discharged after having seen a Dr. Rosa Klein, with whom she was to undertake therapy. She remained on 400 mgs/day for the duration of her hospitalization.

My stay at Mt. Sinai lasted exactly thirty-three days. I kept taking those 400 mgs/day of Thorazine after leaving the hospital, but only for three weeks, until my friend left, at which time I simply went to sleep. I was very agitated about her departure, even trying to stop her (contrasted with that day two months earlier when I cheerfully let her go), and I brooded and complained about it for months, and at least twice expressed my feelings violently (once I poured a drink full of ice cubes down her back when I saw her at a party; another time I broke and entered her new residence, a loft building on Church Street, where she went to live with the young painter who had so avidly pursued her during the previous year). But my essential reaction to this grave turn of events was to go to sleep. The day she left, my big dream came to its unauthorized end. Somehow, just because she had still been there and had gone to so much trouble to sustain me in the hospitals (as well as help liberate me from them) and appeared to be resuming her life with me, I imagined she felt the same way I did about my experience, or at the least had overlooked it, or regarded it as a routine break, like any illness or enforced separation. We never talked about it, so I was free to imagine anything. As usual, I never tried to fathom what lay behind the enigma of her crystal-cameo-Cleopatra facade. I certainly must have assumed that I deserved her protection after my ordeal, for which she shared some of the responsibility. It never occurred to me that she might be scared, not to mention angry and guilty. I never consciously registered people's feelings unless they were very obviously and overtly angry or sad, or thought about them in any way other than stereotypically. People were stuck with one or two feelings for life. They were either happy and well off or unhappy and desperate. They never went *through* anything. While my friend seemed neither happy nor desperate, she comfortably eluded any definition at all by virtue of her great control.

On the one occasion I can remember witnessing her facade crumble significantly (long before the events of August), when she came home one day in a state and sat in a chair crying, having lost a dance studio or having failed to obtain one, or something, I responded coldly and judgmentally, as if she were a mother who should never display her vulnerabilities to a child. Anyway, I did assume that since she was beautiful and educated and from a good American family, and successful at dancing, that she was okay, notwithstanding any problems I suspected she had. But she hardly felt okay herself, despite her fine attributes; and as a result of my crack-up in August—and in fact, more specifically, through my own agency—she went to see a shrink for the first time. That happened the day she left the loft with a suitcase and called me up from a phone booth to tell me she felt like jumping off a bridge, and our friend Laura made an emergency appointment for her to see Laura's shrink. Now two long months had passed, and she had been through some changes about which I knew nothing, one of them clearly involving a decision to run away. The first opportunity to do so was provided by some objection I made to a date she had with a new friend and admirer, though this new friend and admirer was not a romantic interest. One of my big illusions upon leaving the hospital was that my friend would stand by me, if not indefinitely, at least until my crisis had dissipated and my new life had taken shape. But the very essence of my crisis was its function of deliverance from my mother, for whom any intimate relationship of mine at that point would have been a surrogate. At the same time, a new life is a tentative business, and maternal care, in whatever form, is considered imperative to sustain it. During the next few months, sleep became my most reliable companion.

Apart from sleep, I relied on my upstairs neighbors, Les and Atsuko; my friend Charlotte, who lived on East Broadway with her two children; and Dr. Rosa Klein, the shrink who had accepted the responsibility of my early release from Mt. Sinai— none of whom was very reassuring. Charlotte was always kind enough to let me sit around her apartment and complain bitterly, and she always supported my writing, but her smart observations that my intimate friend had left me because she had to save herself were wasted on me. Les Levine was a consistent sort of taskmaster, believing that work cures all, urging me to get out of bed and prove that I still existed by writing something (between October 21 and the end of that year I wrote only four pieces for the paper), even soliciting a magazine called *Canadian Art* to commission an article for me to write about him. But his own obvious industriousness and his manner of pumping himself up unnerved and discouraged me; and in the end, when I did finally get out of bed and mobilize myself, he competed with me instead of crediting me with anything. Atsuko always managed to convey through her Oriental inscrutability that I would be all right if I could just wear the proper clothes and look like a regular girl. Dr. Klein was a birdlike woman, small and delicate yet tough and wiry, very tan, in her early fifties, I judged, her hair graying but in a young style of bob and bangs, her apartment filled with Mexican decor and artifacts, her background Bavarian, a fleer from the Nazis in 1938. I remember her saying something Jungian that I liked after I had described some aspects of my "trip." Her filamentlike, tan, wiry fingers were interlaced in front of her chest, elbows resting on the arms of her chair, body in repose yet seemingly poised for flight, her glance sidelong and coy, her voice shy and tentative, a little girl's voice in an older lady's visage. She said, "It sounds like the creation of the world in seven days." Had I been delud-

ing the slightest bit, I would have seized the remark and run
with it. Anyway, it was the only thing I remember her saying that
I liked. And I'm sure she said it sometime during those first three
weeks after I left the hospital and before my friend abandoned
me, when I felt so optimistic, almost elated, about the future.
When my friend walked out and I went to sleep, I had nothing
to say to Dr. Klein except that I was empty and depressed, and
after she had heard enough of that, she suggested the classic
modern cure for depression: shock treatment. That was the end
of my visits to Dr. Klein. I had never had any luck with these
people and had not expected it now. The following August Dr.
Klein reappeared in my life with a vengeance when my friends
pressed her into service as the "shrink of appeal" in my updated
astronautical crisis. In the meantime, I stayed in bed more or
less until May, when I was invited to make my first trip to the
West Coast.

In the geographical sense, I had traveled very little in my
thirty-six years, not counting the first two years of my life abroad
with my mother, which I didn't remember. I had been holed up
in New York since 1953, first as a poor dancer, then as a poor
wife, mother, and writer. I had left the country once, a madcap
two-day trip to Cuba to try to obtain an abortion, and had been
as far south as South Carolina and as far west as Minnesota. As
a child, at eight, I had spent a winter in Florida with my grandmother. In the early sixties, it seemed like a big deal to go to
Provincetown or Boston or Richmond or Philadelphia. A trip to
Buffalo by airplane in 1964 was high adventure indeed. Yet I
had no great desire to travel, and didn't think I was missing
anything by being so New York bound. My New York life was
exciting enough, even before I became a mental astronaut. As
for England, the country of my birth and my father, it was
unthinkable to me to visit a place where my mother had always
warned me I would be treated badly. It did occur to me, however, sometime after '65, that the artists whom I had so dili-
gently and enthusiastically helped to make successful were
running off to interesting, exotic places and leaving me behind.

Possibly I got that feeling after my first trip to the West Coast that May of '66.

The trip was organized by Steve Paxton, and it was under Bob Rauschenberg's auspices, at the invitation of the Los Angeles County Museum. Jim Elliott, the curator at the Museum, arranged to have Rauschenberg and friends do a series of performances there. Normally I was not one of these "friends"; I had organized, or produced, concerts myself, and Steve and Rauschenberg had appeared in them, but this was the first reciprocal occasion. The reasons, I suppose, were guilt, loyalty, and saviorship. Rauschenberg was well known for his loyalty, regardless of the past, his feelings, and even his lack of personal interest. Evidently I was close enough to his scene, the inner Judson circle at that point, to rouse some sense of responsibility. Shared guilt is usually a feature in any family network. What is perceived to have been done to one may be redeemed somehow by another—not that a simple trip in this case could make up for the loss and injustice I continued to feel. Nonetheless, it got me out of bed, and it signaled the end of my life on Liberty Street. By coincidence, the city's scheduled takeover of Liberty Street to make way for the World Trade Center was set for May. While I was gone, Les Levine found another loft building for both of us on the Bowery.

Before I left, I attended two painful meetings about the trip. At the end of one, at my loft, Steve rose and murmured "Let's get out of here," as if my place had chicken pox. It was certainly huge and empty, and its sole occupant deathly silent. At the other meeting, at Steve's and Rauschenberg's loft, I was just as silent and had the distinct feeling of being out of place, as if my presence on the junket was to make up for something, rather than for who I was or any contribution I might make. I was in fact making up for my ex-friend, now living with her painter and unable to go, and Yvonne Rainer, a most valued member of these vanguard expeditions, also unable to go. Anyway, I accepted the tacit definition of my rank and focused on trying not to embarrass myself further while in Los Angeles by turning in a creditable performance. Yet I defended myself the moment I arrived there when Rauschenberg, by way of saying hello, pounced on me for some criticism of mine that I don't remember about Deborah Hay. I told him instantly to bug off. I said I had just recently cracked up and hoped not to do so again, as if criticism of my criticism had everything to do with it. I was very grateful afterwards when our host Jim Elliott, whom I had never met before, put his arm around me as we walked along a boardwalk from some place to another. It was the friendliest gesture I remember there.

The party included, besides Steve and Rauschenberg and myself, Trisha Brown and Alex and Deborah Hay. We stayed at Jim's place, which was a circular-shaped apartment above the merry-go-round on the Santa Monica pier. The best time I had was riding some bumper cars in an amusement park along the pier and trying to immobilize my colleagues. I didn't do so well at some endless games of multiple solitaire, because Deborah was quicker than I was. I enjoyed roller skating with Rauschenberg in a huge indoor rink that we had to ourselves, rented by the Museum for Rauschenberg's performance. Cruising around the rink, we had the feeling that on skates we could make a good team. Judith, who was living with Jim and just about to marry him, told me years later that she was sure I didn't take off my coat for three days, that the collar was turned up and she could hardly see me. I remember buying a dumb blue cotton skirt and matching bolero jacket to wear in Steve's performance, in which we walked through a labyrinth of a huge inflated clear plastic tunnel, and otherwise carried some tall wooden sticks around that looked like giant lollipops. Rauschenberg at that time liked to skate around these roller rinks with a parachute strapped to his back, giving the impression, I suppose he hoped, of a great American flying eagle. He also liked having tortoises wander around in the dark with flashlights strapped to their shells. The Museum paid for all this, plus air fare for the six of us, board and entertainment for three weeks, and a fee of four hundred dollars apiece, quite a large sum to me.

The performance I turned in at the Museum was better than anything I had done in this vein to date. The vein was something I called a lecture-event, combining action tableaux with tapes of my voice reading passages about art or fragments of conversation or quotes or newspaper items. This was the first one I had done in a year. The last had not been particularly edifying. I had asked Robert Morris to construct a shaky two-by-four structure during the event, which would come tumbling down with me at the end when I hung all my weight on it. This time I asked Steve to help me out by moving sixty Bekins storage boxes around and painting me phosphorescent pink at the end. The effect was dramatically different. The curtain opened on these sixty Bekins storage boxes piled up in a great pyramidic jumble upstage. While Steve moved them one by one downstage, placing one on top of another to form six tall columns straight across the apron, I sat on a dolly that moved back and forth from wing to wing on pulleys, putting on clothes. I started in a slip and finished very overstuffed in a black slicker and slicker hat and boots. As the tape of my voice reading fragments of quotes (interspersed with shouted marching commands) ended, I got off the dolly in all these clothes topped by the slicker outfit and walked downstage to stand in front of the columns of boxes. In a blackout Steve painted me phosphorescent pink (a few of the boxes also glowed where Steve slapped some paint on the parts facing the audience), accompanied by the fully amplified sound of bagpipes, which lasted about three minutes. I never found out what anybody else thought about the event; at the time I myself just thought it was a lot better organized than anything of this nature I had done to date. I did love glowing in the dark to the huge sound of the bagpipes, but the subconscious connections of the piece escaped me. As well they might have, for had I known what I was doing, I doubt I would have needed to do it. The month was May, my birth month, nine months after I had imagined conceiving twins; and my collaborator was the very person I had engaged to be the agent of my conception. Otherwise, the British connection was pretty obvious, but I didn't note the similarity between the setting here and that of a piece I did with Robert Morris in '63 when I had Morris pour water from a watering can over my head as I stood in a black slicker in a round tin tub, downstage center, accompanied by a violinist on-stage playing "In an English Country Garden." Bekins storage boxes still mean nothing to me, but I associate lots of clothes with armor, which, I had been told, was something I very much needed.

Anyway, having "risen" in Los Angeles that May of '66, I descended again quickly the moment I landed in New York. My descent was not the result of going back to sleep, though I continued not to do badly on that score, but of walking into my new loft on the Bowery, found by Levine while I was gone. The Bowery itself, strewn with bodies of filthy drunks, decorated by dark rivulets of pee stain, was something new to me. The loft was perhaps an ideal raw space from some point of view—a hundred feet long and twenty-five feet wide—but raw it was, and broken-down as well, an abandoned hulk of a space, its rough brick walls stuck with many coats of dirt-encrusted white-wash, its pressed-tin ceiling rusted and ruptured and uneven in spots, its wooden floor rotted out and gaping in areas, its windows of translucent wired glass caked and barnacled around the sills in layers of paint and dirt: a space last used as a sweat-shop of some sort. Moreover, I was afraid I couldn't afford the rent, which was a hundred dollars a month, higher than anything I had ever paid for a place. I cried for a week, standing in the rotted-out floor as if stranded in a pothole, wondering if this was my final deposition in life.

But crying was better than sleeping at that point, especially since I had so much to do to be able to live there. The first thing I decided to do was divide the space and rent out the front part, facing the Bowery, to an artist, for seventy-five dollars a month. I used the several hundred dollars the city compensated me for moving out of Liberty Street to pay a crew of black plumbers to install sinks, pipes, stove, and shower booth—a job they did in a day. The only convenience that already existed in the loft was a toilet in a closet. I bought the stove, two sinks, and shower booth for a song at a secondhand plumbing-supply store on Seventeenth Street. My plumbers ran pipes the length of the space to connect with the sink I planned to put in the artist's half of the loft. Dividing the space was a problem because I had no idea how to do it myself, and I had no money to pay to have it done. I tried getting Les, who had moved into the loft upstairs (there were only two in this building), to help me, but he was too busy; he didn't want to, anyway, and he thought it would be therapeutic for me to do it myself. It was therapeutic indeed, because I got so frustrated that I used the materials I had bought or borrowed for construction like baseballs or javelins, hurling them furiously into a mounting pile in the center of the loft space. The more noise I made, and the bigger the pile got, the better I felt. The clatter and mess, mixed with my cries and tears, made a very good Happening on the Bowery that day.

After I calmed down, I was ready to tackle dividing my space. I could hammer nails, after all, and saw two-by-fours, and break up plasterboard; I just had to apply myself to measurements and schema and use a little common sense. In the end, I had built a plasterboard wall and two primitive doors and laid down a bunch of big masonite squares to cover up a large part of the rotted-out floor—and was quite proud of my accomplishment. For the walls and ceilings, Thalia Christo, recently separated from the artist now living with my ex-friend, came over to help me spray them white with an industrial spray-painting machine. During the three years I spent there, I had two Japanese artists, first one and then another, renting the front space facing the Bowery, for seventy-five a month. My own rent, therefore, was twenty-five, which helped enable me to continue sleeping and doing very little, at least for the larger part of '66 and '67.

8

Washed Up

During the summer of '66 I grew steadily better, and gradually lighter and lighter, until by the end of August I was in flight once again, a flight identical in some respects to its precursor a year earlier, but with variations in some features, and wider in scope, broader in depth and magnitude. This time I was alone in my own loft; but the same two people lived upstairs, again the only other occupants of the building, and again in the month of June I was busy turning a raw space into a living area. Moreover, that same month I gave up cigarettes, as I had the year before. And my launching pad, big sheets of masonite coated with urethane, was just as glossy as the floor on Liberty Street preceding the Great Fire. A fire, alas, was the only thing I remembered from the previous year that I wished to avoid. Not even the striking act of giving up cigarettes gave me pause. I had not yet made any connection between my flight in '65 and the withdrawal from nicotine. I didn't make that connection until 1969, when I stopped smoking for the third and last time, in October '68, and took flight after the same interval—two months—had passed. The summer of '66, though I was alone, I did arrange to see two people most closely associated with my ex-friend: Thalia, the ex-wife of her new roommate, and the painter Agnes Martin, who had been a good friend of that couple.

I knew Agnes Martin myself; I'd seen her paintings for the first time in '63 and asked *Art News* to send me to her loft to review them. Agnes was fifty-four in 1966, eleven years younger than my mother, the same age as my teacher in college who brought me out when I was twenty (and who had died in '65). During the sixties Agnes was the only older woman in New York I admired. She had several credentials that were important to me, not the least of them a stay of her own at Bellevue, in 1962. Agnes was known to fall into trances; recently she had set sail on a freighter around the world and had been removed from the ship at Bombay and placed in a hospital. Her fiercely critical and independent nature—she was the only woman I knew in the sixties who was immune to "fashion"—was untempered by worldly knowledge, unsubstantiated by intellect, unrelieved by social adaptability. In her own elements—the wilderness, her painting, her mastery of machines, her fearlessness, her sense of purpose, her supernatural understanding of things—she was certainly formidable. She was not a social creature; she lived very much by herself, and even at that time never hesitated to sacrifice the slightest intimation of friendship for the chance to enlighten or unsettle. In the seventies, when she had retreated to live in the desert in New Mexico, and a number of artists made pilgrimages to see her there, she began to think of herself as a kind of artist's guru. She couldn't imagine why people wanted to see her (she, after all, had no use for them) if not to obtain some oracular knowledge. Until '68 Agnes lived in a loft with a skylight on South Street in Manhattan, not far from the Seaman's Institute, where the artists around there liked to have supper for a dollar.

Agnes longed to be climbing mountains or to be off to some frontier or other, and I think her consolation that summer of '66 was a silly little camping trip that she made with me and Thalia one weekend on a river near Haverstraw. I always hated camping, so I know the outing wasn't my idea, and I would never have gone but for the chance to be in the company of Agnes. Here I could commune for a whole weekend with a young woman (Thalia) who felt as jilted as I did and was, I assumed, sympathetic to my loss, and an older woman who seemed to be above it all, who might tell me what to do with my life, and who was highly esteemed by the other minimalist painters in New

York, one of whom had seized my ex–girl friend. I did hope to find out something. I never expected kindness or encouragement. I remember Agnes sitting naked on some rocks in the narrow river there; I wondered if she was attracted to Thalia, and if so, if Thalia would be interested in having an affair with her. I remember how close to the road we were, how tacky the campsite was from any real camping point of view, the great discomfort of sleeping on the ground (the thing I hated most about camping), and being terrified out of sleep by the commotion of a big animal—a deer, Agnes said—leaping over our sleeping bags.

The only conversation I remember having was about Bellevue. I wanted to tell Agnes what had happened to me, and her message to me when I finished was that "it" would happen to me again. A decade later, in the desert in New Mexico, she liked to tell me that the places we ended up in were the places we had chosen to go to. The last time I saw her out there (she lived on a mesa, miles from the nearest one-horse town), she asked me what I was working on, and when I said a book about my father, she nearly shrieked, "What do *you* know about your father?!" "Nothing," I answered immediately—satisfied that that was the right answer. Agnes liked asking momentous questions in a certain competitive spirit. Though she had no reason to believe I did or didn't know anything about my father (not that she cared, or that fathers or my knowledge thereof was even the issue), she was an important witness in 1966 to the birth of the man who became the subject of this book.

This is not to say that she was in a position to identify the birth or its object, only that she belonged to the cast of characters who appeared, or whom I mobilized, at the end of the summer to assist in various stages of the delivery. Like my mother, Agnes was not the most benign person I knew then, but in the midst of my crisis I found a brief role for her that required only positive action. Her reflections on life were biased completely by her judgment that people were not its best exemplars. She saw herself in a vast universe (i.e., desert) where she alone might master its odds and discern its secrets, overcoming the unfortunate handicap of civilization simply by ignoring it. All this of course made her both admirable and unapproachable. I had acquired the habit of approaching her nonetheless, reading any negative assessment she might make of my life as a just and accurate description of it. One day I bravely and foolishly brought her a few short poems I had scratched off in my loft on the Bowery, for a moment imagining that the slack in my criticism might be taken up by the finer art of poetry—a moment quickly dashed when Agnes told me, and rightfully so, that my efforts were nothing but sentimental complaints, immature yearnings for things past, and that I would do best to forget about both the past and poetry. Echoing Agnes in a way, my mother one Sunday in the country told me that if I didn't get a job I'd have to go back to the institutions. The remark Agnes made some years later about my father—"What do *you* know about your father?"—is also apt here in connection with my mother, whose mission in life, it often seemed, had been to place this very question at the center of my existence.

Not unrelated to the pressing question of a father, as I see it now, was the issue of jobs and institutions—either/or, as my mother put it—raised by her that summer. For if jobs represent the world of men, or fathers, institutions (those defined as holding or detainment centers for the unfit) surely denote the world of women, or mothers, in the sense that the care and protection they exemplify, however infamously, hark back to the maturation periods prior to entering the (real) world. Note that my mother didn't mention marriage as an alternative possibility. Even before I married, she never mentioned marriage. What she had originally hoped for me was that I would be contained by a professional institution as well structured as her own, which was nursing; in my case it could have been teaching, had I kept at it. Having declined to teach, having failed at marriage, having just blown, it appeared, the wonderful career that she had so recently discovered I had (through Marilyn), and having been defined as a "chronic undifferentiated schizophrenic," it must have seemed to my mother that the institutions awaited me as surely as she had made certain I had no father. Broadly, two sorts of people have populated prisons and mental hospitals: men who failed at jobs and women who failed to marry or marry well. I qualified in both capacities. The first represented a failure to *be* a man; the second, to be *with* one. My mother, I should note, had the kind of job that made it possible for her to remain insulated from either choice. She didn't have to make it in a man's world or profession, and she could be excused from serving one man by virtue of serving people at large. Altogether, I had done the two things she had avoided: marriage and a man's career. Obviously I was trying to be different from her, and just as obviously I had failed. Or it could be said that I was trying to be both her and the man she should have married—I mean, the woman she wished she could have been had she married the man she wanted to (who else but my father?)—and that this improbable task had involved a case of mistaken identities. These "mistakes" were at last about to begin to be straightened out. Errors as vast, in a number of senses, as those under which I had labored are often corrected only by an enormous magnification of them. The purpose of a "psychosis," in lieu of conventional therapies or other means of enlightenment, is to do just that. But even before that can happen, the life that has been grounded in these errors must be overthrown. That was my condition the summer of 1966. I was beached on the Bowery, shipwrecked in an old sweatshop. I must have looked very unemployed. I was, in fact, doing practically nothing.

From January of 1966 to the end of June I had written no more than six pieces for the paper (*Art News* had let me go when I came out of the hospital back in October). In July I wrote one piece, called "Pickled Alive," and in August one more, an "Interview with Judith Dunn"—paralleling the previous year even in my writing schedule, one in July and one in August, and even down to the character of the pieces. In July the year before, I had chewed up Kenneth King, a new young choreographer on the scene, for "applying vanguard tactics to a moribund expressionism," in a review called "Horizontal Baggage," a reference to the manner in which he had carted a girl off stage at some point. "Pickled Alive" was an equally jaundiced view of both the ballet and the post-Cunningham Judson movement, as I called it. I quoted Khrushchev as saying that when he heard about the ballet, he thought it was something you ate or something you wore. I said that I'd seen Gregory Peck, Mayor Lindsay, and Vice-President Humphrey at Lincoln Center for the opening of American Ballet Theatre and that I found them as interesting as the ballet. And I reinstated Yvonne Rainer as the leading post-Cunningham Judson choreographer, in fact the only one (I made it sound) worth considering. During '66 I assiduously avoided writing about my ex-friend. By contrast, in '65 I wrote about her in no fewer than five of my sixteen pieces. In hindsight I can see that in '65 I made a subtle (perhaps not so subtle, but certainly unconscious) bid to place her above Rainer in the Judson pantheon. I set this up in January when I summarized Judson activities in '64 with two articles, concluding the second one by calling substantial attention to something my then-friend had done back in June when she was my friend-to-be.

Most interesting in reviewing this review are the last four sentences, which a dream analyst might "read" as highly portentous. I had been describing the event, which consisted of an "audience" watching my friend-to-be out on the street from a sixth-floor window as she sat or stood in various locations according to a tape of her voice portraying the areas so designated. I qualified the resulting "theatrical illusion" as "amazing" and concluded both review and roundup of Judson '64 thus: "A woman passing by was caught in the act. She didn't know it and neither did a fire engine which emerged at the last moment. Quite a dramatic fire engine. So, salut, '64, and more rooms with a view in '65." Two months after this event (not the review), we became "friends." A year afterwards, we had a big room (the loft on Liberty Street) with many windows and views. And no less astonishing, it seems to me, than the reference to fire was the note about "a woman . . . caught in the act" who "didn't know it." What woman, what act, and what knowledge? In my review, I meant simply a woman on the street in the act of being seen without knowing it. In August '65, the week I cracked up, at the moment I was engulfed with paranoia, just when I discovered I had traveled out of bounds and didn't know where I was or how to get back, I became intensely aware of, among other things, the people who worked in some offices across the street, seen through my windows and theirs, and imagined that they had been installed there to spy on us and report our "illegal" relationship to the government, or that in the course of their work they had happened to notice us and had been recording our movements for the same purpose. This observation no doubt entered into my calculations when I decided that an escape from the city was imperative. It should be noted, incidentally, that my medical abstracts from Bellevue, Mt. Sinai, and St. Vincent's all included "homosexuality" as a factor in my condition. The St. Vincent's report ('66) went so far as to say that I was "transferred here after spending one month in Bellevue because of bizarre behavior, paranoid ideation, homosexuality." Later during the sixties, when I viewed psychiatry as an arm of the government, as was chic then, I would have felt vindicated, I'm sure, even triumphant perhaps, had I seen this particular sentence in my medical abstract, linking paranoia so closely with homosexuality and making the latter so explicitly criminal. In the homosexual context, one more prophetic item in my windup review of Judson '64 deserves mention: my "rooms with a view," a naive allusion to Virginia Woolf, for at that time I knew nothing of her interests in other women and her "affair" with Vita Sackville-West. Nor did I know much of my own interests in women or affairs with them, for by August of '64, when my friend-to-be brought me out, I had been "straight" for thirteen years, and my two collegiate affairs were prehistoric and inadmissible. The need to affirm a "criminal" relationship during '65 is one way to read my bid to place my friend above Rainer in the Judson pantheon.

My second setup for this move was to write a review of Rainer linking her with Jimmy Waring—the review was titled "Waring-Rainer"—whose work was often very campy (he was well known to be gay), and by putting her work down for the first time. In my very next review, two weeks later, I further separated her, if you will, from Robert Morris, the man with whom she lived and performed, by linking Morris with my friend in the same hyphenated style in which I had put Rainer together with Waring. In the "Morris-Friend" review I raved first about Morris, whose work was generally acclaimed then, both his sculpture and his choreography, and let him carry my friend along in my enthusiasm for the kind of minimalist work they both did and that I thought he best exemplified. It was May '65; a more detached observer than myself might have noted that I had delivered the goods, so far as my relationship was concerned. There was probably nothing more required of me. If there was, I drew back from it or had no chance to fulfill it. My judgment of my friend's work was not in any case clouded either by this (unstated) condition of the relationship or by my feelings about her. I saw her work as good but still essentially promising. What interests me now are the adjustments and compromises I must have made continually between my aesthetic perceptions and the interpersonal or "family" pressures of my critical milieu. I outstandingly recall Rainer challenging me earlier that year to say something bad about her in print. She might not have been serious—it could have been said at a drunken party, and I might have scoffed at the idea—but doubtless I registered the remark as license for future reference. Using her "permission," in case I needed it, I discharged one duty on her behalf and another on my own. While Rainer felt secure in her position as the superior Judson choreographer, she also felt under pressure to undermine herself. It was an ambivalent position to have, rousing both envy and admiration, and Rainer was as insecure personally as she was confident professionally. In her work she successfully sublimated her problems, and in her everyday style she cleverly dissimulated them. In both domains her manner was cool, contained, calculated, aloof, interested, intense, distantly friendly, and dispassionate. At a later date I would sum up her stance as one of heroic depression. I, for one, knew her rather well, I would have thought, but I saw only her strengths, not any of her weaknesses. Once when I made some remarks to her about the personal difficulties of a dancer we knew called Fred Herko (who later leaped to his death from a sixth-floor apartment window on Cornelia Street), defining him loosely as an orphan—no doubt a thinly veiled projection of my feeling about myself—she snapped back impatiently that we were *all* orphans, a riposte that made her seem to me invulnerable and transcendent. This was of course the way I liked women to be; I didn't accept them any other way.

In the summer of '64 I asked Rainer to do an improvisation with me at a Washington Square Art Gallery concert. I prepared myself by consuming at least half a fifth of vodka beforehand, a measure that I was convinced could only enhance my performance (making me uninhibited and fearless—the two qualities I most sadly lacked in any social, not to mention performance, setting), and the necessity of which Rainer viewed with a seasoned professional contempt. At the time I thought she was mad at me because I upstaged her, but I think she simply found my weakness abhorrent. I could not have performed for an audience of dodo birds without alcohol. It would be hard to imagine *anyone* being able to overlook my own demonstrations of inadequacy. In time this one-sided advantage of mine, the ability to see all other adults as strong and therefore capable of both damning and saving me, crumbled as the panoply of other emotional realities besides my own gradually unfolded before me. Rainer herself was chief among those whose lives cracked and spilled over into public view. And I played my unwitting part in her drama, as she played hers in mine. I never asked her, or even speculated, why she invited me to say something bad about her in print. Certainly I never questioned my own motivations, which at their crudest amounted to nothing more or less than a desire to please all the powerful people around me. Rainer's invitation was tantamount to a command. All I needed to execute it was the proper time and pretext. Then I (ever unconscious) tailored her needs to mine, temporarily at least inverting my friend's position and hers—not that my friend was by any means low on the Judson totem, or for that matter that anything I said about Rainer would seriously jeopardize her preeminence.

The way I helped Rainer evidently in this exercise was by furnishing some, or more, visible proof of her struggle with Morris. Sufficient proof had already been established by *Life* magazine in April '65 in its coverage of the Buffalo Arts Festival, where I had produced concerts by the Judson elite, including works by Rainer and Morris. In *Life's* spread on the festival, Morris's *Waterman Switch*, a brilliant piece featuring himself and Rainer nude and my friend dressed as a man, was amply represented by a large half-page photo, while Rainer's *Terrain*, her major and first full-length work, received no coverage at all. I was caught up in my own problems with *Life's* coverage of the festival (my friend was featured in a lovely color photo of the solo she performed there, on the same page as a color reproduction of a painting by her suitor, my competitor) and didn't notice how the rest of my colleagues fared. Nor was I the least bit aware of the struggle between Rainer and Morris over their work, or their intimacy. The last thing I might have thought was that Rainer had reason to be threatened by Morris's choreography. And in fact it was not his choreography per se that threatened her but the attention he was getting because of it. Morris had been upstaging Rainer with work that seemed bound to arrest the media. Utilizing popular images with romantic effects, casting them in striking pictorial designs as classic looking as Ingres, performing them with great presence and precision, Morris appeared to be making a sweep at that moment in Judson history. Rainer in the meantime, that spring of '65, had come up with a long, cumbersome work (performed in Manhattan) featuring eleven performers and a stack of mattresses and a taped reading of the diaries of an eighteenth-century minister, a work that tried the patience, she has said, of lots of fans besides myself. The stage was set, then, for some showdown between Morris and Rainer that might decide their differences. My own contribution, the two reviews in May, the one pairing her in a bad light with Jimmy Waring, the other extolling Morris in the company of my friend, was perhaps a faint echo of the splash in *Life*, where everything was so magnified and visible, the attention so much more meaningful in its power to affect the larger world. By fall of '65 Morris had stopped performing for good. He was primarily a sculptor, and a leading one at that, and Rainer wanted him off her turf. The way she put it to him was: "Either you have to get out of my field or I have to get out of your life." The way he reported it was that she said, "One dancer in the family is enough." Morris of course was not actually a dancer; and in the end, no matter how open the Judson movement was to work by nondancers, it was the dancers who prevailed and claimed the field—not a surprising development where choreography was a secondary medium for all the nondancers. Nowadays a lot of that work would be called performance art, to which its practitioners can be expected to have a primary commitment. Back in the sixties, three of the outstanding nondancers making "choreography"—Morris, Rauschenberg, and Alex Hay—were living with or married to dancers. Rainer, it could be imagined, having disposed of her main competition and apparently saved her relationship, might have been free to pursue her choreographic ends happily and unimpeded to some glorious conclusion or other. But a year after Morris quit the field, she succumbed to the first of a series of near-fatal intestinal attacks, resulting in as many major operations. During October and November '66 we were both laid up at St. Vincent's, she in the medical wards, I in the psychiatric pavilion.

As the men left the field to the women, the women fell apart anyway. In Simone Forti's case, she had already abandoned choreography to play Bob Whitman's wife. (Simone, incidentally, had been married to Bob Morris before meeting Whitman and before Morris got together with Rainer.) My ex-friend "married" her painter and ceased to dance or make choreography for several years. She left her painter in two years, after being laid up in the hospital with a toxic reaction to penicillin resulting in a sort of elephantiasis, a huge enlargement and discoloration of the legs.

In December '65, a month after I'd been left alone in the loft on Liberty Street, Bob Whitman diabolically paired Simone and my ex-friend in a theatre piece called *Prune Flat,* mixing live performance with screen images, including a *third* female in similar but separate duplications of herself; and I dutifully commemorated the event in my last review of the year and my final notice of my ex-friend. I often used my column both to invoke people and to decathect them, though in this case I have no doubt that my wish was to reinvoke the object in question. I wrote:

The two women appear in white standing up against the screen to blend with a sky-blue ground on which a succession of big succulent fruits are projected, cut open to spill out ball bearings (from an orange), glitter (from a tomato), and feathers (from a pepper). This fruit scene is capped by a persimmon oozing red squashy all over the large screen, later suggested in a shot of visceral matter following a close-up of pubic hair. The two women continue to blend with a still-life of house plants, red and green; then a sudden shift to a fall scene of rocks and leaves at Palisades Park. At this point the stage action and the movie become more complex in a series of duplications. . . . As country becomes city, barren streets are briefly populated by the two women turning corners in winter coats and again duplicated as they walk slowly across stage in the same coats. A striking effect is achieved by one woman flying slowly diagonally upward in a green dress on a black void . . . the whole event . . . a quiet color fantasy of women at home (fruits, plants), in themselves (organs, secretions), in and out of their clothes, and moving around in the city and in the country.

Such audacity on my part—and public masochism, I think —were possible only through my continuing ability to separate art from life, another fatal, however acculturated, trait of mine, which gave way to life (for a long while I hated art) in the late sixties. In retrospect I think Whitman may have been sentimentalizing my lost relationship; but whatever he made out of it, he made it his own, and my ex-friend and his wife were now in the same boat.

Another "wife" casualty would be Steve Paxton, who washed up on the Bowery in '67 after breaking up with Rauschenberg, living in a tiny triangular room a block south of my loft, where Canal Street, the Bowery, and the Manhattan Bridge form a big, busy intersection on the edge of Chinatown. The Judson soap opera included a scene in October '66 when Rainer had her first serious intestinal attack (in the middle of the night), and Morris called Steve, who ended up being the one to carry her downstairs to a taxi and the hospital. Steve was a rescuer of mine too, but I saw him as a persecutor also, as he clearly saw me. His struggle with Rauschenberg paralleled Rainer's with Morris, though Rauschenberg's flair for "choreography" was not nearly as developed as Morris's. It was Rauschenberg's social and professional connections that tended to obscure Steve; even so, Rauschenberg's roller-skating-parachute act, a big flying-eagle umbrella image, had the numen to dominate Steve's more modest designs. At any rate, Steve has told me that when he went to live with Rauschenberg, the people he had known began communicating with Rauschenberg through him. Then too, issues involving work and friends were in all cases complicated by extramarital affairs. After Morris left the dance field, he was fully capable of causing Rainer great pain through revelations of his sexual exploits and serious interests in other women. In my own case, I played the girl in relation to a girl who dallied with somebody outside our union. The power of the man was felt as strongly by me, however more indirectly. The painter who captured my ex-friend was as intimidating professionally as Morris and Rauschenberg.

It may have seemed as if the other women I knew needed men more than I did, simply because they got them or hung onto them or languished over them or went swiftly from one to another of them, but this, I believe, was not at all true. I think that I actually needed them more, even to an inordinate degree, to fill the vacuum of the huge absence of them in my background. Yet this very absence made their reality fairly impossible. By the summer of '66 my connections with men had become especially weak, thus creating the opening for the appearance of another supracultural figure. The important kind of man that was missing for me then was a mentor, patron, manager, business guardian, or the like. To the editor-in-chief of the *Village Voice* I was just an arts contributor; I never saw him, and the first conversation I had with him was that fall on the telephone. To John Cage, the most influential man of ideas in our art world, I was mainly a supportive critic, just nominally a personal interest. To Walter Gutman, the stockbroker and patron of artists, I was one of many party friends and recipients of his small grants. As a result of cracking up in '65 I was more remote than ever from the men whose power meant something to me. Having lost credibility and confidence, having retreated in deep embarrassment, I found that the last people I wanted to see were those who meant the most to me. For males the summer of '66, I saw my younger-brotherly competitor upstairs, Les Levine. Otherwise I briefly saw Larry Rivers, who invited me to the Hamptons on Long Island to talk to some people about art. I remember driving out there in a big black car with Larry and Saul Bellow and seeing Larry's wife, Clarissa, in their summer house. By late August, however, when I had departed this world again, I made sure to see a number of men who might play a part in my new cosmo-drama and to attend the birth of the man who might make all of them seem as unnecessary as my background had led me to believe they really were.

The most important man for a girl is her father. Men at large become comprehensible only by comparison. Only a father who has been known can be lost to any advantage. A father known and lost can be found again in essence. The best kind of father to have is neither of this world nor too much of the other. Christ, for me, was too much of the other—not functional enough between God and the gods of my world. I lacked the figure who could mediate between me and a world governed by men. I had acted in many ways like a man but was still only a girl. I had no male language or business skills. I was intellectual but had no understanding of the codes that rule male transactions and communications. I couldn't step back, for example, into a position of equanimity when my sense of parity was threatened, or identify the one-upmanship that pervades and defines male thought and expression, or, more profoundly, recognize the grid upon which male games were played, those set norms for preferential treatment—class, sex, age, race, subsected by standards of beauty, fame, power, achievement, wealth—including mysterious codes governing mobility and exception making, all subject to changing fashions and political climates. I was the kind of girl who rushed in over and over to play games she didn't know were being played, in which the cards were already stacked against her. Other sorts of girls, who never played, may have looked less battered, but they too believed that whatever was wrong with them, making it difficult or impossible, say, to play, was their own personal, individual fault. These kinds of girls most likely had fathers, but just as likely they had no knowledge of what their fathers represented. Those who did were a tiny, strictly educated minority. I knew none myself, or if I did, they kept the news to themselves. Had they told me about it, I wouldn't have believed them anyway. As I discovered in 1970, I had the enormous resistance of a girl without a model upon which to draw to infer the larger picture.

The "father" I would create in '66 was to be surpassing. He would allow me to jump (social) games completely, to be exceptional, to be free of the class and sex that bound me, to make work that broke all the rules, to be successfully antisocial, to become what "crime" had made of me, to join all the little kings in the art world who never grew up. The man I invented would mediate between myself and the art world exclusively. Later, in 1970, the rest of the world (American feminism) found me, and at last, at the age of forty, I left home, as it were—home where the father is primal, all-powerful, and never openly acknowledged.

In the late sixties, I would be like a girl who felt she could do anything because of her rich, powerful father. This defense would weaken in 1969 when I met a girl whose father appeared to be more powerful than mine. That, I believe, is why the "rest of the world" found me in 1970. The comedown was terrific. I left home, the art world, to join thousands of women who found fathers disappointing. Now I can look back and say I had a wonderful romance, which lasted four years ('66–'70), as long as my mother's with my (real) father.

9

Coup

My real father, as such fathers go, was not a disappointing sort of man. He wasn't the king of England exactly, but he came pretty close, as much as I could determine. The first picture I ever saw of him, when I was twenty, featured him standing between King George and Queen Mary. That's pretty close. And I had been telling people about him for years. I told everybody I knew about him, even casual acquaintances. I impressed people too, but I think they were impressed more by my story about how I never met him and how my mother deceived me by always telling me he was dead than by anything he represented. Anyway, only the royal family itself, and a few selected other English folk like Winston Churchill and G. B. Shaw and T. E. Lawrence, meant something to Americans. And anyway, what do bastards know, and why did I need to try to impress people at all? I impressed them enough just by saying I was born over there myself. The father business sounded too farfetched. Fathers can be anybody, especially if you never met them. Nonetheless, I was telling the truth. And the truth never got me anywhere. It was only a story, after all. I never made it sound like much more. I had not really taken possession of the man, and I told the story blandly and a little sadly, as if the story had ended, and the ending was not great. I had my mother's attitude about it completely. The difference between us was that she kept the story to herself; after she died I learned that her best friend for seventeen years had never heard of it. And the only reason I found out about it myself (apart from the man's name, profession, and nationality, which I knew very early) was that my mother feared I would see the obit in the *Times* when he died in 1950, so she sent me the clipping along with a cover letter updating her story, turning herself into a divorcée instead of the widow she had always said she was; and that a few years later, when I was twenty-six, I happened to discover the rest on my own when I saw *East of Eden* and got the idea that my mother had never been married at all, which she subsequently confirmed.

At this point, the story was as embarrassing for me as for my mother, but the need to expose my mother was stronger than my instinct to protect myself. When I told it, I always hooked people by saying, ". . . and I never met the man!" Then they would look incredulous and say "Really?" And then I would have to tell them the particulars, or the essential outline. In the end, they would invariably shake their heads slowly, side to side, over the way my mother had handled the situation. It was a lot more satisfying than just having a dead, important father who wasn't Winston Churchill or G. B. Shaw. Yet it did somehow rob me of an original pure fantasy: that no matter what people thought about it (and what did Americans know, anyway?), I did in fact have the kind of father a child might make up. Indeed, I never had to make one up. Fantasy, in my case, was reality. But after 1950, and his actual death, and my mother's unfolding perfidy, and the growing subliminal realization that this ideal father could not have been so ideal; having clearly caused me and my mother a good deal of pain, I gradually approached the position of a child who might finally have that classical need to make one up.

For this I was well prepared by the example of my mother. Not only had she invented a father for me, in the important sense of establishing an identity for someone she never produced, but to protect her status she had made up two vital statistics about him that could only make me very doubtful about the nature of reality. The truth had never worked for *me*, and my mother seemed to have done all right living out lies, I might have inwardly reasoned. Also, since my mother was so bad and had discredited herself so thoroughly, I would naturally want to invent my own reality and be done with hers. I no longer wore her kind of clothes, lived in her kinds of spaces, ate her sort of food, had her kind of manners, knew her kind of people, or read her kind of books—why should I go on sharing the same kind of father? Of course, I didn't think about these things; I just happened to be living in an environment that made an insurgency like this possible. I was angry enough, too, about what had happened to me in '65 to make me want to blow up America. Yet as the month of August '66 drew on, I had not the slightest thought or plan for the future.

I was simply as high as a rocket en route to the moon, once again riding along on waves of ether, blissfully content with my unhappy surroundings, amazed by the beauty of simple light bulbs and patterns on the wall made by cracks or leaks and stains, thrilled by such incidents as bank tellers handing me twenty dollars for a ten-dollar check, knowing that they "knew who I was" and wanted secretly to help me out. That I was not yet "who I was" made no difference; I had that big feeling inside me that something was about to break. In fact I was much better off with just this big feeling inside me; when things did break, I was in a whole lot of trouble.

The pattern was familiar from the year before. First I left earth very gradually, like a slow glider leaving the ground at an imperceptible increase in altitude. Then I floated along deliriously, taking in the sights and reveling in eternity. Then I realized I was gone and got scared and paranoid, though instead of moving desperately to reverse my course, as before, I attempted to steer my way through to the other side and to avoid being brought down before completing my mission, whatever that might be. Several striking features of my trip in '65 were absent from this new excursion. While I had given up cigarettes again, I had no Great Fire in my loft, and I recall no particular sensations of heat in any part of my body. Nor did I hear a voice ordering me to give up criticism, or anything else; and I had no labor pains, therefore no excuse to bring Christ into the picture to explain an immaculate conception. Having been already conceived thus, it seems that my new project was to develop some identity. The essence of this new trip was to uncover a personal ancestry. I did focus on Christ again, but only to contemplate his historical role.

I was obsessed for a while with Christ's importance. I wanted to know how or why he had become so important. I was still amazed over his appearance in my own life. The importance of Christ to Jungians, as symbol of the self, was not yet clear to me. Early drafts of this book were full of inchoate speculations about Christ, including a certain blasphemous identification I made with Simone Weil, who had an experience in 1938 in which "Christ came down and took possession of me." Weil was twenty-eight at the time. Her biographer, Simone Petrement, said, "The possibility of such a divine-human encounter had never occurred to her, and she thought it providential that she hadn't read the mystics, so that the experience could not be part of her fertile imagination." The identification I made with Weil was as an outsider. She grew up in a French Jewish (unorthodox) family with no awareness of being Jewish; I in an American Protestant (unorthodox) family with no awareness of being Protestant or even what "Protestant" was. Weil's experience of Christ, like my own, gave her no inclination to enter the Church. Her rationale, however, was a lot more religious than mine. She said,

> When I think of the act by which I should enter the Church . . . nothing gives me more pain than the idea of separating myself from the immense and unfortunate multitude of unbelievers. I have the essential need, and I think I can say the vocation, to move among men of every class and vocation, mixing with them and sharing their life and outlook. . . . There is a Catholic circle ready to give eager welcome to whoever enters it. . . . I do not want to be adopted into a circle, to live among people

who say "we" and to be part of an "us," to find I am "at home" in any human *milieu* whatever it may be. . . . I feel that it is necessary and ordained that I should be alone, a stranger and an exile in relation to every human circle without exception. . . . This may seem to contradict . . . my need to be merged into any human circle in which I moved. To be lost to view in it is not to form part of it, and my capacity to mix with all of them implies that I belong to none.

A very modern view—one succinctly summed up by the "obscene" comic and martyr Lenny Bruce, who died, incidentally, that month of August in '66. Bruce expressed relief at what he said was a trend of people leaving the Church and going back to God. Anyway, I had no rationale whatever for not entering the Church; I simply wondered why I had no inclination to do so. Weil, after all, was a precocious social worker at the age of twenty-eight: I was just a local critic of the avant-garde, at an age advanced enough to have become a failed mother and a mental case as well. (Weil died, by the way, at thirty-three.) My experience of Christ never sent me back to the Bible either. It did, however, send me back to Otto Rank—a man born the same year as my father—the disciple of Freud best known for his work on the trauma of birth.

The work of Rank's that I now remembered was his long, well-known essay called "The Myth of the Birth of the Hero," in which Rank applied psychoanalytic techniques to an examination of myths about great culture heroes and savior gods, including, of course, Christ. Ultimately this essay became a key to my understanding of the "family romance" and the myths or delusions I had created or invoked to explain my own. Back in '66 I was looking more exclusively for Christian references to support the question of Christ's importance. Finding Christ treated on a par with fourteen other "heroes" helped contribute to my grasp of him as one of the Year-Gods, like Dionysus, annually and seasonally sacrificed to ensure life, etc. But I never satisfied myself with related questions of Christ's historical role and his position as the *last* of such sacrifices. Finally, in 1977, a book called *The Passover Plot* by Hugh Schonfield gave me a historical perspective I was missing, if not a clue as to how this one sort of Year-God had escaped his milieu to become the symbol of that sacrifice for so many different peoples. My general knowledge of the zeal of followers and missionaries in spreading the word, and of later institutional pressures, seemed to me just to beg the question. Anyway, in August '66, by the time I had definitively stepped out again, I was simply raving about this material, asking questions about Jews and Christians that had never concerned me before. It had finally occurred to me, for one thing, that Christ was a Jewish man. I became deeply agitated over the antiquated split between Jews and Christians and, by association, all other sorts of splits. I raved about my friend Charlotte's son, who happily combined, I thought, East and West, Jew and Gentile, in his immediate heritage (his mother being Jewish, his father Chinese and Irish Catholic). And later on, during September, when my bag of myths opened once again, making me this time encyclopedically genealogical, I bestowed a Jewish heritage on myself too. I suppose this was how I resolved my questions about Christ's importance; by personalizing the issue through a contemporary Jewish man, a more realistic "father" than Christ. Later, when sane, I reintellectualized the pursuit.

Looking back, I can't remember any other issue that consumed me prior to the eruption of my "genealogy." Nor am I very certain of the exact sequence of events that August, or just when I went aloft or informed myself I was gone.

I do know that I knew by August 20, because that was the date of a particular concert at Upper Black Eddy, in Bucks County, Pennsylvania, where I happened to be, and where I remember knowing I was not myself again. After that, things moved swiftly toward the collapse of personality that always precedes restitutive measures of invention, classically called delusions. In Upper Black Eddy I reached the empyrean heights of my glider trip aloft. The occasion was a concert by LaMonte

Young, whom I drove out there in my heap with his wife, the artist Marian Zazeela, and some of their expensive electronic equipment. I must have picked my moment. LaMonte was the composer of "eternal music" in New York. Since his arrival from California in 1960, he had become well established as an outrageous character and respected innovator. In '64 I wrote a piece about him for the *Voice* which opened with the words "Welcome to This Presentation of Dream Music"—the first sentence on a sheet of program notes for three of Young's concerts that year. LaMonte had exotic origins as a descendant of Mormons (e.g., Brigham Young) in Idaho, born in a log cabin in the center of nowhere, the eldest child of a man who was a shepherd. His apocryphal story about how he first discovered an interest in long-sustained tones, music of infinite duration, had him hugging telephone poles as a small boy out on the Idaho plains, listening to the steady hum of the poles' wires. LaMonte was a slight man with dark, curly hair and glasses and a strong nasal twang to his voice; he usually appeared in public in a black woolen cape that fully encompassed him. I remember only his head, carried along by the black cape. LaMonte's work was distinguished by the lack of contrast, variation, and climax that define Western music. His Theater of Eternal Music consisted of a group of singers and instrumentalists using microphones and electronic stuff to produce long-durationed pitches, which changed only subtly, highly amplified, accompanied by light shows of Marian's calligraphic drawings, in concerts lasting several hours at least. LaMonte's dream was to have Dream Houses in which musicians would live and execute music lasting forever as constant and continuous sound. His own loft on Church Street never stopped humming; a low monotone always emanated from his equipment, mixing with the aftersounds of performance. His goal was to get you, like himself, inside his sound. I had no trouble getting inside it; it was a mind-blowing experience, to use that cliché aptly, but the experience of the work meant less to me than its intellectual references. I liked the idea of the work. The polymorphous perversity of the sixties found exquisite expression in this kind of oceanic womb music.

LaMonte was very fashionable. At Upper Black Eddy, other fashionable art-world people congregated to hang out and hear the music. Playwright Sam Shepard; art mogul Henry Geldzahler and his friend Christopher; drama critic Michael Smith; Yoko Ono's second husband, Tony Cox; and my friend the critic David Bourdon are those I remember.

I doubt that I went to the concert itself, which took place in an amphitheatre a quarter of a mile down the road from a house where we all stayed. I could have gotten lost for good inside the sound that day. As it was, I did nearly get lost, sitting outside the house there on the lawn in a white wooden armchair facing a dense thicket of tall trees, LaMonte's music floating up from the amphitheatre down the road. I had advanced from paintings, curtains, and light bulbs to trees. My eyes fixed themselves somewhere in the center of this forest, causing the trees to lose their individuality and create one organism united by an intricate mass of webs and woven lace, Ariadne's thread fashioned by a glance into a shimmering green-and-golden gossamer network. Perspective had vanished, along with individuality. The mass enveloped me because the elements of the spectacle— leaves, trunks, branches—had left their position at a distance of some thirty or forty feet and wandered up against my eyes. I was entranced enough to want to stay there forever. I remember how difficult it was to snap out of it. I think that was the moment I knew I was in trouble. Yet I enjoyed the rest of the weekend there. The company was gay and happy, the weather sunny and dry, the swimming pool made me feel rich, the indoor music was the latest Beatles extravaganza, and Tony Cox decided to seduce me. I was indifferent to the sex he offered, but not to the possibility of good sex. The potential for some kind of tantric experience now existed. My body was swamped in libido. Conventional sex left out the vast periphery, which consumed the center; the fire was everywhere. I had a revolutionary body, no respect for genital primacy. Orgasm was the least of my concerns—i.e., as a relief of tension. I was constantly relieved.

The shimmering trees in my eyes were all through me. The music the trees the people the pool the me—all one single throbbing organism. I had fused with my environment again. And this was my problem. I was losing, or had already lost, the critical sense of being separate. I drove LaMonte and Marian back to Manhattan; we had some trouble on the road, but I don't remember what it was. I think I had to strain very hard to stay on course; possibly we ran out of gas or oil or something. The old heap I was driving was not the right vehicle for a woman in space. Soon I found a good excuse to abandon it. By that time I had abandoned myself too. Cars and other possessions reflect their owners precisely. But before all was lost, I had a very high, sociable week.

Tony came to see me and brought a book called *You Are All Sanpaku*. He said it was about how you could tell what was wrong with people from the whites of their eyes. Then he brought Yoko over, and the three of us had dinner at Sloppy Louie's, the fish restaurant on South Street. I drew diagrams on napkins and paper place mats. Yoko was very quiet and impassive; Tony said they were going to England in a couple of days by freighter from Montreal. That week in August I drove Les to Rhinebeck, New York, to visit Wynn Chamberlain, who had a pool and a wife called Sally; on the way home I slipped into infinity again as we rode along engorging the center white highway line. The line took up the whole highway. It entered me like the trees. It was a comet streaking me through the empyrean night. It had no end and no beginning. It was God's white line, the ultimate guide to no-everywhere. I was losing sleep again. The world was so incredible. There was no need to sleep in order to dream; I was dreaming up the world. The days and nights were filled with amazing events. One day I added red silk to my expanding repertory of visuals. The artist James Lee Byars unrolled a carpet of the stuff one mile long down the Central Park sidewalk of Fifth Avenue, the side uninterrupted by cross streets. I stood at the bottom of the silk on Fifty-ninth Street and transfixed myself by gormandizing the long red trail through my eyes. Byars was more outrageous than Young. His own "eternal" projects were much more public and at that time entailed the legal cooperation of the city. Personally, too, he exemplified the stereotype of the antisocial artist. He was never drunk or unruly; he simply overwhelmed you with his own interests and questions. He was a kind of walking encyclopedia of questions. He asked questions continuously. For Byars, questions were a way of life. He made a living asking them, too: for a while he was installed at the Hudson Institute, a private think tank for "futurology" at Croton-on-Hudson, about thirty miles north of New York City, where he "performed" a piece consisting of a search for "the one hundred most interesting questions in America at this time." He went to Oxford and spent a week there asking the dons questions. He appeared to have no life apart from his art and questions, and he assumed that others had no life apart from their interest in same. I suppose he was actually crazy, and he got away with it by constantly reordering his depersonalizations and calling them art. I was beguiled by him, and I never saw him long enough at a time to worry about having to do something—go to the bathroom, for instance—that might bring a disconcerting slice of life into his cerebral, symptomatic world. Probably I loved his questions because they subliminally invoked my own. But where Byars apparently satisfied himself with unanswered questions, I was interested in answers that led to more questions—in the detective-story tradition leading to the "scene of the crime." All the male artists around me were making a living transcendentally. I transcended *everything* by going crazy, then sank back into the morass of my "story." But later on, by the end of '68, I lived more like the males around me, having succeeded in transforming my criticism into a personal and stylistically outrageous column. The prototype for this eventuality was a piece I wrote about a Happening by Bob Whitman out in Amagansett, Long Island, that very August of '66, when I was perfectly crazy.

The Happening took place in a swampy meadow the night of August 27, one week after the Young concert in Bucks

County. The review I wrote appeared in the *Voice* September 8. This was a dramatic and unprecedented moment for me. I was beside myself before submitting it for fear of what my editor would think. I was afraid of my editor anyway; she could be jolly and uproarious one moment, then fierce and reproving the next. She never edited a word of copy (of mine at least—a practice I later viewed as a handicap), but she could make you feel as if you and your copy were completely dispensable. She sat like a tiger hunched over in her lair (she had a long mane of beautiful strawberry-blond Ginger-Rogers-colored hair) in a tiny office on the second floor of the tiny, triangular two-storey structure on a corner of Sheridan Square that once comprised the *Village Voice* office building. I had a huge stake in this review. It had gushed out of me in ten minutes, a most unparalleled quota of time (I usually worked on these things for several hours at least). I knew I was crazy, and I felt inarticulately that its publication would help me to stay in the world (in both senses: out of the bin, and no more insane than I already was) and/or at least justify my conviction that it was possible to function, and even brilliantly, while insane. I had a lot to prove, to myself anyway. After a year of dead, uninspired work, what little there was of it, I had suddenly come alive. And I wasn't too crazy to know that the review pushed the limits of the *Voice*'s, or any newspaper's, idea of criticism. That was my covert hope, to push those limits. I wanted to show how controlled crazy could be. I went over to my editor's office prepared to fight for the review. And I had to, too. She read it while I sat there, excited and apprehensive; then she looked up big-eyed and bushy-tailed and ready to pounce and roared, "What *is* this?" or "What is *this*?"—and after I remonstrated a bit, she tried to dismiss it by saying that another reviewer on the paper had already written about the Happening. At last, after about forty-five minutes of wrangling (why didn't I write for a literary magazine? she asked), she pointed her finger at me, arm fully extended, and said all right, she would take it, but I'd better watch my step and not do anything like that again. I was fantastically relieved . . .

then greatly worried over whether it would come out looking the way I had written it, without the typos for which the Voice was notorious.

But I don't think its publication helped me, in the short run, at all. It just gave me more fuel for my flight and made me feel like the incredible photograph of Lee Harvey Oswald that had appeared on the front page of the Voice just a week earlier: that moment in Dallas when he was shot in the gut, a spooky, dramatic reproduction in which the shocked bystanders were developed in negative, accompanying a review by Mailer of Mark Lane's book *Rush to Judgment*. I mean, I felt too exposed. The Oswald photo triggered my paranoia. I did a tremendous take on it; the photo loomed up out of the page and seemed to enlarge itself like a video projection arching across the sky—or penetrating my body. The photo was animated, and I was the victim, though I couldn't have said so or thought so.

After my review of the Whitman Happening appeared on September 8, I managed to stay free in the world ten more days, but otherwise I was pretty far gone by at least the 12th. I know, because by then I was consumed by my amazing genealogy, which I felt obliged to broadcast to everyone I knew or encountered. As in '65, the last stage of my trip was superimposed on one of the *Gemini* flights, this one number eleven; but unlike the previous year, I never consciously tuned in to it. Only two news events grabbed my attention, as I remember now, and they were both photographs: the one of Oswald, and one of LBJ on the front page of the *Times* August 19, laughing and waving at a crowd of students reaching out toward him.

The way I read the LBJ photo, when I was fully deluded in the middle of September, was that the whole country, represented by these students, was laughing at the President, and that he would soon be deposed through a plot involving the successful contamination of the White House water supply with acid. The people were laughing at him because they knew he had gone crazy, and they were just humoring him along. I created quite a coup, then rearranged the government to suit my own idea of what the world should look like. Assassinations, after all, were part of the American way of life. The only events of the sixties that made me seriously read the papers were the big assassinations, King's and the two Kennedys'. I especially devoured details of the assassins' backgrounds. In 1981 I clipped and collected everything I saw on the assassin manqué John Hinckley, Jr. But other types of murders interested me too; on August 2 of '66, Charles J. Whitman gunned down a crowd of people from a university tower in Austin, Texas, killing twelve and hitting thirty-three others, and before he did that he slew his wife and his mother at home. The *Times* reported that he was a "nice, uncomplicated guy," a "typical American boy" (former altar boy, Eagle Scout, Marine, etc.) who "hated his father with a mortal passion." His father was in Florida at the time. His father-in-law said he was "just as normal as anybody I ever knew." Whitman wrote a note explaining he wasn't sure why his wife and mother had to die except to spare them the embarrassment of what he was about to do. On August 16, Ted Kennedy urged a curb on the use of guns. The Chappaquiddick incident, much later on, was also of great interest to me. But of course the whole population becomes engrossed in these tragedies. Even the accidents—sometimes especially the accidents—rouse the public imagination. Politics I followed just barely; I knew what was going on in the world in very broad outline. There was a war, there were race riots; this much I knew. The war was unpopular and everyone hated LBJ; that much I knew too. I can only assume that my fantasy of deposing the President reflected sentiments of the people at large. But the war didn't interest me. Somehow the public attitude about the President and his policies dovetailed with my personal mythology. I had a father to depose, and LBJ was a convenient symbol. This must be the equation in any (real) assassin's incentive to kill. And like any assassin, I made no connection between symbol and personal reality. The symbol is unconsciously invested with attributes of the real thing, or that which it symbolizes. Consciousness deprives people of certain feelings, wishes, and deeds. I would have scoffed at the idea that a man like LBJ, with his big, droopy ears and rough, leathery face, had anything in common with my father.

I made no association whatever between the impact of this photograph, the interpretation I made of it, the fantasy of a new government, and the father I was so busy inventing just then. Killing off one symbol (my real father was as symbolic as LBJ) and replacing it with another is surely the most transcendent of exercises. But as I've said, the symbol I had been given, my impressive English father, had ceased to function advantageously, if it ever really had done so, and my new life demanded a better archetype. Underlying this demand was the accumulated evidence (evident to my unconscious) of my mother's possessiveness. A father who belonged so definitively to my mother—a father, that is, whom she had never produced, and whose reality she had further manipulated (killing him off twice!), and about whom she had guarded information so fiercely—was a father I might best do completely without. I never tested or questioned my mother's possession of him. I did make a token gesture that September; before going over the edge, I called her up and asked her for the one picture I knew she had of him. Her voice wavered on the phone, cracked a little, receded in surprise, and I withdrew. Even when she was dying in 1978, or perhaps because she was dying, I let her have him. I tried to pry information out of her, but whatever I got left her possession of him intact. Above all, what she possessed was the unmodified view that she had made a big mistake. It was fitting that in September '66 she was the last person I visited before taking charge of her "mistake" and blowing it up into a mistake to end all mistakes.

10

Threshold

My visit was really to see my children, who were staying with her that summer in a cabin on a lake in Lakeville, Connecticut. I judge I saw them Sunday, September 5, but I can't be sure. I only know that the Young concert and the Whitman Happening and the review I wrote of the latter were behind me by the time I got there, and that I usually saw them Sundays; and I couldn't have seen them the following week, on the 12th, because I was incarcerated the 18th, after spending at least seven days in Rauschenberg's building on Lafayette Street. By the 5th I was already very blown away, and had been since August 20, the date of the Young concert in Bucks County. I was determined this time to elude any captors. But after my visit to Connecticut I no longer wanted to be alone—a sure sign that the end of freedom is near. The visit that Sunday was remarkable not for anything my mother did but for the revelations my children afforded me. My mother certainly unsettled me, but she always did, and on this occasion I noticed only three things about her that reinforced my negative opinions. One of them was the way she treated my son over lunch, threatening to take his plate away before he was finished and even to eat what was left herself. Another was the way she played baseball with them on the lawn, forgetting completely that she was a grown-up, whacking the ball as hard as she could (which wasn't bad for a sixty-five-year-old woman), then laughing just as inappropriately over her advantage. These were useful observations for me. I remembered that she had competed just as fiendishly with me when I was small, and I assumed she must have been as neurotic about food—not a difficult connection to make if I paused to consider my own anxieties with my children and food; I too disliked making and serving it and was unreasonably upset if any of it ended up on the floor. The third item that loomed up that summer was sex. I observed my mother teasing my son when he happened to be exposed; at a later date he complained rather bitterly that she had succeeded in shaming him and his sister. Being more contemporary about sex than I was about food, I was mortified by my mother's repressive Victorian behavior, but I felt it was not possible to say anything about it unless she said something herself —e.g., complained about my son's enuresis. Then I would defend him fiercely, attacking her in turn for not understanding him. Of course it was easy to defend my son when somebody else was taking care of him. But the opportunity to defend him against a common oppressor created a bond of sympathy between us that paid off that Sunday the 5th, when I visited them in my dilapidated spacecraft, the Oldsmobile heap.

After lunch I asked my kids what they wanted to do that afternoon. I never did that; I always scooped them up, put them in the car and took them someplace, assuming that they had no ideas of their own, or that if they did, I wouldn't be able to take them there. Already I was having a revelation. The moment I gave up my prerogative, I noticed a certain intelligence in my children. A very basic underlying supposition I had about life was shattered that day. I had actually lived with two beings whom I had assumed to have no center of feeling, consciousness, spirit, or intelligence of their own. I had, in other words, never looked in their eyes. But I had never looked into anybody else's eyes either; and if anybody had ever looked into mine, the look had been wasted. I had grown up in an objective world, in which experience counted for very little. Inner life was never acknowledged; it simply didn't exist. The evidence of it that I had read in poetry and novels had been filtered through academia. It meant this or that, and it was good or bad literature. The evidence of it in the art around me was similarly processed. The evidence of it in people one knew, the occasional testimony one heard, was smothered in a certain criticism of it. The very need to express oneself subjectively was considered symptomatic of something being wrong. Sensations were privatized, feelings inadmissible, intuitions ignored, and thoughts subordinate to belief systems. People were isolated, yet paradoxically communitized by vast, underlying, hierarchic assumptions. If people counted for little (I mean the individual experience of people), children counted for much less; animals and plants, of course, for nothing. The sixties was the decade of revolt against this state of affairs. The uprising of victims—blacks, Native Americans, women, old folks, homosexuals, the handicapped, finally children and even animals (Save the Whales, etc.) and plants (Plants Have Feelings Too)—was the political expression of this revolt. In uncovering the individuality of my children that day, I launched myself on another great course of error, also typical of the times: that we were all equal and free before the law. As I had despised my own authority, this was quite a convenient twist of affairs for me. I now assumed that my children knew as much as I did— possibly more, since they were closer to the source of our origins —and that the three of us could therefore be great friends and forget about who was who.

I discounted experience once again, this time in the evolutionary sense: i.e., life character development, which implies seasoning and wisdom with age, like the cultivation of such old-fashioned virtues as patience and acceptance, and the ability to perceive social values in manmade rather than God-given terms. In the sixties, authority was vanquished, or at least successfully challenged, and subjectivity reigned wild. Liberation became another kind of excuse to disregard the experience of others. Manners, for example, were ditched, because they belonged to the ruling class, the class of our parents. With the newfound subjectivity, all other realities became suspect, even those belonging to "comrades-in-arms." People felt free to confront everybody else's reality. For me, this mind-set came to fruition in the early seventies, when I joined the anarchy of the women's movement and went running around the country telling as many women as possible what to do and think and being told by them in turn. The savagery unleashed by liberation went unchecked until around 1975. In its nascent form, back in the mid-sixties, or whenever during that decade it seized different people, it was an apocalyptic feeling of seeing the world fresh immediately after a disaster. I was a great candidate for "liberation." Not only was I living in a convulsive city and in a milieu that was already antisocial, but I had recently become one of society's choice victims. My huge subjective experience of '65 had been invalidated by doctors, friends, and family. Now, one year later, I received evidence that I was not alone. Being open to the subjective world of my children, I could see, with staggering implications, that realms and realms of experience were systematically excluded from "normal" life. And it was such a simple afternoon.

There was nothing much to it, really. First the three of us went more or less dancing off into the woods together to find a certain Tarzan rope swing that my son had been talking about. The day, of course, was brilliant; what else could it have been? Stepping lightly through dappled pools of sunshine, noticing leafy, woodsy, mossy shapes as if I'd never seen them before, the chatter of my kids sprinkling the air in bright confetti notes— this was the world in its splendid innocence before (after?) the disaster of civilization. The threshold was the entire eternal space of things. At the site of the Tarzan rope I was faced with an abyss. The proposed swing went way out over a deep, plunging pit. Here was the first big test. I had to hold on to this Jack's-beanstalk rope and swing into infinity. I was much too high to further dematerialize myself. But of course I didn't hesitate to do it, or to complete the requirement by swinging out there with each kid in turn, with a finale consisting of all three of us together hanging on somehow in a defiant and triumphant squealing sort of entwined tubular clump. On the way back my son told me a long, involved story (he said it was a ghost story), which unfortunately I didn't hear or record for its plot; I was too completely caught up in my amazement that he was telling me a story, that he should have a story to tell, that he knew how to tell one, and that I was so very attentive to him telling it to me.

This is sad but true. I was not in the habit of listening to people, much less my children, for my mother had never listened to me and nobody had ever listened to her or to her mother either. On the principle that a child should speak only when spoken to, a number of children grew up not really speaking to each other, having accustomed themselves to the belief that nobody was there to listen to them. By the time I was "grown up," my mother treated me like a mother who had never listened to her. We were both mad at each other for the same reason, though we played a different game over it. When I wasn't listening, she sharply reprimanded me; when she wasn't listening, I asked her to repeat what I had just said. The only thing we could share was family gossip, which terminated when my grandmother died in 1952 and my mother lost touch with my grandmother's family. My conversation with my mother consisted essentially of her remarks and occasional vain attempts on both sides to relate something of our lives to each other. She usually commented on my appearance, asked questions of a practical nature like "Where do you live now?," and sometimes summed me up by observing that I was unstable or prone to lose things or, more homiletically, that if I was unable to work, I would have to go back to the institutions—the remark she made this summer of '66 that stands out from all others. Children who grow up without listeners learn to talk to themselves and will find their own children distracting. Like my mother, I had been so preoccupied with my inner unconscious thoughts that the demands of my children were intrusive and disturbing, and the demands over and above the basics of food, clothes, sleep, transport, affection, etc.—specifically, those for loving attention

to the developing mind and psyche—tended to be especially upsetting. Affection itself was a borderline category. How many
parents love their children but never think or learn to demonstrate it? And then stop loving their children when a lack of affection makes their children rude and unpleasantly demanding?
Up until 1966 I had been ever busy inculcating my mother's self-involved heritage in my children, simply by being detached enough to make them feel that I wasn't really there. Now,
ironically, I was so detached, so very removed from the world of
disturbing and disturbed relations, that I was able to pay a great
deal of attention to things in their pristine state, before they
became so disturbed. There was no ideology or program here.
I had just regressed to a better time. One year earlier, when I
had so regressed, I had not seen any children. But then one
doesn't when being born. And now my children were older than
I was in the archaic sense. Following them around in the country that afternoon was a natural enough thing to do.

After returning from our rope-swing adventure, they both
suggested a trip to Bash Bish Falls, about a fifteen-mile drive
from my mother's bungalow on the lake. Bash Bish is located in
a spot in the northwest corner of Connecticut where three states
—Connecticut, New York, Massachusetts—meet, in the foot-
hills of the Berkshires. Parking in a clearing along a moun-
tainous road, the descent to the action is a long trek through a
pine-bed forest, clambering down rocks and gullies, sliding, sink-
ing into the deep spongy carpet of lengthy brown needles to the
pool at Bash Bish Falls. The pool is not big, but it's deep,
and the water booms down in a narrow cascade from a height of
about seventy-five feet. Lots of daredevils jump or dive from the
cliff where the water begins to fall. This was the second big test.
My son, our leader, was not interested in jumping or diving,
but he did want to climb up there to the top with his sister,
leaving me to quail down below. It wasn't the sort of expedition
I had ever allowed them. I had always been vigilant in exposed
settings. It had never been clear to me where my vigilance might

end and their survival instincts, or capabilities, take over. I had
no real confidence in the latter—especially since a terrible moment one afternoon when my son was four. He had darted out
into the street from where we were both standing on the sidewalk outside our apartment building in Washington Heights—in
order to cross the street, he later informed me, before I had a
chance to stop him. He had been struck instantly by a moving
car and flung onto his back, his eyes rolling up in his head—
whereupon I had raced away down the street screaming, then
looked back wildly the way terror-stricken people do in war
movies or famous old rape paintings and staggered back in
shock as the driver of the car (as it happened, a nurse at Columbia Presbyterian Hospital) was picking him up gently and carrying him round to the passenger side and placing him on the seat
to drive him to the hospital. I had jumped quickly into my own
car, my then heap, a '55 Ford, to follow her there. There was no
serious injury. The left side of his face was swollen and black
and blue for days. The incident didn't make me less confident in
them, only more watchful of myself watching them.

But now they were much older, and this confidence, or its
lack, was on the line. I reclined on one elbow there on a rock by
the pool, looking deceptively nonchalant, I can imagine, all too
aware that the real adventure here was the waiting I had to
make for them to climb safely and return. I developed confidence on the spot. I had no training or trial period. A frontier
was established and crossed in a few moments. I may have been
"younger," but I had a "history" of being older. It felt very
dangerous, making this kind of passage, so brilliantly illustrated,
or exteriorized, by the event of the climb. It wasn't that my kids
were not old enough (my son was eight and my daughter six)
but that they were still small enough to be perceived as helpless.
In truth, I had no developmental sense of them whatever. I had
only been aware of such obvious transitions as the ages for walking and talking. This big day in the country did nothing to clear
up my ignorance in such matters; it just served to reverse my
previous conceptions: from now on I saw them as competent

and wise way beyond their years, especially my son, who was suddenly so verbal and interested and interesting. Climbing back up through the pine-bed forest to the car, he regaled me with memories of having been born, of when he had his first pair of shoes put on, of his days in a nursery school when he was three, of secret moments with his sister when I was busy typing or cooking or daydreaming or whatever—disconcerting evidence that lives had been going on right at my feet that I knew nothing about, and that my children had a past, a past of their own, not just my parental memory of them. My daughter conveyed the past, and perhaps her hopes for the future, differently. Returning from her climb to the top of the waterfall with her brother, she picked up a used Coke can and a stick and tried bashing the can in in its center so both ends would flare up at the sides like a fat ribbon tied in the middle; after she made a dent in it, she got me to finish the job. Then we had to fashion the can back into its cylindrical shape, then fit it into another used can open at one end. I don't remember if we succeeded or not, but we both worked at it for a while, until, I suppose, the metaphor of some meaningful relationship was exhausted. I took it to be our bodies, rent and crushed, resurrected and reunited: mother and child endlessly separated and dismantled and joined together again.

For the past year, my children had lived with their father and his new wife. I had become a Sunday-afternoon visitor, the creator of brief and empty diversions (park, movies, zoo), a guilty outsider to the inner plan of a family—an abandoned grown-up child visiting her "adopted" children. I always felt numb and bad going to see them. We went through the motions, but our emotional life together had been suspended. This day in the country was a kind of mystical, symbolic reunion with them. I had "let them go," it's true, just as I had imagined I had to a year earlier in the Church in Garnersville, but none of us had been happy with our new earthly arrangement. On the road driving back to my mother's cabin on the lake, I was certain my son had something else in mind for us when we passed a sign that read End Speed Zone and he yelled, *"Mommie, go faster, go faster!"* I saw the three of us back in the hospital where we had all started together. Possibly this was the third and last test. I pulled over to the side to catch my breath and have a calm conversation about safety and speed zones.

My son hated to see me go that day, and I hated leaving them with my mother. I told him to take good care of his sister and drove slowly off through the narrow dirt road crowded by trees blending in the evening dusk to Route 22 and the return to New York. Approaching Brewster, a big town halfway home, I decided to ditch my heap and call for help.

After leaving my mother's summer cabin, I lost radio contact, as it were, with the world in particular and at large. Driving along Route 22, passing mammoth shapes dimly outlined against the murky night sky (like the awesome complex of buildings known as Harlem Valley State Psychiatric Center, its tall, heavy brick smokestack standing sentinel and marking the site), I beamed into some celestial frequency. I had a kind of dialogue with my dead grandmother about the pros and cons of remaining on earth, and I imagined that somehow I would marry my son in heaven. I felt pulled or magnetized off the road, and as if I couldn't define the directions of other vehicles or gauge their speeds or proximity, or be sure that I myself was on course and not drifting left across the center line or right across the shoulders into the grass. My vision was blurring. I decided I wanted to live—that my grandmother, if that was to whom I was talking, had to wait. She had seemed to be beckoning me; the pull was very great. Her birthday was August 22, and I had begun to wonder whether she had recently decided to manifest herself around the time of her birthday. In 1966 she would have been ninety-four.

At Brewster I pulled into a gas station and got change to make a phone call to the city. I was afraid of the attendant there. I had begun translating everything—looks, gestures, postures, movements—into digestive or sexual terms. A suspicious glance could mean I looked edible. A friendly smile could mean mur-

Above: Single mothers and their children:
Jill Johnston, Charlotte Bellamy, Jill's son
Richard, Ann Wilson; Charlotte's son Miles,
Ann's son Ocean, and her twin daughters Ara and
Kate. *Photo © Les Levine.*

Right: Jill's daughter, Winnie.

Below: Richard and Jill. *Photo by Peter Hujar.*

der. A hose or a hammer picked up that rape was imminent. A cash register opening and closing that something had already been devoured. I was fairly frantic. But I managed to get a dime in the black box and call Agnes Martin: I suppose I thought of Agnes because she was older and because she knew about Bellevue. The thing to know about Agnes was that her impulse was to save and to slaughter at once. Fortunately, in this case at least, it wasn't difficult to sort the one from the other. I wanted her to do two things: obtain a vehicle and come and get me, and to tell me what to do about the cache of Thorazine I had on me. I have no memory of how or when I obtained this vial of the deadly Thorazine, but I can imagine it was any time after August 20, when I knew I was flying away and wished to have an uninterrupted flight plan. Now the big moment had arrived. If I couldn't cool out somehow right away, "they" would come and get me. I had to be able to keep calling my own shots. I asked Agnes in a freighted sort of monotone how much Thorazine she thought I should take. She asked me how much I had, and when I explained I had this whole vial full, she said perfectly blithely that I should swallow the entire thing. This I knew was patently ridiculous. She did, however, agree to find a vehicle to rescue me—not a small thing to do late in the evening and from that far away, about an hour-and-a-half drive. Hanging up, feeling certain she would come, I parked the Olds in a remote corner of the gas station, took 400 mgs. of Thorazine, close to the amount I knew I had been given in the hospitals the previous year, then sat down on a curb close to the car to wait, trying to maintain the semblance of somebody who was sitting on a curb naturally waiting, though the pills made me feel delirious and nauseous and faint. And I had to wait an eternity. It seemed as if I had to concentrate to the utmost to magnify hugely the tiniest amount of consciousness I had left, to stay awake and remain cognizant of where I was. Finally Agnes arrived, with Thalia, in a yellow convertible Volkswagen bug they had borrowed from a male friend of Thalia's. I fell into the back of it, swooning might-

ily in some kind of Thorazine delirium. (I never saw the Oldsmobile heap again; a couple of months later I heard that state
troopers had reported its whereabouts to my mother in Connecticut.)

I might mark that as the moment I definitively separated
from my body. My booster rocket had fallen away; I was untethered to the planet, just a mind floating—like a balloon
without its ballast or a kite its string or a capsule its mission
control system—into the vast reaches of sayonara. I was very ill,
in a coma perhaps, lying in a tepee (the back of a yellow convertible bug), like Black Elk of the Oglala Sioux when he was
nine and his legs had crumpled up under him and he couldn't
walk: "I was sick . . . both my legs and both my arms were
swollen badly and my face was all puffed up. . . . I was lying in
our tepee and my mother and father were sitting beside me."
Was I not enacting some Caucasian girl's version of the Black
Elk story? I spent three days in New York at Thalia's place in
my delirium, a cocoon of gray fevers, a miasmal, penumbral
vortex of mental vegetation—the seat of chaos, where genies or
jinns take shape and rise up in filmy, smoky, tornadic, sepulchral
splendor to bewitch the sufferer. Sometime during these three
days I gave birth to my wondrous genealogy. Black Elk said, "I
could see out through the opening of the tepee, and there two
men were coming from the clouds, head-first like arrows slanting
down. . . . Each now carried a long spear, and from the points of
these a jagged lightning flashed. They came clear down to the
ground . . . and stood a little way off and looked at me and said:
'Hurry! Come! Your Grandfathers are calling you!' " Of course I
heard no such thing, and saw no such beautiful apparitions. But
I did generate ancestors, who kept coming and coming, or kept
naming and naming themselves, in a self-producing field of absurd interrelationships. Once begun, it had no end, and of
course no reasonable design. Its design was the logic of dreams:
a fabric woven of that mythological mix of lies and truths which
reveals so much more than lies alone or truths alone are able to

convey. And in any design like this, a central figure emerges—the totem in person, so to speak—from which the rest radiates or to which all the rest refers. For Black Elk, it was a council of six Grandfathers who had called him to teach him. For myself, it was a dead Frenchman called Guillaume Apollinaire.

11

Totem

Guillaume Apollinaire! Imagine! A dead French poet who had
never meant anything to me, whose existence I had barely been
aware of before 1966. I had been "called" by the spirit of a
foreigner—a man of Italian birth and Polish ancestry—who had
died over a decade before I was born. But his very remoteness
apparently made him an appropriate subject. For if a man like
this had never meant anything to me, neither had my own father, in quite an important sense. Then, you might say, any man
would do. But Apollinaire was not simply a random choice.
He had a life and a background that my own curiously echoed.
Had I been searching for a father, narrowing down the suspects,
I might easily have picked him out of a lineup for some striking
similarities. He was the critic and champion of the avant-garde
in Paris before World War I, during the Belle Epoque, those
seething years of anarchy and disruption in the arts—the period
that we all seemed to be reliving somehow. Mysteriously, I had
divined that Apollinaire was the man of our century who best
represented my heavy transitional life in the sixties. I have to say
"divined" because I would never have selected him, or anybody
else for that matter, consciously. To have found myself in any of
the old masters would have been high presumption, a little like a
female painter identifying with Picasso or imagining she could
be anything but his mistress or model.

The way I got so close to Apollinaire was by a certain sleight
of mind. In 1963 I had read all about him in a book by Roger
Shattuck called *The Banquet Years*. While I was reading, I never

thought, "Aha, here is somebody just like me!" or anything like that; I merely filed the information, and the photographs, in a mental drawer marked To Be Used Later. Apollinaire was featured in Shattuck's book along with three other French culture heroes—painter Henri Rousseau, writer Alfred Jarry, composer Erik Satie—and I have no memory of finding one figure more interesting than any other. Satie, actually, should have interested me the most, considering that he was one of John Cage's dead mentors, and everything that interested Cage was supposed to be interesting to his followers. Certainly no one in the sixties commemorated Apollinaire the way Cage did Satie, honoring him by a marathon recital, eighteen hours and forty minutes, of a piece by Satie called *Vexations*. And certainly the writings of Apollinaire were of no interest whatever next to the entire oeuvre of Gertrude Stein, honored in numerous productions of her work and marathon readings of *The Making of Americans*. But everybody understood that Apollinaire was one of the luminaries. In some circles he has the reputation of a great poet; in my own circle he was known to have been the colorful promoter of all things innovative. I seemed like his logical heir, or so I thought after his name erupted in my mind with all the force and voltage of Christ's the year before. But the case for his actual paternity seemed no less persuasive; and in fact at this time I simply told everybody he was my father. I wasn't just fooling around, either; I really thought he was.

Had he been alive in 1966, he would have been only eighty-six. The fact that I never met him of course made him as eligible as any other man. But more impressive was the rumor that he was dead. Beyond that was the important datum that he was European. These three items in themselves were demonstrably convincing. Moreover, he had a mustache and he was dashing and debonair, just like my mother described my father. He was also a king, as shown by Picasso's drawing of him. But perhaps my chief exhibit rests, or rested, on a concussion. On March 17, 1917, Apollinaire, a lieutenant in the French army, was sitting in a trench in the south of France when he was struck in the head above the right temple by some shell splinters; a military surgeon removed the fragments. Later on, he had an operation called a trepanation—the opening of a window in the brain to relieve a certain pressure that was causing symptoms of dizziness and paralysis of the left arm. He was thirty-six years old. He died in Paris of the flu, during the big epidemic of 1918. Ages and dates are very important in legitimacy suits.

At any rate, the best way to explain Apollinaire's unlikely new role as my father was to point to his concussion as the germinal factor in a big hoax. Many folk heroes are known or said never to have died, or to have returned from death: Arthur of England and Joan of France are good examples. In our time, some people say that Anastasia is alive and well in New Jersey and that Amelia Earhart is driving a BMW in Cincinnati. As for Christ, of course, his resurrection is still big news. I'm not being entirely funny. Celebrities aside, lots of regular people, men in particular, are known to leave spouse, job, and town one day and never return, resuming life elsewhere with a whole new identity. Apollinaire sustained a blow to the head. Life begins with quite a bit of pressure on the brain. A concussion is a kind of birth. A blow to the head is a typical castration symbol. I could reopen my case, starting my book in some such way: "In the beginning was a concussion . . ." In itself a concussion is just an unfortunate accident; it may also provide an explanation for an inconceivable birth, or the perpetration of an identity hoax. A woman might experience it as amnesia; a man might drop out of his own continuum.

It was the famous photograph of Apollinaire with his head bandaged that gave me this bizarre, but not unreasonable, idea. Photographs always meant everything to me. My father's very existence was synonymous with a photograph. It was the *most* famous portrait of Apollinaire in a derby that stirred my paternal imagination, so fertile for symbols by which I might identify him. The mustache; the derby; the dark hair; the stiff white collar; the aloof, proud, bemused, urbane gaze; the handsome, debonair appearance—this was the image I had of him in that region of the mind where ideals coagulate. This was the sort of man who could be found posing between the king and the queen. The trinity of the king and queen with my father in between was for me the Holy Family. I had been carrying that image around with me since I was twenty. This new one of Apollinaire in the derby was just a kind of blow-up, an enlarged detail, of the same man. The photo of Apollinaire bandaged was something different, representing perhaps that moment when his identity as my father was conceived. He looks very mischievous in the photo, as if he is going to put something over on us, not at all the way people normally look in pictures of themselves wounded. And I have to stress his age, which was thirty-six in 1916, when the photo was taken—the age notorious for a so-called midlife crisis, give or take a year or two. Other notables known to have experienced life crises at thirty-six or thereabouts are Dante, Shakespeare, Beethoven, Goethe, Ibsen, Voltaire, Margaret Mead, Michael Harrington, and Timothy Leary. Others, like Van Gogh, simply died at thirty-six. I always ask people I know who are older than thirty-six what happened to them then. It could be anything: accident, illness, divorce, bankruptcy, revelation, a benighted pregnancy, the death or departure of a loved one—such events may alter a life direction sensationally. Some new existence always heaves into view. It may happen earlier or later; there are those who perceive their entire lives as a midlife crisis. For myself, I was right on target: in '65, at thirty-six, I went completely mad. My theory about Apollinaire was that he had some prescience concerning his fate that moment in the trenches in southern France (when he was struck, incidentally, he happened to be reading a copy of the *Mercure de France*, to which he contributed a column called "La Vie anecdotique"), and that as the first big war shuddered and screeched to a halt, he arranged a certain outrageous revision of himself. He calculated the time of his demise and made preparations for the disposal of his body. There was a funeral with military honors all the way to the grave. His mother held his officer's cap between her two hands in front of her as though it were on a cushion. He was buried, by record, at Père Lachaise, the final resting place of many French heroes, on the outskirts of Paris. And then he disappeared. He didn't go away like Gauguin to sunny Tahiti, or like Rimbaud to darkest Africa; he went across the Channel to Merrie Olde England, where his life was resumed under another name. The prospect of migrating with a new identity would not have been unfamiliar to Apollinaire, who had already been living under an assumed name. In fact, his name had been changed twice, the first time by his mother shortly after his birth. Like myself, Apollinaire was born with a name other than the one by which we know him and raised in a country other than the one where he was born. More than anything else, it was the circumstances of Apollinaire's birth that had prompted me to adopt him—or to imagine that before (or after) he disappeared, he dreamed me up. Our similar careers, compounded by the same kind of background, must have seemed too extraordinary to overlook. In order to become my more conventional father, the very proper Englishman, he would surely have had to have been the most resourceful and versatile of fellows. Having had no father himself, Apollinaire was a man of few restraints or inhibitions. Once identified with a man like this, anything would seem possible. The field of paternal candidacy itself was wide open and uncharted. With my instant kinship to a man whose own paternity has never been resolved (and who reputedly was not certain himself who his father was), I naturally superimposed our genealogies, dovetailing fact and speculation on both sides. Everyone who saw me between September 5 and 18 has said that I was busy making up charts and talking incessantly about the names that went into them. Around the 12th, I ended up at Rauschenberg's six-storey building on Lafayette Street, where I was held for a week, more or less under house arrest, and from there forcibly removed to Bellevue. I left a whole pile of these charts in a big wooden

drawer in Rauschenberg's kitchen. I may have recovered them
(he says I did), but if so, I subsequently lost them. I'm a historian of the memory of some lost ruins.

My mind of course was a shambles, which I reorganized by
cultural models in order to imagine I still lived. I had brought
civilization down; the ruins were my raw material, the stuff with
which to refashion a life that might better meet my needs. As an
analyst of this sort of ruin, I could reconstruct its history by
joining fact and fancy to make a true (psychological) picture of
a disenfranchised person. A person who felt outside civilization
to begin with might be expected to dabble in ruins one day.

Once when I was an art critic, I went to review the work of a
young sculptor called Dan Flavin who became well known for
his neon light assemblages. All I remember from that particular
show was a smashed, flattened, corrugated, and rusted small can
(a "found object") that he had titled *Apollinaire Wounded*. In
general I loved all destruction art, as well as occasions when
violence creatively erupted. A few years later, at a "Destruction
Art" symposium, Charlotte Moorman, the avant-garde cellist
and collaborator of Nam June Paik's, was performing a certain
piece that called for her to stand at a table and raise a violin
over her head very, very slowly until it reached a full height, at
which moment she was to bring it down forcefully, smashing it
to smithereens on the table in front of her. The piece was called
One for Violin. A man in the audience wanted to make it two:
as Moorman raised the instrument over her head, he tried to
stop her by stretching himself out in front of her on the table and
arguing with her—he wanted her to give the violin to some poor
kid who could use it. At one point he removed his coat and
offered it to Moorman in exchange for the violin. When he refused to desist, she eventually just bashed him over the head.
The din had been terrific, everyone yelling different things, and
I'd added my bit, hollering, "Give it to him!" At the time I
thought I meant *hand* it to him (or so I wrote, in an enthusiastic
review of the event called "Over His Dead Body"), but I can see
now that I could as easily have meant "Give it to him" in the

violent sense—i.e., bash him—without realizing it. This was 1968. Not for a moment did I associate the key event of the performance—a man struck violently on the head—with that loaded motif of mine: Apollinaire wounded. Not even when I found out the following year that the man who had so foolishly interposed himself between Moorman and her instrument had in the meantime died. (Whether or not his death was linked to the incident, I have no idea.) But art and life remained disjointed for me right into the seventies.

It was always exciting to have art bisected by life, as in this Moorman-violin-intruder event, but I would just incorporate the distraction into an ongoing art frame. The only way to get away from this was to abjure art, and then I went overboard for life, which included art only in the form of my own writing—as though to make up for the many lost years when I had almost no personal reality. It was this very lack of reality that made me so creative just then. With one or two bare facts at my disposal, I felt free to embroider quite a large picture. I assume that this is what people do who know or have been told very little, and that I had done this all along, but had until now kept it to myself, and *from* myself as well. In some sense, a psychosis is nothing but the *exposure* of hitherto concealed thought constructs. The essence of my story was that my dead father had never really died, even though—or I should say *because*—my mother had once told me he had. The mischievous image of Apollinaire with his head swathed in a bandage suited my needs perfectly. If my mother had put something over on me, I now had a man who could (have) put something over on *her*. Imagine what might have poured forth from a head in which a *window* had been made when the surgeons did their operation! Is not a poet, in any case, considered a fountainhead of languages and identities? It took me just a few days to establish the bulwark of Apollinaire, a highly placed operative between me and my mother. To do it, I drew on both families and a few others as well.

12

My Napoleon

If my own father had never died, neither had my mother's. So the man I put together was a triumvirate of her father and mine and Apollinaire, with Apollinaire's father in the background, and several important accessories. My mother's father had a clean-cut, well-trimmed, tall, lean, and self-possessed look of his own, at least before his declining years in his forties, when he began to resemble the rugged, furrowed, earthen-faced farmers of his background. His age when he "died," forty-six, fit neatly into my new genealogical scheme, for the father my mother said was mine was forty-five when I was born. Back in 1966, I was altogether fuzzy on dates of death, birth, marriage, etc., but I knew the outline, the essential features. Had I been clearer, obviously I would have had less, or no, basis for my new story about myself; yet the facts were belied by some ancient familial truths, which I could perceive very clearly in my altered state, and the facts in any case had striking appositions in them. It wasn't difficult at all to conclude that my mother's father and mine were the same person. First, as noted, they were the two men my mother had told me were dead. She never mentioned the death of any other man except her father's father, whom she never knew and who manifestly had to be out of the running, even to my deformed way of thinking. Nonetheless, he was surely a key figure in our family mythology. In 1896, at the age of sixty-three, he ended his life by putting a bullet through his head. His son, my mother's father, was twenty-two at the time and was living in Manhattan, where he met my grandmother, marrying her in 1900. My mother always thought her father was a much younger boy when his father killed himself, possibly because she assumed that the suicide occurred immediately after the death of her father's mother, at which time both her father and his sister may have been given up for adoption by their father, though it is certain only that the girl, who was nine when the mother died, was actually adopted.

In reality the mother died in 1888 (at the age of forty-nine), when my mother's father was fourteen. Yet my mother, like me, though fuzzy on facts, had the basics straight: that her grandfather's suicide could not have projected a great model for her father, who was not yet established in the world and who had already been "abandoned" by his mother. A man like this would not seem the best paternal material, but my grandmother was clearly drawn to somebody whose circumstances reflected her own, for when she was fifteen, in 1887, both her parents had died. The correspondences here were quite close—which tells plenty, but doesn't readily explain how or why my mother's father and mine turned out to be the same person. All I had to go on, besides the lie that they had both died, was a similarity in appearance and the striking but not too unusual fact that when he met my mother, my father was old enough to have sired her. (Actually I had something very concrete, had I thought of it, in the identical nature of my mother's maiden name, and *my* surname, at birth.) When I was so crazy that September of '66, drawing many wild but not improbable conclusions, I had the good sense to keep this part of my story under wraps, making a big fuss essentially over Apollinaire alone, whose paternity I claimed only for myself. But that was my design, to have a father I could call my own. My "good sense" here was probably just the appropriate flight from the awesome reality of incest, which was the model that made a third party like Apollinaire possible.

Surely incest was the best explanation for my mother's decision to keep me in the dark about my father. Grounds of illegitimacy alone hardly seemed enough to explain such exsanguinating secrecy. It's true that many children of my circumstances have been told that their fathers were dead, but I had no way of knowing that (I never knew anybody else of my circumstances, or if I did, I had not been told of it), and the significance of legitimacy in a patriarchy largely escaped me until the feminists found me. Had I seen *Chinatown* in the early or mid-sixties, I might never have imagined Apollinaire; instead, perhaps, I would have been convinced that I was stuck with a history of incest, which would have meant that the necessity of separating out from my mother had a worse prognosis. As it was, I was able to downplay the incest, make it a shadowy sort of reality, by adding an extra character who cast doubts on the awful literalness of the two men my mother said belonged to both of us. *Chinatown*, the film by Roman Polanski starring Jack Nicholson and Faye Dunaway, which I saw in 1975, showed a woman desperate to shield her daughter from the man responsible for her daughter's birth, her own father (John Huston)—not only to protect her from the shameful knowledge but to defend her from another such plunderous act. The end is purely Oresteian; the mother is killed, the daughter is faced with her mother's father (and her own), who presumably once again has the field as he fawns lasciviously over this blooming sixteen-year-old (her mother's age at the time of the incestuous conception). The mother is shot by the police while trying to get away with her daughter; she was wanted as a suspect in the slaying of her husband, who actually has been slain by her father. It seemed clear, however, that she was paying for the crime of incest, which only the detective/lover (hired by her to find her husband's murderer, and by her father to find her daughter) had found out about. It was the detective who caused her death, by inadvertently leading the police to her whereabouts. Was this the fate that my mother had tried to preserve us from? I don't know. But if it was, fortunately for her, an ocean lay between her and the man who might have pursued her daughter, a war ended the possibility of travel, the man himself had long made another life abroad, and he died before his daughter had the chance to travel herself.

War and travel were high on the agenda of my paternal

scheme. A back-and-forthness across borders and large bodies of water is the transitional image I have of creation. On one of these trips I was conceived. The occasion was a clandestine meeting between my mother and her own father, though she thought the man was a perfect stranger when she met him, and continued right on thinking so. They met on a transatlantic voyage to America when my mother was bringing a patient from the American Hospital in Paris, where she had been working, to Boston, and my father (and hers) was on one of his business trips between London and New York and other U.S. destinations. My mother was twenty-five, this father forty-two, though they might have been twenty-six and forty-three, or twenty-four and forty-one; but there was assuredly a seventeen-year difference between them. According to my mother, her father died in 1920, in his forties. It's unlikely she knew his exact age, since he was two years younger than my grandmother, and he lied about that on their marriage license, making himself two years older than he was, thus the same age as his wife. She said he died in Huntington, Long Island, of tuberculosis. She told me that *my* father died (abroad) of pneumonia. Influenza, tuberculosis, pneumonia—it was evidently all the same to me: one big lie. My theory about this father of my mother's was that his "death" was actually a departure abroad. A departure, after all, had everything to do with the "death" of the father my mother said was mine. I mean that when I found out he had not actually died (in 1950, when he actually did), it became apparent that my mother had always said he died because he had abandoned her, or, for all I knew, she him. Departure and death amounted to the same thing. And I had never seen anybody dead. I doubt that I believed in death at all. Death certainly never meant a loss, simply an absence. My mother's lie about the death of these men became my truth. The real truth lies someplace where the two intersect. The extent to which fact and motive blend or diverge is the measure of my story. I had enough experience of my mother and her mother to know that my mother's father was a henpecked man. He was not the best provider, he never found a profession, he was withdrawn and taciturn and finally sickly, and he had a hobby, mathematics, that must have seemed to my grandmother like a real waste of time. My mother said her father married her mother only because she was beautiful. My grandmother had a number of fine qualities, but forbearance was not one of them. She would not have been easy on this discouraged husband of hers. And here is a major condition for departure: the discouragement of a husband compounded by a wife's lack of confidence. This was a typical, perhaps classic, sort of couple. The man was intelligent but unschooled, worthy but self-damned; the woman beautiful but ignorant, hardy but insecure. The nurturance my grandmother had to offer would have been largely domestic. She accepted domestic enslavement, and she toiled for a man who didn't amount to anything or whose services as a provider were frequently in question. Clearly they decided on their own that they would do better apart. But there was no divorce in those days; there was death, and there were mysterious exits. Socially speaking, there was only death. Any other kind of separation was too embarrassing to report. The way I saw it, then, was that after my mother's father had had enough of his nagging wife, and perhaps his disappointed daughter (though my mother always said only the nicest things about him), he shipped out to Europe—around, say, 1915—where he turned up in France as—Guillaume Apollinaire.

No—this was too wildly improbable. But I did have to get him abroad if he was going to turn into the man who met my mother on a transatlantic crossing in 1925. And I couldn't have him going directly to England first, for I already had Apollinaire traversing the channel to become that same man. Somehow Apollinaire had to be the man in the middle, the medium between the other two. Three in one: Apollinaire a kind of Holy Ghost. He was in fact plunk in the middle by his age. The births of the three men spanned exactly ten years—1874, 1880 (Apollinaire), and 1884—dates about which I was conveniently murky that September of '66. The charts I drew up, the obsessive diagrams, were crowded with names, not dates;

there were no inconsistencies, only agreeable juxtapositions. My
mind had ceased functioning linearly; it was moving by aggre-
gates, in the realm of collage. This is how dream sequences
transpire. A good collage (dream) brings disparate elements
convincingly together. Specialists will call the kind of thinking I
was doing paralogical, or "side-by-side" thinking. The way it
went, I achieved identity, making various persons the same or
interchangeable, on the basis of identical predicates—i.e., common qualities or parts. This can result in an orgy of identifica-
tions. Any part of any person may suggest identity with another.
The object is possession. Apollinaire was mine, or me, for open-
ers, just by virtue of his first name—never mind his profession or
background, or all his other names or how he got them, or his
career in the army and his concussion. By a little swift etymolog-
ical figuring, I could see my own first name embedded in his.
"Gill," I thought, which is a common English spelling of my
name, was simply an Anglican contraction of "Guill." Why else,
I asked myself, had I been called William in boarding school?
There was never an explanation, but I suppose they wanted to
nickname me Gillian (Jillian), and since I was boyish, William
sounded close enough. And in fact, as I found out years later,
Gill and Jill and William and Guillaume and Wilhelm (as Apollinaire was born) are derived from some common source.

The conclusion I would draw, from seeing my name embedded in Apollinaire's and remembering at the same time that
I had once been called William, and amassing other evidence
that clung by association to those two items (I got William the
Conqueror in there, another famous bastard, and a man who had
once crossed the Channel in quite a big way), was that I was a
part of some Design, and that an Intelligence outside myself had
been guiding me toward my fulfillment in it, in fact my central
role in it, and that that Intelligence might be manifested in those
around me—for instance, in my schoolmates who dubbed me
William—because they must have known all along "who I was."
If in September '66 I had had information recently acquired
about my mother's family in America, I would have swept it right

along into those proofs of identity, paralogically accomplished, by which I sought to establish connections, uniting my mother's and father's families and Apollinaire's. There was a William and a Juliana, to name two, back in my maternal grandfather's genealogy near Buffalo. But identical parts of names were especially pregnant with synergistic possibilities. An outstanding connection was provided by my father's middle name and my maternal grandfather's first name, which were the same. (John Hinckley, Jr., the would-be assassin of Reagan, pointed to the identical letters in his surname and that of Travis Bickle, the hero of Martin Scorsese's *Taxi Driver*, to account for his attempts to duplicate Bickle's movie exploits in real life.) My mind raced from one synapse to another, drawing this new picture of my past, not unlike the way a child might form a picture by drawing lines between numbered dots, a picture already established (by a superior, outside Intelligence) but made explicitly visible only when its nodes, or dots, are linked up. I like to think the whole life is created this way; the picture is already there, and as we go along filling it in, we see the design we were meant to be. We may pull the image this way and that, bend it out of shape if we can, screw it up sometimes, skip a corner here and there, stumble over an unsuspected color, dare to alter something very intrinsic, confuse a choice with fate, and so on; but in the end we have only made what we could never imagine might have been otherwise.

The "collage" I was working on in September '66 was a rapid-growth product. I was having one of those spurts—the kind a child has from time to time when it adds a few inches in height over quite a short period. The additive and composite method of collage, the bringing of many things into focus at once, has the creative advantage of aligning elements not ordinarily thought to belong together—a great opportunity for the displaced and disenfranchised. Apollinaire himself, a man of dubious ancestry, of complex civil status (French by language, upbringing, and occupation; Russian and Polish through his mother; Italian by birth), without citizenship in his adopted country until 1916, two years before his death, and a man to whom extraordinary things always seemed to happen, was the champion of Cubism (that art of fractured images, laid "side by side") and a poet who enjoyed the dislocations and odd juxtapositions of words, images, and meanings typical of the painting he espoused. But Apollinaire laid claim to things by simpler methods as well: he would just say this and that was his by virtue of some special intelligence or by association (he would point out) to his name. In 1907 he was reported by a newspaper in Paris as having entered a cafe a little drunk and called for Apollinaris water, crying, "C'est mon eau! C'est mon eau!" His American biographer, Francis Steegmuller, said, "For Apollinaire, Apollinaris water was 'mon eau'—anything Apollinairian was his and had importance. Born in a corner of Trastevere, assigned a name out of an alphabet by a clerk, reassigned the Slavic name of a more or less nobly born adventuress mother, his father a silence and an absence—this French poet needed a name of his own." In 1974, passing through Mechelen, Belgium, I ordered Apollinaris water and called it "mon Bruneau" —the maiden name of my father's mother. In 1966 the rumor that Apollinaire was my father was as firmly established in New York as was the rumor once rampant in Paris that Apollinaire was a son of the Pope.

For reasons perhaps not unlike my own, Apollinaire was loath to reveal his actual father's identity to his art-world friends, preferring to allow the rumor that connected him to the Church hierarchy to flourish. By so doing, he achieved a certain confusion (if not in his mind, in the minds of others) between the identity of his own father and that of his mother's, for his mother's father was indeed a papal chamberlain, a mostly honorific position. While the identity of Apollinaire's father may still be in question, there is no doubt whatever that his maternal grandfather was one Michael Apollinaris de Kostrowitzky, of some lesser Polish nobility, who had been a Polish officer in the Russian army and had seen his family property in Poland confiscated after his two brothers participated in the anti-Russian uprising of 1863. His brothers were sent to Siberia, and he moved to Rome with his wife, Juliana Floriani, and their daughter, Angelica Alexandrina, Apollinaire's mother. Papal chamberlains were recruited from *"signori rispettabili e cavalieri laici,"* respectable gentleman and secular knights—Romans, Italians, or foreigners who offered proof of religious attachment to the apostolic seat. No doubt he primarily submitted proof of noble Polish lineage: in 1851 he and his brothers had qualified for listing in a Polish almanac of heraldry. In Angelica, he had, evidently, quite a rebellious daughter. She was kicked out of a Roman convent school ("extremely difficult child") and gave birth at a young age to two sons of father "N.N." (*non noto*—unknown). The paternity of Alberto, her second son, remained even more mysterious than that of Apollinaire, her first. There was no indication one way or another, according to Apollinaire's biographers, that the two boys had the same father. The man most generally conceded to be Apollinaire's was one Francesco Flugi d'Aspermont, born in 1835, descended from an ancient Swiss clan which was ennobled in the seventeenth century.

Only four other things about Francesco seem certain: he left home; he had a brief career as an Italian army officer; during the 1870s and -80s he spent some time in Rome; and in 1884 he was provided with capital and persuaded by two older brothers, one of them a prelate, to emigrate to America because of his gambling debts and romantic entanglements—one of them reportedly with a Russian woman whose child or children he fathered. He was at least twenty years older than Angelica de Kostrowitzky. It might be imagined that an older man, a foreigner to boot, in an army officer's uniform, would have been quite an attractive item to this rebellious daughter of a Polish exile in Rome. Angelica's father had himself been an officer, and she never really approved of Guillaume until he became an officer in the French army. No proof has ever been adduced to account for a single meeting in Rome between Angelica and Francesco Flugi d'Aspermont, and the case for his paternity rests on just two reports: Angelica's mention of his name to one of her women friends, and Apollinaire pointing to a photograph in his mother's house and saying to a friend, "That is my father." *Francesco was little more than a photograph.* According to Anatol Stern, the Polish surrealist poet, who in 1959 put forward another candidate for Apollinaire's father, Francesco was merely one of the numerous lovers of Angelica (who became Olga, by the way, when she left Rome with her two sons in 1887). Stern's candidate was a grandson of Napoleon, which happily for me brings Apollinaire's paternal design quite close to mine. As in my own case, there was some confusion between his earthly fathers, his own and his mother's (if not in his mind, then in the lore of his time and the later accounts of his life)—a confusion concretely rooted in being born with the name of the maternal grandfather—and a third, more impressive, figure emerged to complicate the issue and to mediate between the other two. Apollinaire was my Napoleon, if you will, though Apollinaire was content to let it be known that his father was probably some Vatican dignitary. If he himself strongly suspected that Napoleon figured in the picture, he was smart enough not to say so or to mask it in his fiction, the descendants of Napoleon being perhaps more numerous in mental hospitals than in history.

In 1966 I knew nothing of Napoleon in Apollinaire's story, nor did I register Francesco Flugi d'Aspermont. When I read Shattuck's *The Banquet Years,* in which Francesco is allotted several lines, I had not consciously identified myself with Apollinaire. Such a lack of information, I suppose I don't have to point out, served my purposes quite well. It was, after all, a mythology that I was missing, not a real father, whom it was my fate never to have, or whose time had passed me by. As I had confused my own father with my mother's, it was not difficult to superimpose Apollinaire on his, whoever he was. Father or grandfather, it was all the same to me. I didn't know that Francesco had emigrated to America in 1884 (such a wonderful fact!), where he could so easily have met my grandmother, born in 1872. So I had my grandmother going abroad somehow to meet his son; and for one moment at least during my seizure in September, I imagined that my grandmother was the English governess Apollinaire knew in Germany when he was twenty and wished desperately to marry. (He met this young woman, Annie Playden, in 1900, the year my grandmother met my grandfather, and courted her till 1901, the year my grandparents married. In my "dream" it was very easy to move people around. This Annie Playden, incidentally, subsequently emigrated to America herself, ending up in California as Mrs. A. P. Postings.) Had I known about Francesco's emigration, I might have been wildly intoxicated by the mere thought of his almost certain meeting with my grandmother in New York, and the birth of a son who would somehow have been spirited back to Europe, there to be known as Apollinaire. However, if Apollinaire did indeed cross the Channel, as I surmised, at any time after his "death" in 1918, subsequently to meet my mother in the form of an Englishman on a transatlantic voyage back to America, this would make him my uncle and my father; and I was already constrained to think that it was my grandmother's husband, Frederick Crowe, rumored to have died in 1920 at the age of forty-six, who turned up in Europe, later to meet my mother on one of those return trips in another guise. Possibly Frederick was actually Francesco, I could have reasoned, in which case my mother would be Apollinaire's half-sister, and Apollinaire my father and grandfather and uncle-in-law, which is rather improbable. Anyway, the dates are not compatible: Francesco was thirty-nine years older than Frederick, according to the record. Nonetheless, it isn't inconceivable that Francesco met my grandmother at some point in New York and fathered a child by her. He would have been fifty-two when she was fifteen. If no proof exists for a meeting in Rome between Francesco and Angelica before Francesco emigrated to America, there's no reason to assume he didn't meet anybody at all. And imagine what he would have been up to once his brothers provided him with capital and he arrived in the great land of opportunity, fleeing his gambling debts and his series of entanglements. He would certainly change his name to begin with from Francesco to something like Frederick.

Possibly Frederick was Francesco's son, but Frederick was born in 1874, and Francesco didn't arrive in America till 1884. So much for Francesco—a man who, by family account, was never heard from again after his departure for America, the type of man who succeeds in dropping out of sight while still in this world. For me, perhaps the most interesting thing about him is that he was forty-five when Apollinaire was born, the same age as my (own) father at my birth. But of course the most interesting thing overall is his disappearance, and the disappearance of all these men, and their failure to be or to become fathers. A long history of paternal failure in my mother's family was the background for my legitimacy suit. A founding father called Almond Crow, born 1793 in Pennsylvania, became a successful farmer upstate in New York and had ten children, but he died in 1849, at the age of fifty-seven. His wife, Olive, survived him by twenty-two years; she died in 1871 at seventy-seven. Of their ten children, only two survived their mother, and one of them was my mother's paternal grandfather, Chauncey Crow, the one who committed suicide in 1896. Not a single male in this family, from the nineteenth century on into the twentieth, emerged away from the land. They may have become carpenters or painters or handymen or blacksmiths, but Frederick, my mother's father, was the first to leave the rural landscape and seek his fortune, as is said, in the big city—a fortune that turned out to be my grandmother, whose ambitions were limited to motherhood and domestic service. Frederick added the e to his family name, making it Crowe, hoping, perhaps, to shake off any stigma that might cling to a name associated with the "bird of death." But it didn't matter. The men of his family seemed as doomed as those of the Kennedy clan, though in the latter case a prominence was implicated in the fall of its men, while in my mother's paternal clan it was a very lack of prominence that made the men so vulnerable and weak. It was my mother's fate to garner all this subdued animus, cast about across

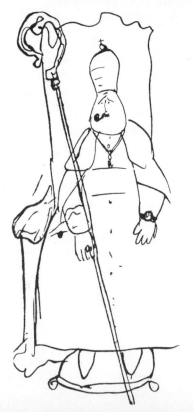

The animus image—Guillaume Apollinaire. *Above*: Wounded in World War I, 1916 (*Photo: Harlingue-Viollet*). *Left*: As Picasso drew him. *Opposite*: As a young dandy. In *Les Peintres cubistes* Apollinaire wrote: "One cannot be forever carrying one's father's corpse. It must be abandoned with the other dead." He was Jill Johnston's choice of father in 1965, a man whose own father had been merely a photograph.

*Photos by
Phyllis Birkby.*

the ocean, project it all in one big swoop onto a certain distinguished Englishman, withdraw it under severe pressure of
disappointment, and reinvest it in me. I then had the problem,
like her, of how to get rid of it—or, from a more advanced point
of view, how to objectify it, analyze it, flesh it out, and rein-
corporate it as a viable psychic function.

Obviously my mother was more vulnerable than I was to a
living, concrete father; at the same time she was not prepared to
take one seriously or to assume responsibility for one, in the
sense of any sustained relationship, thus missing the chance to
find out what fathers were really all about, and the opportunity
for converting an ideal into a pragmatic reality. She had been
left stranded by her own father, who returned to subdue her and
leave her the victim of a disappointed ideal, always the condition
for maintaining it intact. This is an ancient sort of story. In the
chapter bequeathed to me, the ideal was more rigidly enshrined,
in the hopes, I believe, that this time it might be left that way,
that I might be spared the same disappointment of reaching for
it and seeing it evaporate. And, like my mother, I displayed all
the signs of a *compensatory* masculinity. The quality of masculinity in any woman for whom the male is absent or rejected
can be very marked. Such women may be the *least* masculine of
women. I don't think this is well understood. But perhaps certain
men who call any glamorous or acceptably feminine type of
woman "one of the boys" understand it quite well. The part I
played in the art world as one of the boys was purely functional:
I had a specific service to offer. It had not nearly the significance
of an image. The glamorous or aggressively feminine guise is,
after all, a manmade product. Women of my mother's tradition
exist in a sort of no-man's-land between the sexes. Their own
attempts to appear feminine are as contrived as their more masculine attributes are compensatory. Service itself is an in-
demnification, a payment, to make up for not cutting the proper
image. Every wife makes this sort of payment; if she cuts the
proper (feminine) image as well, she qualifies as a "token
woman"—a particular subspecies of man. But imagine several

generations of wives who work for men who themselves are improperly formed—that is, who fall short of the standards set for males. Such women might end up trying to do it on their own. My grandmother, at the age of forty-eight, was in just such a position. Her dead husband became an "ideal," and both she and her daughter entered the work force as independent women. My mother, in the course of her work, had the misfortune of encountering their ideal in the flesh and once again losing him before she had the opportunity to know him. For her he was twice dead, and she made him the same for me: first, she said he was dead soon after I was born; second, she said (and confirmed by newspaper clipping) that he died when I was twenty. In its updated form, this ideal family man had become completely abstract, no longer rooted in living memory. The advantage of avoiding disappointment, and therefore of leading a life of even greater independence, was modified by the ominous psychic reality of possessing an unrecognizable ideal. The chances of *knowing* such a man would be very remote indeed. My mother had upped the ante in our family complex. Since 1965, when I began thinking about these things for the first time, this has seemed to me a very interesting case, posing special questions and introducing curious solutions of women in relation to the patriarchy. Not that these questions and solutions have not been raised and tried already, but that the known tradition to which they belong has been specifically male—the quest of the fatherless son, the subject of that famous essay by Otto Rank "The Myth of the Birth of the Hero" and, of course, the Grail legend and of many folk traditions throughout the world. The main question that dogged me was what a girl could do with a similar type of background. In Apollinaire, for a brief time at least, I believed I had my answer. All I had to do was be like him.

13

Mathematics

But before I could do that, I had to survive the insane state in which I had conceived him. My credibility plunged to a new all-time low, and for another year I spent most of my time in bed. For a while it seemed I might get away with it—I mean, not have to pay the heavy price for this kind of breakthrough. But I didn't really have a chance, and even had I stayed out of the hospital, I was due to have a giant case of postpartum blues. The time it seemed I might get away with it was the week I spent at Rauschenberg's place on Lafayette Street, where, until I realized I was under house arrest, I felt fairly secure and, under such unusual protection, was able to spin out my dream to its fullest. Rauschenberg's building seems in retrospect as wildly appropriate a place to have wrapped up my trip as the Church in Garnersville had been a year earlier. Huge letters on the exposed southern side of the building read ST. JOSEPH'S UNION / MISSION OF THE IMMACULATE VIRGIN—HOUSE FOR NEGLECTED CHILDREN, meaning that before Rauschenberg bought the building it had been an orphanage run by Episcopalian nuns. But Rauschenberg himself was, I think, the ideal host in these circumstances. His place in the art world in America seemed to me roughly akin to that of Picasso in France between the wars—not Picasso the painter but Picasso the innovator and collagist, the man championed by Apollinaire as the inventor, along with Braque, of Cubism. Rauschenberg was never the painter so much as the master of mixed media, forcing painting into what he called the "combine," enjoining paint to mingle freely with photographs and print and found objects and sometimes sound, confusing painting with sculpture and then again with theatre. Along with Jasper Johns, he also looked like Marcel Duchamp's heir or beneficiary in America. Duchamp was living in New York and had been actively lionized by John Cage, the intellectual leader of this Neo-Dada revival, who had been close to Johns and Rauschenberg since the mid-fifties. Cage, obviously, was the man in the middle. He was a lot younger than Duchamp, quite a bit older than Johns and Rauschenberg. Johns was far more the painter than Rauschenberg, much more the purist in both realms, paint and Dada (his tendency was to keep them separate); he didn't have the defiant and daring, large-scale, scrambling, ubiquitous sort of outrageousness that Rauschenberg had, which made him seem to me a Picasso of our time. Not that Picasso ever scrambled, but he did cover plenty of territory, and the work often looked big and refractory, and wherever he went he appeared to lead the way. At any rate, Rauschenberg had been developing a comparable sort of reputation, the first reputation of a painter in America not ascribable to the medium of paint itself or rooted in the European tradition of fine art. A typical American upstart, very Texan and capitalistic. He came from Port Arthur, Texas (also the hometown of Janis Joplin), and he had great credentials as an outsider—his father's mother was a Cherokee. I made plenty out of his background the week I spent in his building.

Nobody remembers how I happened to stay there, but I suppose I just went to visit and ended up being "the (wo)man who came to dinner." The previous week, unable to be alone, I had gone around visiting other folks, but none of them had the facilities or wherewithal to entertain me on any indefinite basis. Nor did Rauschenberg, actually, for he and Steve were at that moment in the midst of preparations for "Nine Evenings: Theatre and Engineering," to take place in October at the Sixtyninth Regiment Armory, the first big collaboration between artists and engineers organized by Billy Kluver of Bell Labs. But there was plenty of space in the building on Lafayette Street, and Rauschenberg was the kind of guy who was accustomed to having a lot of people around him. The tensions that had existed between us had eased in the past year because I hadn't been actively vying with him and Steve in domains of Judson leadership. I had been largely sleeping and complaining and licking my wounds. And as a single person, I now could be perceived as living, if not with a man, at least with a proper neutrality. A paranoid way of looking at their sudden hospitality was that by helping to get me out of the way, he and Steve ensured my absence at the upcoming "Nine Evenings," which I might easily not have covered to their satisfaction. That was David Bourdon's mischievous idea when he came to visit me in the hospital in October. At the time I thought there was some truth in it (after they consulted my ex-shrink and called the cops, I had, in any case, plenty of reason to be angry at them). But I hardly had the power or credit at that point to be very damaging, even had I wanted to be; anyway, whatever their motivations, nobody forced me to spend time in their building in the first place. It's conceivable also that I would have been a lot worse off someplace else, which could have been the hospital, before I had the chance to complete my fantastic genealogy and unravel my great plans for the future.

The genealogy, of course, was my mandate for the future. By then I had English royalty all mixed up in it too. One of my "charts" was nothing but a list of all my Christian names, written out one after the other horizontally across the page, and including Mary and Elizabeth and Anne and Jane and Victoria and Eleanor and Margaret and Catherine and all those names of English queens—and finally *Jill*, next in line, I hoped or imagined. A name like mine, which was embedded in William (or the French Guillaume), the English hero second only to Arthur, seemed eminently like the feminine name of the future. It was the easiest thing imaginable to mix myself up with English royalty. Why had my father been posing between King George and Queen Mary (in 1925, the date on that photograph) if not because he knew them intimately? What was he to them? What were they to him? Why were the two men dressed alike? Which one was my father? Where was my mother? Was my mother one of *them*? Was this not a picture that raised lots of questions? Surely I must have been asking myself these kinds of questions over the years.

Now in a flash I had it all sorted out. This father of mine was obviously some kind of international philanderer. The reason he was posing with the king and queen was that at that very moment he was having an affair with one of their daughters, or rather a daughter of the king, a secret bastard daughter, maintained in style somehow but unknown to society at large, or identified if necessary as a remote cousin or friend of the family. The product of this union, another daughter, I reasoned instantly, had, like me, been spirited to America along with her mother, thus sparing the Crown any embarrassment and letting my father off the hook. She grew up in Manhattan, her mother married another man, and eventually she bumped into me, her half-sister, and we became lovers, not realizing, of course, that our fathers were the same man. This was my ex-friend, whose mother, I now registered, was a very regal-looking, English-royal-related sort of person, a double for Elizabeth I, a quintessentially unemotional, elongated, upright WASP. (Years later I confided this fantasy to my ex-friend, who told me her mother's family did not in fact have some royal connection; she had never mentioned it when we lived together.)

But my fairy tale thickened; it could hardly escape me that Rauschenberg was "one of us." There I was, living with him (indefinitely, it could seem); he had that tall, lean, distinguished appearance, that look unmistakably identified with my various fathers; he was frightfully successful; his hands and mine, the long, "artistic"-type hands, were cut from the same mold; we roller-skated together like Siamese bananas; neither of us cared romantically for the opposite sex; he had once changed his first name from Milton to Robert (Robert was the father of William the Conqueror); and his background had some wonderful flaw in it. Surely his German grandfather had not *married* that Native American woman who gave him the kind of profile that used to be on one side of an American nickel. I don't know if he did or not; it didn't matter—the association was enough. Like me, he was not a regular American, and he had a past that when you were growing up you were not supposed to brag about. I instantly made him a half-brother. That father of mine was a busy, ubiquitous man; he visited America many times during the twenties and thirties; there was absolutely no reason not to assume that he had other serious involvements besides my mother. He was forty-two or thereabouts and still unmarried when he met my mother on shipboard. Rauschenberg was born in '25, a peak time in my father's career. It must have been a dream of mine to meet my English half-brother and half-sister, both younger than me. But since England was barred to me—I would be treated badly, my mother always said, if I went there—there was clearly no chance of my ever meeting them. Now I just transposed their nationality, liquidated their English identity, gave them a couple of mothers, adjusted a detail or two, and presto! I had two American siblings, conveniently a part of my own world in New York. This didn't mean I no longer had my English half-siblings. I was simply doubling and multiplying everything. Anyway, now I had the makings of a new kind of government, which would ensure a better future for people like me, bastards all, and thus for the world.

It was the photograph of LBJ on the front page of the *Times*, waving at a crowd of students who were reaching out toward him, that stimulated my dormant king-maker tendencies, hitherto limited to small exercises in the art world. Having interpreted the photo as meaning that the President was about to be deposed, since the acid-contaminated White House water supply had caused him to go mad, I immediately rigged up a government to replace him. One day at Rauschenberg's I was sitting in a metal swivel chair in the middle of the living area, adjoining the kitchen, on the third floor of this six-storey building, swiveling round and round this way and that like a little kid, exclaiming on the exciting times we lived in. Steve and Rauschenberg were sitting nearby, attentive and receptive as usual, yet impassive and detached, and by later account increasingly exhausted by my energies. Possibly that was the moment I conceived my grand plan for a new world. Or else it was another moment, when Alex Hay was there, equally interested and disengaged, but more bemused, when I deployed a certain momentous question about my own place in this new world: Should I go on writing and lecturing, or should I become a child shrink? I had read Erik Erikson that summer (*Young Man Luther* and *Childhood and Society*) and had just had the experience of entering into my children's domains; two other critical experiences with children followed right afterwards—one with a three-year-old girl whose mother and father had recently separated, another with George Segal's sixteen-year-old son, Jeff—in which I similarly entered their spheres and seemed to have conducted Erikson-type therapeutic encounters. So I imagined a whole new career, working with children. I did not imagine training or preparation. I felt infinitely powerful, instantly masterful. I became whatever I had read. My big books that summer were Erikson, *Black Elk,* and Norman O. Brown's *Love's Body.* Evidently I thought I could be a queen and have a career as well. Actually, I never imagined myself a queen—or, I should say, "queen" was not the word I used. I saw myself as part of some kind of quadrumvirate, like four figureheads, consisting of myself and my ex-friend and Steve and Rauschenberg. In '66 this was rather a pre-emptive vision. But visions of this nature are compensatory formations; they make up for a lack of consciousness and signify revolts of the unconscious. I had no "gay" consciousness at that time at all. But gay kings and queens are not a bad idea, and there have been quite a few of them anyway.

Essentially, my plan for a new world was an International State, a functional League of Nations. There was nothing insane about that. I believed in it when I was sane, I imagined it while not sane, and I continued to believe in it afterwards. I saw a

United States of the World, run by a viable United Nations, with rotating heads, the first one being Chinese (the Chinese were still excluded from the U.N. at that time), and elected presidents or prime ministers of all the countries, equivalent to the governors of all our states. I saw Robert Kennedy as our first prime minister. His brother Jack had provided the first and only occasion that got me out to vote. I used a prime minister because I admired the English system; I thought America suffered from the lack of continuity and stability that royalty represents, and that the Kennedys were a wild projection of America's yearning for that kind of family—not a unique observation. Nonetheless, I made royalty gay. I suppose I drew some unconscious analogy between homosexuals and bastards, and it was the latter, after all, whose interests besieged me. Fatherhood was the merest cultural contrivance. I could hand out fatherhood myself. I was involved at that moment in a veritable orgy of father making. Either people had no fathers at all or their fathers could be anybody. I had made my own case the standard. This was my finest moment. The world was revolving around the centrality of bastardy. An international state would mean the end of fatherhood in quite an important sense—that is, the propriety of nationalism. Surely this was the wonderful outcome that fatherhood had been established to make possible—the end of fatherhood prefigured in its beginning. Warring fathers of various kingdoms, city states, had created mergers resulting in nations, which would at last unite peaceably, having understood the real goal of all their wars. That week in September, I felt I was living in the midst of this bloodless revolution, that it was actually happening. I had another role for Rauschenberg: I imagined him chief or minister of festivals, an important cabinet post, like the minister of culture in France, but with much more power and influence, since the "new world" would be one of celebration, a constant reminder that Armageddon—that final convulsion of warring fathers, the two big superpowers—had been cheated and bypassed.

Outside, I saw signs of this "bloodless revolution" everywhere. I made something out of every name, letter, and image posted on buildings, scratched into sidewalks, advertised on billboards, displayed in newsstands, exhibited in store windows, evidenced on license plates and street signals and fluttering in garbage cans or flashing in neon or just moving invisibly through the charged revolutionary air. I felt it in the air. The city seemed muted and suspended, its huge busyness arrested by silence and changelessness. At the axis of change, all parts are held in perfect and timeless symmetry. I had hallucinated a new world, and it was absolutely real. For a moment I was living in paradise. The "real world" and my dream of it had merged. I had not so succeeded a year earlier. The Passion play represented birth and death, not a world into which one might like to be born or which one might be pleased to leave. For what would one be happy to die if not a perfect world? Death in a straitjacket at Bellevue was purely abortive. The symbolism of the crucifix wasn't lost on me, but the sacrifices of "mental patients" are lost on society. They leave or are forced to leave a world they never had. Now, for one week anyway, I had a satisfactory world that I did not want to leave. When my friends called the cops I was furious—but at least I was leaving a world that I might somehow reconstruct in the future. I had evolved something in my imagination that contained a blueprint for the hereafter. But first I had to be walked out of my solipsistic condition. No world is perfect that isn't well coordinated between individual and State. I could have walked out of this monologue on my own (three years later I did); but in our present society, withdrawal from the *omnium consensu* is a thought crime, equivalent to the criminal *act*, thus subject to that arm of the penal system called Institutional Psychiatry. Criminal acts are at least subject to due process. People caught in "thought crimes" are apprehended without legal recourse. Their confessions are instantly wrung from them, their judgment and sentence imposed on them by "medical" people with full constitutional sanction. The term "mental illness" remains a euphemism for crimes of thought against the State. Despite the greater protection afforded the common criminal, there's a very instructive correspondence between the two kinds of crimes, of thought and of deed—that is, they share the same motivation to wrest something from a State that they feel has denied them a certain basic right; this feeling or conviction is emotionally deep-rooted and unacknowledged. Most criminals are men; most "mentally ill" people are women. The model: men act, women withdraw. In some cases, of course, the two categories merge and overlap. Criminals may be judged insane, and the insane can become dangerous. Both kinds of people make front-line revolutionaries when the conditions for revolution exist, and a consensus develops for revolutionary action. At such a point, that which was unacknowledged is laid bare. The victim is no longer alone. An ideology of oppression is enunciated. Remedial group action is prescribed. Programs for change are applied to the State, and separatist schemes are hatched. In 1966, I was five years away from this kind of consensus. In lieu of revolution, some victims may be helped by individual psychiatry. But all too often victims are maintained by representatives of the class or classes by which they are already oppressed—e.g., female clients by male shrinks. But to quote Thomas Szasz, one of the great critics of the psychiatric institution, "What is called 'mental illness' (or 'psychopathology') emerges as the name of the product of a particular kind of relationship between oppressor and oppressed." Having denied their oppression in the first place (they think that what's wrong with them is purely personal, something for which they are individually and solely responsible), victims don't choose these oppressors. They end up in some shrink's office by default, in desperation or under pressure.

By 1966 I had had a number of encounters like this, and after 1966 I had several more. My encounter with Dr. Rosa Klein in November '65 was under institutional pressure. It was by her jurisdiction that I was released from Mt. Sinai. At Mt. Sinai I had a young male shrink whose job, of course, was purely inquisitional. At Bellevue I had a succession of testers and questioners. There was never a difference of opinion about my "thought crime" (whether I had committed one or not), as my medical abstracts testify, only certain differences in terminology. Not every record, for instance, judged me a "chronic undifferentiated schizophrenic," a term that appeared to relate to my age and to various "denials" I made about my history and condition. "Patient was admitted from 8/30/65 to 9/22/65—brought in by roommate. History of being at psychiatric hospital before . . . denied previous psychiatric admissions. . . ." Had I been sixteen or even twenty-five, this denial might have been believed, or at least confirmed. My most damning denial, however, was "no insight into her condition." More fully, "She denies hallucinations . . . denies being suspicious . . . denies suicidal ideation . . . no insight present at this time." The fictions peppering these reports are due to various preconceptions: people of my age, thirty-six, *must* be chronic; people facing their questioners have already been judged and therefore cannot be believed. Szasz is eloquent here, drawing many parallels between the medieval treatment of heretics and witches and the contemporary treatment of mental patients. One example: "Like the accused heretic, the accused mental patient commits the most deadly sin when he denies his illness and insists that his deviant state is healthy. Accordingly, the most denigrating diagnostic labels of psychiatry are reserved for those individuals who, although declared insane by the experts, and confined in madhouses, stubbornly persist in claiming to be sane. They are said to be 'completely lacking in insight.' " The hospital doctors at Bellevue took great liberties with the information I gave them. "Had recently gone to New York Hospital but was not admitted there. Her two children (five and seven at the time) were in treatment there." What I had told them was that prior to '65 I had had periodic attacks of crippling pain in my chest, and that I would go to the emergency unit of New York Hospital, where X-rays would be taken, after which I would be sent home. (The first time it happened, in '61, I was admitted, and diagnosed as having viral pneumonia.) I also told them my two children were born at New York Hospital. I might have told them that in '59

I had consulted doctors there about a legal abortion and was turned down. I had no reason to make any of this stuff up. For their part, they clearly did. And the stuff I *had* made up, about Christ, Apollinaire, LBJ, English royalty, the International State, etc., I kept strictly to myself. I described my somatic symptoms, I gave away plenty of my history, I was manifestly disoriented—but I knew I had been nabbed by the "thought police." Even at Rauschenberg's, as at the Church in Garnersville a year earlier, I was careful to edit my divulgences and to try to give, at Rauschenberg's at least, an appearance of being creatively possessed. For this I was provided with reams of large paper and plenty of Magic Markers, pens, and colored pencils.

I was writing in a large, clear, even script. The world was mine on paper before I felt it outside. There were several projects: the one I've described, to outline a genealogy or ancestral mandate; one to align myself with Black Elk by diagramming his Great Vision; one to align myself with Jung by drawing many renditions of a mandala figure Jung had described in his book *Psychology and Religion*; and one to establish myself as a mathematician, the discipline from which I had naturally been excluded. My "contribution" to mathematics consisted of a twelve-page book, made in about an hour, called "Squaring the Circle." I suppose it comprised various squared circles, or encircled squares, but I don't remember how or what exactly. I put holes through the pages and tied them together with a string or a ribbon just like an assignment for grade school. My math fantasy was fairly overblown. I figured I was descended from at least one famous mathematician, from another who might have been great had he been academically attached, and from another who was known to have conducted "mathematical" experiments in connection with his business. The latter two were my grandfather (the hobbyist) and my father (entrepreneur, philanderer, etc.), respectively. The ancestry of the first, the famous one, was most dubious, but at the time I was convinced of some direct lineage.

Years later I learned that a direct lineage from almost anyone in a common gene pool (e.g., Caucasian) is not inconceivable. Out of such a pool supposedly one in twenty-four people is related to you in some way. Counting right backwards from two parents to four (grand)parents to eight, to sixteen, to thirty-two, to sixty-four, to one hundred twenty-eight, to two hundred fifty-six, etc., by about the tenth generation any child has one thousand twenty-four (great) (grand)parents. The most comprehensively recorded genealogies remain very exclusive. Incidents of bastardy, forgery, and abandonment abound in every history; the records of aunts and uncles and cousins are lost in the tiniest disappearing tributaries, if they were ever recorded at all; and the genealogies of women are much abridged or truncated or for that matter omitted. Nonetheless, of course, my claims were improper, for the silly reason that I had no proof. To date I had not made any investigations of this nature, and at that time I still didn't even know who my paternal grandfather was. In the misty sense of things, my "animus" mathematician was perhaps a better ancestral claim than Apollinaire, on the principle that the further back you go, the wider the field of possibilities range; but Apollinaire was the man close enough in age to be my father. This mathematician, one Evariste Galois, another Frenchman (though French by birth), was born October 25, 1811. I had heard of him in the most fleeting way. In '63 or '64, around the time I was "storing" such figures, my friend the sculptor Mark di Suvero, whose father had been among other things a mathematician, while discoursing to me one day upon one matter or another dear to him, happened to mention Galois. What he said about him I don't remember, but the name stuck in my head. The only mathematician who had previously meant anything to me was A. N. Whitehead (1861–1947), whose essay called "God and Mathematics" I had once prided myself on understanding. I had read Whitehead deliriously at the age of about twenty-three. (I understood the English philosophers very well; and had it not been for the Germans, Hegel, Kant, et al., whom I found turgid and dense beyond belief, I might have immersed myself in philosophy and forgotten about dance.) Whitehead

was quite young enough to be my father; but, like Christ, he was
of no consequence to my art-world friends—and, anyway, he
belonged to a former life, one that had been illuminated by my
college philosophy professor. That was a life of old men, or men
who died old and white of hair: Plato, Whitehead, Russell, my
philosophy professor, the father of my dance teacher. I met them
all around 1950–51, right after my father died in England. The
men who meant something to me now, in '66, were those who
died young—"before their time," as is said. And of these, Galois
was my most dramatic choice. Apollinaire, after all, was practically middle-aged at thirty-eight. Galois was only twenty when
he died—from wounds received in a duel. His fame rests entirely
on posthumous manuscripts and a letter to a friend written
feverishly on the eve of his fatal duel, outlining the content of
three mathematical treatises. One concerned elliptic integrals of
algebraic functions; the other two, one of them completed, dealt
with the theory of equations. The completed treatise was on the
"conditions for the solvability of equations by radical expressions." Knowing a few critical facts about Galois and his family,
it's tempting to read something both personal and political into
such a phrase, especially since I have no idea what this stuff
means in numerical terms. Galois's father, the mayor of their
town, had championed the villagers against an oppressive priest,
who in turn attacked the mayor so badly that he committed
suicide. Galois was sixteen at the time. Despite, or because of,
his genius, Galois was a difficult student. He carried on the most
difficult investigations almost entirely in his head; in general he
antagonized his teachers and examiners, who tormented him
with the trivial conventions of the subject. He failed twice in the
entrance examinations to Ecole Polytechnique; he was accepted
at the Ecole Normale in 1830 but expelled the same year for a
newspaper letter about the actions of the director during the
July Revolution. In 1831 he was arrested for a threatening
speech against King Louis Philippe, but acquitted; then he was
sentenced to six months in jail for illegally wearing a uniform
and carrying weapons. He died the following year, 1832. Now

consider the phrase "conditions for the solvability of equations by radical expressions." Surely my "feverishly" dashed-off book of squared circles was in the same spirit or tradition. Where a boy like Galois had been denied recognition of his mathematical genius, I had been denied mathematics, period. In both cases, the culprit was "the father" or father State.

My education in mathematics stopped resolutely at X. With algebra, in the seventh or eighth grade, I gave up on math. I passed geometry only because I liked the figures and learned the theorems by rote. Problem solving stumped me completely. I think somebody pulled a string or two to get me into college, because long before college entrance examinations I developed the habit of closing the book as soon as I saw questions about apples and oranges and the like, to be solved by signs and numbers. Much later, after I had a master of arts degree and wanted to matriculate at Columbia for a degree in philosophy, I took what was called the Princeton Graduate Record Exam. When the results came in, I was asked to explain myself by some university official who informed me that I was in the lowest percentile in the country in math, while in English I was in the highest.

I had nothing to say, of course, but I could have blamed it all on X. When confronted with X in the seventh or eighth grade, I was unfathomably angry. It made no sense to me that you might want to solve something by positing an Unknown. It was this entity called the Unknown that made me mad. And I think, though naturally I didn't think it then, that X, or the Unknown, represented my father, whose existence or whereabouts I was not supposed to "solve." Now consider again the phrase "conditions for the solvability of equations by radical expressions." If X symbolized the unknown father, the solution to an algebraic equation would signify understanding or knowledge of that father. X and its machinations had passed me by; now I just took matters into my own hands (the mission, after all, of going "crazy"), lined myself up with a young boy whose problems, in their own way, must have been as dire as mine, and closed the book on mathematics by squaring off a whole bunch of circles. That doesn't mean I suddenly "understood" my father —only that I had indicated to myself that my ignorance was no longer acceptable. At any rate, I had not been pursuing this father of mine or trying to find out anything about him (I had been living under a tacit injunction not to do so); thus my "solution" at that moment was purely transcendent, not grounded in reality at all, as befitted my generally altered state. The youth of my new animus figures clearly served this purpose of soaring above the State, as it were, to grasp unities, equalities, etc., *denied* to youth and to other minorities or hapless individuals, who have traditionally resorted to violence, or violating the State, to obtain identity. In the squared circle and like configurations, all opposites, all differences, are reconciled.

This was all very well while I was inside, enclosed and protected; but outdoors, the inflationary aspect of my new scheme ran away with me. A unified world was one thing, my place in it something else. While the city felt wonderfully silent and suspended, as resolved, ordered, and whole as my drawings, I was personally in a different state of suspension: the kind in which you are dead certain that everybody knows "who you are," but no sign of that awareness is yet plainly manifest. The signs I did see remained those I kept making up. The rainbow was very clear; the "pot of gold" was not. It was as though a meeting with the king and queen, imminent and announced, kept failing to take place.

14

Freud Too

The meeting that did take place was with my ex-shrink, Dr. Rosa Klein, who had returned from her vacation in Mexico, having been eagerly awaited by Steve and Rauschenberg. On our way to her apartment, I thought the cab driver knew who I was and had perhaps even been sent to pick me up, as if I were a visiting diplomat or ambassador with a palace appointment. I believe I thought Steve was just "softening" the blow of this imminent sudden exposure to worldwide fame by *pretending* we were going to see Dr. Klein. Once we saw her, I rationalized the visit as clearance, or sanction, for my new role, whatever that was to be. I felt I was being watched, followed, awaited, protected, and indeed I was; I was wrong only about the extent of the surveillance (I thought the whole world was in on it) and the reasons for it (*they* thought I was mad)—not inconsiderable errors. No basis for consensus had been established between myself and my friendly captors. I had passed that threshold where it's possible to see oneself exiting the common reality and entering another. I was now normalized in this "other" reality, which I then naturally assumed to be the common (and only) one. "Common," to anybody driven mad, has not been nearly common enough but rather much too exclusive; thus the new world or reality of "madness" is to make up for that deficiency and restore the sense of belonging—to make it, in other words, truly common. This is what is meant by the "self-healing" aspect of a so-called schizophrenic episode. The common shared reality is shot through with inequities, which people cast in victim roles have understood, if at all, only personally, not politically. The "truly common" world of madness—everything equal, commensurate, in balance, harmonious—is antithetical to the State, except, of course, on its own terms: stable class relations, the peace that follows victory, the sense of belonging achieved only by having enemies, etc. The "thought crime" of madness is the hallucination of wholeness, more properly the estate of religion or of art. The crime here is seeing through everything, parting the veil—the *maya* of politics. The danger lies in the confusion of power. Having withdrawn from the world, I had rushed back into it with my dream figures, populating it with mere symbols. The effort was to avoid object loss at all costs. My confusion was between symbol and letter, a literalism equating symbol and original object—that which I had withdrawn, internalized, and made potent. The powerful company into which I expected imminently to be received was the "original object" converted into a symbol and thrust back outwards. What mightier symbol of social authority than royalty? I expected to be saved by the couple who flanked my father in my immortal picture of him.

I could have sustained this expectation for a long time. To do it I just had to keep seeing *signs* of it everywhere. But the "thought police" in the form of my ex-shrink had now been alerted to my delinquency. I wasn't living at home, I wasn't working, I was talking a great deal and exhausting people, I was taking drugs on my own (400 mgs. of Thorazine daily), I wasn't sleeping or eating regularly, and I didn't appear to have any plans. But most damaging, I was making things up. Dr. Klein was also informed of my genealogy. A picture was conveyed of someone drifting along inconsequentially and precariously and making things up. Yet what really mattered were practical things: Where would I go if I left Lafayette Street? What would I do if left to my own devices? Would I sleep and eat at all? Could I take care of myself? Would a car knock me down? Shouldn't my drug intake be supervised? Would *they* feel or be held responsible if I left and something happened to me? And so forth. These are questions that typically assail people unequipped to deal with a case of bicameral relapse. This is a critical juncture in the passage from person to patient, from person at liberty to patient stripped of civil rights. The onset of this passage, as Erving Goffman has described it—"effected through a series of linked stages, each managed by a different agent"—was the moment I no longer wished to be alone. The first "agents" were my friends Thalia and Agnes Martin, who had picked me up in Brewster several weeks earlier. Next were assorted folks: Charlotte, George and Helen Segal, Trisha Brown, Deborah and Alex Hay, to whom I had paid intense visits and who would inform the network of friends and acquaintances that all was not well. Now Steve and Rauschenberg became the link to the authorities. As Goffman put it, "As the prepatient may see it, the circuit of significant figures can function as a kind of betrayal funnel." They had to get me on something practical. On Sunday the 18th, a couple of days after the visit to Dr. Klein's office, I gave them the excuse they needed to call her back, letting her advise them to summon the cops. I had decided to rent a car.

The Bellevue report reads: "Dr. Klein advised hospitalization after she learned of the patient's plan to rent a car and take her two young children for a ride in the country. It was her feeling that due to her severely impaired judgment at this time, there was a real danger to herself and the children in permitting her to carry out her plan." In December 1982 I went to see Dr. Klein to ask her what she thought of this report and what she remembered of the incident. She looked just the same except that her bob and bangs had turned white. She wore a dusky green corduroy suit; and though she had changed apartments, her new office cum living room seemed identical to the one I remembered: same size, low but roomy, and atmosphere, gloom lit with Mexican artifacts—another basement outpost. I felt she thought I was coming to see her as a patient again, and this pleased her. She fluttered a bit, smiled and chirped, hopped more or less from the door where she greeted me to a comfortable chair, where she sat receptively, still and expectant, arranging herself after a few quick nervous gestures, birdlike as before; tanned, bony, delicate fingers interlaced in front of her chest; keenly interested in me. I sat on the couch in the corner closest to her chair, aggressively clutching these various reports.

She disagreed with the hospital diagnosis of schizophrenia. She said when she saw me I had suffered a "classic manic attack." She would diagnose me as manic depressive (the profession has never agreed on the symptomatology and diagnosis of these states, schizophrenia and manic depression). She said, "One thing typical of a manic attack is the development of delusions." She said my mother had reluctantly gone to see her at that time and expressed a certain helplessness, and recalled her as saying, "I've done everything I could do. . . . It's caused me a lot of trouble." (Rauschenberg would recall his "shock" that my mother seemed so willing to let "strangers" take responsibility for me.) I asked Dr. Klein if she remembered that I had stopped seeing her after she recommended shock treatment for me. She vehemently denied recommending any such thing, then asked me if I had had shock treatment at Mt. Sinai (where I had spent twenty-five days before beginning "therapy" with her). I said no, I didn't. "One doesn't remember things," she retorted, strongly implying that people in my mental state have unreliable memories, if any at all. Her conclusion was: "That could be checked." (I had the full Mt. Sinai report in hand, but for some reason I didn't try to make her read it to prove her wrong.)

As for the Bellevue report concerning my plan to rent a car, she now added quite a ringer to her original testimony. After I read the above-quoted passage to her, she told me that I had said I wanted to "take them [my children] with me and kill us all on the turnpike." It was my turn to protest. I told her she must be mad, that I had said no such thing, nor even thought it. I pointed out that this was not what she was quoted as saying. "It's the same thing," she said. Ah! she had given herself away. Here was a classic bit of psychiatric double-talk. She didn't challenge my protest or insist she was right; she simply indicated that it didn't matter whether I had said it or not, because her fears for me, and for others, as expressed in the report ("a real danger to herself and the children") were identical in her mind with my own intentions—which *she* imputed to me! Medical experts, as Szasz would say, know the "minds" of their patients better than do the patients themselves. What one fears another might do becomes, in the hands of the law (handled here by psychiatry), an excuse for arrest—i.e., a projection of one's own violent intentions. I suggested to Dr. Klein that she needed a better excuse to lock me up than that I wanted to rent a car. She demurred tacitly.

The *real* reason I tried to rent a car, apart from the fact that it was Sunday, the day I usually drove to the country to see my children, was that I sensed I had already been judged and condemned, that I was no longer safe on Lafayette Street, and my instinct was to get away. Three years later I replayed this scenario beautifully, I must say, setting up (unconsciously) some of the same elements, but correcting history, as it were, by making a grand and conclusive escape. On September 18 of '66, I got about as far as the telephone.

According to Steve, after I announced my intention of renting a car, he called Dr. Klein, who told him I should be remanded to Bellevue. Bellevue sent an ambulance, I balked, and the ambulance was sent back. When they came again—I remember a couple of big attendants dressed like cops—I agreed to go in a cab. The Bellevue abstract, 9/18/66, quotes me as saying, "I went by myself but with a gun in my back, and I didn't sign in." In other words, I became an "involuntary" patient. Certainly I walked in differently than I had the year before. I knew where I was going; I had much more control over myself (I had been at large longer); I wasn't just being led like a lamb to slaughter; I was appropriately furious; I looked reasonably serious, carrying a few books and journals under my arm; and while waiting to be interrogated I drew mandalalike diagrams of St. Mary's, the boarding school where I had spent six years in my teens—a single-structure red-brick building like Bellevue, but, unlike Bellevue, a castellated palace built round a courtyard and a lily pool on top of a hill. I had also done my best, before being led away, to frustrate their design for me. My instinct to get away was correct, but I had denied any treachery to myself; thus I wasn't clear about *why* I was trying to get away— or, I should say, I was not trying to escape per se. I just thought I wanted to go to the country and see my children. I was truly surprised when they sprung Bellevue on me. At that point, I called two friends who I hoped might intercede on my behalf. They both came over—Charlotte and John Giorno—but added only their presence as witnesses. My impression was that they were both captivated by the scene and transfixed by some awe for Rauschenberg.

My three-week stay at Bellevue was much less eventful than the year before. I did nothing this time to cause the authorities or aides to abuse me beyond the normal conditions of incarceration, which remained terrible. Just two months earlier, on August 29, the *Times* had printed one of those periodic sensationalist exposés of the bad conditions at Bellevue—a long front-page report. The usual protests were made: "Hospital officials continue to hope that Federal officials will enforce minimal health standards, which would raise the level of patient care. . . . The hospitals are troubled by consistent reports of patient abuse by the aides, whose salaries begin at $72 a week. . . . 'We take people with a tenuous hold on reality [said the outgoing hospitals commissioner] and then remove all trace of reality by placing them in a stark, barren environment—it's inhuman.' . . . 'My feeling is that many, many patients regress because of the environment [a second-year resident asserted]. They become more withdrawn, more depressed. Their sensitivity to the environment is one of the reasons they are patients.' . . . 'Our greatest strength is our greatest weakness [said Dr. Zitrium, medical director of Bellevue, who kept a mousetrap on his desk to symbolize the institution's losing battle with packs of mice that scurry through the wards]. This is the institution that never says "No, we're full." The buck stops here.'" Dr. Zitrium meant that everybody is welcome—all races, colors, etc. The place is free, therefore it's naturally inhuman. Sixteen years later I made three tours of inspection and found the place exactly the same. Most apparent, when the door to a ward is opened, is the stale yellow odor of air that's never been let out.

To the visitors I saw in September '66, I had nothing to say except that I had nothing to say unless or until they facilitated my release. My most interesting visitor was my informant, Dr. Klein, who brought me a lovely book of drawings by children and told me it was not in her hands to release me—it was up to the hospital authorities. Finally it was Rauschenberg (featured during that time, by the way, on the cover of the Sunday *New York Times Magazine*) who arranged to have me transferred to St. Vincent's, where I remained for seventy-nine days. Rauschenberg had been pressed into service as my reluctant guardian. In December 1982, when I interviewed Dr. Klein in her office, she reminded me of a precious detail: I had imagined she was Anna Freud's sister. She said that I had asked her if she had told them who she *really* was. Then it became very confused. She and I became sisters; Anna Freud became our mother. Clearly I thought that if she told the hospital authorities who she really was—i.e., Anna Freud's sister—they would let me out of there. Now I recalled that I had Shattuck's *The Banquet Years* with me in the hospital, which I had showed to Dr. Klein, open to the pages about Apollinaire, excitedly trying to explain my descent from the great poet. I freely associated Annie Playden, the English girl Apollinaire had loved in his youth, with my grandmother and Anna Freud, mixing up relationships to suit each new shake of the kaleidoscope: my mind clinging to the wreckage. The connection between Anna Freud and Rosa Klein was not difficult to make. The latter was a Bavarian Jewish woman, also an analyst, whose father had likewise been a doctor; she was close enough in age; she too had escaped the Nazis; etc. But underlying this connection was an idea already developed: that Freud was my Jewish ancestor, the only "old man" in my new pantheon of fathers.

It may seem curious that I chose Freud over Jung to represent my psychoanalytic animus, but there were several good reasons for it. I think, for one thing, I was desperate to be Jewish. My closest friends in the early sixties were Jewish, and they often teased me about being different. I adopted their style and manner and tried to be as Jewish as I could be. Anyway, at that time I was much more familiar with Freud's work than with Jung's, and I had read Ernest Jones's big devotional biography as well as work by other disciples. But most recently at hand were Norman O. Brown's visionary reinterpretations and dilations of Freud, *Life Against Death*, which I read in '65, and *Love's Body*, in '66. Before I got to Lafayette Street in September '66, passing that threshold marking some common or neutral territory between this world and the "other," I felt overwhelmingly that this "Freudian" thing of the unconscious becoming conscious was happening to me. I felt flooded by all these unconscious contents, actually inundated by personal and archetypal history that had been buried within me—as if a lid over me had been nailed, bolted down, to cover a natural geyser or volcanic crater which had burst through these rusty nuts and screws and blown the top of my head off. Madness, it can be said, is an excess of information. Anyway, I thought Freud had a special patent on this sort of thing, therefore he must be personally responsible for what was happening to me.

To make it as personal as possible, I imagined he had somehow sired my grandmother. I didn't decide whether it had happened in America or in Europe (location was not important), nor did I give him a woman for the purpose (all that mattered was that Freud had fathered my grandmother). Freud was a very sexy guy, I reasoned, and he didn't marry until he was nearly thirty. And I had that model of my father, who sired at least one child before he got married. Freud was sixteen when my grandmother was born in 1872. Later, when I correlated their ages and remembered my grandmother's fixed abode and poor circumstances in America, as well as Freud's entrenchment in Vienna, I thought the connection was doubtful. Had I known, though, that Freud's father had a son, Freud's half-brother, at seventeen, I might have prolonged the fantasy. Had I known that Freud himself was conceived before his parents were married and that Freud's birthdate had been altered, a fact concealed from him (along with the vital statistic that his father had had a second wife, Freud's mother being the third), I might never have let him go. But the point of my fantasy, as I see it now, was to make the great Freud responsible for this unusual eruption of mine. If *he* had something to do with it, it had to be creditable. Better, I thought there was a real design in it—that Freud in his scientific wizardry had participated in arranging my birth as a kind of experiment to see what a human of my circumstances might do under conditions of stress. I thought genetic and social programming were at work. I still think so. While I stopped imagining that Freud had anything to do with it in any specific personal sense, I realized that I was at least a child of the psychoanalytic age. Because of Freud, insanity has obtained new purchase on the human estate. Insanity may still be treated archaically, like a crime or a disease, but many scholars and analysts and people who have been there have created an enlightened vanguard literature according insanity the status of a language, and raising important questions about the nature and evolution of mental processes. Freud's glossary, the designation and targeting of victims, has been succeeded by terms like "strategy" (Laing), imputing sound motives to victims, and "double-bind" (Bateson), describing human transactions that create victims or place them in untenable situations, evolving a tensile context: family and social structures. Archaic views isolating victims have given way to views in which families and society can be seen as responsible agents. I began reading the more advanced literature in 1968 with Laing's *Politics of Experience*. Then I began seeing myself as a child of our time.

Everything I had imagined was not false, but cast in metaphor. I *was* programmed by genetic/social forces, and I *was* acting out a part in some prefabricated design; my job now was to take charge of the experiment that was me and to stop being used by the impersonal action of history. I could trace the design to some of its sources, undertake a report on the "success" or merit of the experiment, become the author of a life that had previously been sanctioned by others.

While Freud was good at designating victims and keeping them in place, he also set precedents for self-analysis and liberation. My "Jewish connection" was an unconscious alignment with another kind of victim. Women and blacks and Jews have had special affinities in America. I inherited these affinities just by walking into the predominantly Jewish society of East Broadway in 1961. There was only one black in that extended family, and I wasn't close to him, but my East Broadway friends had black friends and alliances and mingled black vernacular with their own. And I was captivated by Mailer's "The White Negro," a popular essay then and the only thing by Mailer I ever really liked. We went to black hangouts to dance and listen to jazz, and I liked to think I could dance as swingingly as a black. In retrospect I saw that period, the several years preceding breakdown or breakthrough, as one of intense identity conflict. I was split in two: one part aspiring to be Jewish (incorporating black elements), the other stuck in my post-Victorian background. I could never be Jewish, and I was no longer my mother's daughter exactly, either. Freud, I assume, played a role in apposition to my Jewish friends similar to that of Apollinaire in relation to my art-world milieu. The project was an identity theft—an enterprise for which I was clearly well prepared by my mother, who had given me an embezzled name. As an agent I once had put it: "Your mother stole your father's name." That may seem an odd concept, but only perhaps as it lays responsibility squarely on the mother for a lapsed (patriarchal) condition of identity.

In 1966 I duplicated her act in spades. Not, of course, that that was what I thought I was doing, nor that it had any immediate beneficial effect. On the contrary, the most immediate effect was highly punitive. If my mother had gotten away with her own brand of theft, I seemed to have been making up grandly for her presumed innocence. Obviously I secretly thought my mother was culpable, and it was my job to pay for us both. The displacement of my mother's "fault" onto myself could only happen through my mother's failure or inability to take responsibility for it herself, and her willingness to let her father or fathers make her pay through her daughter. In the deeper recesses of thought, I had contrived to obtain a father in some manner akin to the way I perceived my mother had. I was her dream child, the product of a man who existed in imagination only. She would have fit very well into Freud's seduction theory post-1896, when he decided, fatefully for psychoanalysis, that the patients he once believed to have been raped or molested by their fathers, because they had told him so, had really made it all up: their own incestuous fantasies. (My mother would not have put him to the trouble; she would have denied any seduction.) I did well, I think, to make Freud himself the object of an updated fantasy! In another environment I might have picked Jung, Freud's Christian counterpart, a man three years *younger* than my grandmother, a man equally committed to a theory of the unconscious, equally devoted to fantasy, and a man with a choice rumor of illegitimacy in his background. Collecting bastards is a hobby of mine (the well-known Jung story made his grandfather Carl Gustav Jung an illegitimate son of Goethe's—one of Jung's heroes—through Sophie Ziegler Jung, wife of Jung's great-grandfather Franz Ignaz Jung), but in '66 my collection consisted of Apollinaire alone. He was the first. Anyway, I had no outstanding Swiss connections at that time, while I did think I could be Jewish because of my grandmother's German father, whose name was Seibold (I suppose it was Seiboldt before he landed at Ellis Island). My grandmother's sisters had married German men in America: one a Rohloff, one a Staudenmaier, which I thought sounded suspiciously Jewish. But my chief exhibit was an entrée my grandmother made when

I was a child called "ball soup," consisting of soup with bread balls floating in it—my mother's favorite. I thought it *had* to be matzoh ball soup. I also thought my cousin Eddie Staudenmaier, whom I hadn't seen in years, could pass easily for Jewish. This Jewish fantasy lasted at least until I got to St. Vincent's, where I was admitted October 10, after the customary three weeks at Bellevue.

15

Argh

Seventy-nine days later, when I was released from St. Vincent's, I walked out into a grim world with no fantasies at all. Unlike the previous year, when I left Mt. Sinai after twenty-five days (under the care of Dr. Klein), having nagged and beseeched all my captors to let me go, this time I didn't care so much. I had adjusted to the protected dormitory life at St. Vincent's and was thoroughly institutionalized; there was nobody at home waiting for me. The worst things that happened there were watching patients being carted off for shock treatment or robotized by high drug dosages; seeing an older lady brought in crying who died of a heart attack later in the evening; and having a doctor called Scardino come to see me about five minutes once a week. Dr. Scardino had a mustache and stooped shoulders and a sharp nose and dark, beady eyes that were too close together. He was the one who wrote in his report: "Transferred here after spending one month in Bellevue because of bizarre behavior, paranoid ideation, homosexuality." He called me some other names as well: illegitimate, unkempt, giddy, inappropriate, ambivalent, a poor judge, fixed delusional, etc.

Once I left the hospital, I was on a kind of parole and was required to keep seeing Dr. Scardino as an outpatient once a week. It was the only thing that got me out of my loft on the Bowery, apart from crossing the street most afternoons to pick up the *New York Post* for the crossword puzzle. I walked across town to the hospital, where I saw Dr. Scardino in an office on the ground floor. Five minutes, just as before, was the limit of the visit. He would ask me what I was doing. I would say I was doing nothing. And he would tell me I'd better get a job. It had a familiar ring to it. Although he knew I was a writer, he never asked me about writing. Writing wasn't a job; it was a pastime. In any event, I had little inclination to write; I felt my career as a critic slipping away, and I wondered idly, then more seriously, and at length frantically, what sort of work I could do. "You'd better get a job," he kept saying. It sounded vaguely threatening, like my mother the previous summer when she told me that if I didn't get a job, I'd have to go back to the institutions. I would say to him mordantly and defensively, "What do you want me to be, a waitress?" And he would shrug indifferently. It didn't matter to him. He was a man with one line.

Sometime during that year I got a taxicab license, one of the hardest things I ever did. I had to learn dozens of addresses whose existence and locations I cared nothing about, spread all around the five boroughs of New York. Passing the test I considered a great accomplishment, but I never used the license. I was in fact doing some writing, even heroically (or vainly) trying to strike back by submitting seven pieces in a row to the *Voice*, printed on successive weeks—beginning December 15, while I was still in the hospital. Then, between February 2 and April 27 nothing appeared at all. Evidently the effort was too great. There were two pieces in May, three in June, then nothing again until October, when my career received an unusual boost.

The piece I wrote out of the hospital was about "Nine Evenings: Theatre and Engineering" which I had missed at the Armory in October. I said the event "proved to be a sensational failure . . . which I was unable to attend." I equated its failure with the 1913 Armory show, a blockbuster of early Cubist and Futurist paintings that were ridiculed at the time. The title of my piece was "Post-Mortem," and I can see now that I unconsciously screened the event through a portrait of my own condition. I wasn't there, I was saying, and it was not well received (possibly because of my absence), but we would all get our due in the end—or something like that. Certainly there was an attempt to put myself back on some equal ground with my friends, the whole Rauschenberg outfit. Next I wrote a dumb piece about Cunningham, saying how great he was and how passé in one breath. Again I tried to re-establish a footing with my friends by pushing the idea that Cunningham had been ripping off some Judson ideas. Next I put down Paul Taylor, who had long defected from any vanguard position. Then I retreated into history, writing about a woman dance scholar who I thought was neglected, no doubt because I never heard from my friends, who in any case were recuperating from "Nine Evenings" and not doing any theatre work around town. Yvonne Rainer in particular would have been recovering from her near-fatal intestinal attack, sustained in the middle of "Nine Evenings," at which time she ended up at St. Vincent's, her stay there overlapping with mine. A general dispersion of the Judson/Rauschenberg scene was underway during this year. Couples were splitting up; individuals were stopping performing; several were getting ready to leave the city. Yet the scene staggered on, and I never heard from anybody, despite the fact that I tried to let them know I was ready for business.

The pieces I wrote were truly uninspired, right up through October, but seeing my name in print was the only thing that made me feel I was alive. The newspaper always appeared on the stands on Wednesday, and when I had something coming out, I would take a bus Wednesday afternoon from the Bowery and Grand, where I lived, up to Fourteenth Street to buy a paper, secrete it back to my loft, and read the piece I had written over and over until I knew it by heart and could recite it to myself all week long, or longer, until the next one came out.

But my main activity was sleeping. Around two in the afternoon it was impossible to remain in bed anymore, and I would go across the street for the *Post* and do the crossword puzzle. Then I would find distraction in television. I watched baseball and reruns of "I Love Lucy," "The Honeymooners," and "Perry Mason." I've always had a favorite detective, the man who unfailingly solved everything and lived to do it again on the next show. My childhood model was Dick Tracy. During the seventies I liked Jack Lord in "Hawaii Five-O"; the eighties brought me Tom Selleck in "Magnum P.I." Not until Jack Nicholson in *Chinatown* did I find my hero in the movies. Anyway, back in '67 I watched Perry Mason defeat poor Hamilton Berger, his rival the prosecutor, day after day in rerun after rerun. Many hapless victims were exonerated by Perry's brilliant courtroom pyrotechnics. Had reruns of "Dr. Kildare" been playing, I would have watched Richard Chamberlain save everybody in the hospital.

I had one other diversion during that period. Sometimes I went to the Figaro, a well-known café in the Village, where people played bridge every evening in the basement. I had played bridge fiendishly in college, where it was integral to college life, but nobody ever played cards in the worlds I knew in New York. Going to play bridge with strangers at the Figaro was sort of a desperate thing to do. Several years earlier, when I was depressed over the end of my marriage, I would tool out to some wilderness suburb in New Jersey to play bridge with my friend Pat, who had two small daughters and was a Pepsi-Cola addict and whose husband was a high-school history teacher. Pat was somebody I met as a mother wheeling babies in the park. The charm of it was that they knew nothing about my New York scene or anybody in it. They were the kind of folks who bought everything on credit from Sears Roebuck; their small 'burby house was a study in middle-class motel plastic and hardship funk. They were deep in debt, their marriage was floundering, and they belonged to a bridge club and played competitively in tournaments. I found them reassuringly depressing, and I'm certain they viewed me the same. In '67 I was not so blessed, but strangers at the Figaro perhaps served a similar need. One evening I played with a very youthful, good-looking *New York Times* editor who took me home and made excellent love all night. He reminded me of my ex-husband, a great lover and a handsome fellow who was unaware of my existence. In the morning my bridge partner / lover walked me to the subway, and as we separated I wondered if something more was supposed to happen; but he said nothing, and I imitated his blank expression. So far as I remember, that was my only sexual encounter of the year.

Nor was I looking for it. I still thought my one true love was my ex-friend, that she was probably lost forever, and that I would never find anyone like her again. One of my favorite monotone deliveries was to complain of her loss or of her betrayal and defection. It was an empty complaint, though. I was not really feeling anything. Typical of the kind of depression I had is a total lack of feeling or interest in anything whatsoever. Reading, for instance, one of my conspicuous interests, was out of the question. The sentences on the page just didn't mean anything to me. I saw letters and words, but they failed to ignite a connection in my mind. This was a dramatic reversal of my state months earlier when a single word would fragment explosively into meanings galore, a falling star showering through the universe in atoms of significance. Likewise, where before I couldn't stop talking, one thought tumbling over another so rapidly that I felt seriously handicapped by the linear nature of speech, I was now struck mostly dumb. I could sense things going on outside or around me, but the noises and images were like echoes and apparitions, very far away, nothing to do with me. In company, which was rare, I sat dumbly or mumbled cynically. Nothing mattered—we were all going to die anyway. And the sooner the better, I frequently reflected. Suicide was definitely on my mind. What were the best ways to do it? I wanted to know. I asked Les upstairs about it. He didn't know, or care. He just thought I should get up in the morning like everybody else and begin writing to prove that I existed. From February through April, when I wrote nothing, Les usually called on me once a day to belabor my condition and tell me about all the great things he was doing himself. He didn't have to tell me. I could hear him upstairs, running for the telephone, letting people in for deliveries or interviews, using some incredible gabonga-gabonga machine he had to stamp or imprint thousands of plastic shapes he called disposables. I would lie in bed listening to all the commotion, thinking he was going to die anyway, so why bother? Yet I suppose it deepened my depression, since I knew he was right; as long as we continued living, we might as well do our best. But my own best just then was lying in bed. I had a course to run lying in bed as surely as I had had a trip back in September with a definite time and shape to it. Neither course looked very good, but lying in bed is a prominent sign of giving up, a warning that the body is on the verge of growing cold. I was still young enough to see myself stuck eternally in one course or another. I had no sense whatever of passing through things. I was now depressed for life. When I felt happy, I was happy for life, and so forth. I never counted on change. The seasons changed, but not me. The weather changed, never me. If I had happened to reflect on my history of changes, which I had never done, I would have said I changed for no apparent reason, or that forces impinging on me made me change. I took no responsibility for changes myself. My presumption was that life simply happened to me, and so it was natural to lie in bed until something or other moved me. I cannot remember now what finally did move me, unless it was the changing season in April or May. But I did have a very important friend at that time who kept throwing me a life preserver in the form of a telephone call about once a week to invite me to have dinner or ice cream or to see a movie and who therefore, I could assume, seemed to think I was worth saving for something.

Otherwise, I occasionally saw Charlotte and her close friend June. I was mad at Charlotte for not trying to rescue me at Rauschenberg's the day I was hauled off to Bellevue, a feeling I would try to communicate in such a way as not to alienate her completely. I would say that people in general had not been helpful. Possibly I also attacked her personally. Conceivably she already felt guilty. But it was June who rushed to her defense, and the defense of everybody else, conveying the opinion that Charlotte and the rest of my friends had put up with a lot and done their best for me and that I was a real ingrate to be so unappreciative. June was unsympathetic from the start. She saw me as quite self-centered, someone with little or no sense of other people's realities. That seems pretty accurate. The realities of others meant as little to me as my own. I perceived others as more or less powerful (if not in any sex or class/politic sense), but I never, never perceived them apart from myself in conditions of their own: their histories, their reasons for doing things or having feelings or acting different ways. Thus when my expectations crossed with needs that had nothing to do with me, making people unavailable, I reacted inevitably with paranoia, mixed with anger and frustration, to which I felt unentitled. Then I would probe further, testing their love and limits, trying to find out if my paranoia was justified, ultimately driving them away, satisfying the foregone conclusion that I was not worth the effort I had elicited in the first place. My relations with people were definitely disturbed. I counted absolutely on my position as critic to command reliable attention. I was one of those people whom Freud characterized as "exceptions"—those who feel they have the right to privileges in compensation for some serious disadvantage caused by an adult in their earliest childhood. I was very demanding, and I pressed every advantage beyond all rules of mutuality. Then I would crash into each extremity of a particular demand, ending up lying down somewhere in a daze, wondering what had hit me, whereupon I would withdraw completely, hurt and sulky, back at square one with no mutuality in sight at all. It may be thought that at this point the whole thing would have come clear to me. But this was not to be the case. I now distanced myself from my mother, resolving insofar as possible not to see her, but that was not the same as making her culpable for my problems. I did blame her, to be sure, but only in the most childish sense: the way grown-up children make their parents wrong but have no insight into the problems of their parents—i.e., a feeling for *their* reality. And while it may not be thought to be the child's responsibility to understand a parent or parents who have made them wrong, the child who cannot, by herself or with help, break the cycle of wrongdoing through identifying its sources, and forgive the parent, who has been unable to ask forgiveness, is a child who will remain wrong. I continued protecting my mother and stayed wrong. I didn't see her as a person until 1976 when she was ill and dying. What was to be avoided at all costs was my mother's devaluation in my eyes. My criticism of her really left her power intact. To perceive that I was rejected unjustly would have deprived me of my "original object," to paraphrase Gregory Bateson. And the only way to accept the fact of rejection was to continue giving my mother, and everyone else, ample justification for it. I was "that . . . schizophrenic [who] has devoted years to preventing his parents from seeing their own actions except within the frame of his misbehavior." But by the mid-sixties a real forum for "misbehavior" had developed, in America and around the world. If before 1965 I had been a prepatient, after 1965 I became prepolitical. I was a vaguely liberal political sort of person, sympathetic with the various causes I knew about but personally remote and uninvolved. I would say I was more apolitical than even liberal. The event that made me *pre*political was my incarceration. The axis of change was my anger. Until 1970 a target for this anger remained undefined; I simply found a good channel for acting it out. It was my anger, identified as ingratitude, that made Charlotte's friend June indignant. If June herself was a victim—as woman, as Jewish, as whatever else— she was a lot better assimilated than I was. Even when relatively repressed, before '65, I was less assimilated.

There was a certain irony in connection with my Jewish women friends. My background—without father, heavy with secret—had alienated me from the dominant culture in which I had been raised and of which I was supposed to be a part. My Jewish friends were more thoroughly conditioned to patriarchal realities. Who was the more "illegitimate" here? It was a nice question—and not one that was ever discussed. I just used the franchise I got from them (freedoms of speech, dress, manner, sex, intimacy, etc.) to become a rebellious adult. In this I exceeded all our wildest imaginations, becoming some sort of Gentile travesty of a *shtetl* Jew. I suppose my Jewish friends watched my progress throughout the sixties and into the seventies with a certain horror. In the early seventies I met Jewish feminists, better educated on the whole than my Jewish friends of the sixties, who regarded my behavior with even greater astonishment. On my side, they seemed more WASP than thou. For a while I was considered the distaff version of Jerry Rubin and Abbie Hoffman. And indeed, Jewish men seemed to understand me better than Jewish women did. Even Jewish lesbians (politicized and all) tended to be more conservative. At root, I believe, was the depth of my anger. Of course, at that moment I was too depressed to look upset or anything at all. The only reason I gave June to be indignant was a murmured comment or two to the effect that my friends had not been helpful. I suspect June secretly felt I had good cause to be upset, but wanted no part of the responsibility for it, especially as she had not been a participant in my drama. But the small society in which we lived condemned its victims as bitterly as did society at large, and June was always outspoken. Through her, I learned more or less what everybody thought. At any rate, neither June nor Charlotte was more helpful at this time than I felt the cast of characters who had collaborated in locking me up had been before. Nor was anybody else I knew sympathetic to my case. Unless it was that friend who kept throwing me a life preserver by calling me up once a week to go out for dinner or ice cream or a movie. Or Les upstairs, who kept urging me to get out of bed and write.

Les was a Dublin-born-and-raised Jewish man, on his father's side, with an Irish Catholic mother. I had met him in 1963 in Toronto, where he had emigrated seven years earlier. When he came to New York, I introduced him to a few people, one of them being David Bourdon, who had now undertaken my rescue by calling me up and asking me out so regularly. David had worked for the *Village Voice* and was currently at *Life*. His name means "big bell" in French, and his father owned a lumber company in California. He never talked about his origins or family or past or even himself in the present much. He did talk a lot, though, and fortunately for my part I was expected to say very little. David always decided where we would go, and when we got there he held forth with vast amusement mostly on his own about favorite art-world topics: who was who and who had just done what and what everybody thought about it. Popular items then were Warhol and his "superstars"—Viva, Ultra Violet, Bridget Polk, Edie Sedgwick, Naomi Levine, Baby Jane Holzer, Billy Name. David knew all of them quite well. There was a period of time when he gossiped on the phone with Warhol every day. He was a good friend of Christo's and Ray Johnson's and fast becoming one to Les, who was enamored of Warhol's reputation and diversity.

I was always surprised when David called, since I had virtually nothing to offer. I must have assumed, remembering that remark he had made back in October, with great mischief aforethought, that Rauschenberg and his gang had probably wanted to get me out of the way before they did their "Nine Evenings," that he felt I had been unjustly treated as a critic—something, perhaps, with which he could identify. In 1983 he mischievously accused me of *believing* the remark. But whether or not it was true, he did mean he was on my side, and I certainly needed somebody on my side. For a couple of years, right through the spring of 1968, David and Les were the only people I knew who acted like friends. In November of '67, as my dreary year slowly unwound, and my newspaper shocked me out of my complacency as their one and only (however delinquent and discouraged) dance critic, David said the most reassuring and supportive things and was perhaps even instrumental in making sure the paper maintained me. One of his friends was Voice photographer Fred McDarrah, who kept him informed of Voice politics and gossip. Then, later, in May of '68, when I was well launched on a new course of writing at the paper, David introduced me to a man who was so rich and powerful and momentarily so interested in me or my case that he transformed me overnight into a Cinderella—abruptly ending my depression, catapulting me out of my former life, and overturning my mother's ancient injunction against visiting the fatherland.

I have to say, though, that I did come alive in November '67—on November 9, to be precise, when I picked up my paper and found a long, serious dance review in it by an unknown woman. I could tell that it was serious, not just a singular contribution. My editor's threat of the year earlier to find another dance critic had materialized. By chance, I had happened to submit something that week too, but it was very short, not more than five hundred words, and placed tellingly on the page following this large curveball, the surprise new dance review. Not much mystery about the placement: the paper was growing bigger and more successful; its need for a dance critic who was serious and wrote consistently and wrote about everything was based on satisfying the market for advertisements. I was no longer serious, I had never written consistently, and I rarely wrote about things I thought were not exciting and new. Since January '66, however, with the exception of the one crazy piece about Robert Whitman's Happening in the Long Island swamp, I had written pretty consistent detritus, though I had lamely been trying to demonstrate a certain seriousness by covering a variety of work. But I had no heart in it really. I stopped writing criticism long before I stopped. I got a taxicab license because I knew I was not really doing it anymore. I tried desperately to imagine what other sort of writing I could do. I had not read fiction since my twenties and was certain I could not make things up (!), and I thought poetry much too arduous and demanding and difficult to consider.

But curiously, just two weeks before that awful November 9 which proved in the end to be my great opportunity, I wrote something odd enough to suggest new tangents. I had already written some odd things—notably that Whitman piece, but even before my astronautical trip in '65 I had written two or three things that could later be said to prefigure the future. One was an outrageous review of an outrageous concert by the

Fluxus people in July '64, which I titled "Fluxus Fuxus." Another was a review in October '64 of a Happening by German composer Karlheinz Stockhausen called *Originale,* which I reviewed both from without and from within looking out, analyzing the work and my own performance in it as "free agent," titling the review "Inside Originale." Another, in December '64, was a kind of blow-by-blow outline, very Dada in feeling, of the plot of a grand opera, pure spoof, by Dick Higgins, enterprising publisher of the Something Else Press, the press that represented the spirit of the wildest and most precious and hermetic art of that time. In these three reviews I attempted to match the form and spirit of the work I was reviewing. The Fluxus and Higgins pieces were virtually collaged. They were both cast in a single paragraph, prototypical of later work that I considered "all-over" writing, like all-over painting, so called for its lack of focus or emphasis or reference points or central subject or transitions between loci of importance. All-over meant everything was equally important. In the Fluxus review I introduced bits of extraneous material: my life outside the theatre, other things of note going on in the world, historical allusions, cryptic reflections inspired by the concert—e.g., "Is Child Art on the stage any different from Child Art in the home? Of course it is, and Fluxus Fux any notion of value attached to staying home or going to the theatre." Three years later, in October '67, after a three-and-a-half-month hiatus during which I wrote nothing, I did something in a similar vein, though shorter and broken into paragraphs and a lot more naive in tone. I took a child's stance to the work at hand, which was itself much less sophisticated than the childlike work of Fluxus. The occasion was Charlotte Moorman's annual avant-garde festival, which took place on board the *J. F. Kennedy* ferryboat, plying between Manhattan and Staten Island all afternoon, carrying both artists and regular passengers. In my report, called "Ship Ahoy!," I mixed up art and setting, artists and people ("Two bunches of white balloons fly away to the sky. A tug tows a barge carrying rusty old scrap metal"), quoted remarks of friends, strung images together like beads, and placed myself in the center of the event. At the end I said, "Oh, what a beautiful day." I seemed to be launching myself, on the *J. F. Kennedy* ferryboat. A week later I pressed my luck with a "review" of a dance concert at the New School by several choreographers. My title, "Dancing Is a Dog," told all. "Funny how you see a thing when it isn't there," I wrote, "and when it's there you don't see it anymore." I continued: "I don't clean my house but I polish my boots. Much of theatre occurs on the stage and much of it occurs in the heads of the audience. Dancing is a dwarf lady, Yvonne said once. Or dancing is a dog. Steve Paxton had a friendly dog on stage with him. . . . If the world's a stage nobody should mind showing off. Theatres are special gaping places, like monkey houses. . . . Well, who did we come here to look at anyway? So sometimes an audience gets to look at itself. . . . Once Steve did a dance in which he snapped pictures of the audience. . . . Dancing is questionable. Dancing is sometimes not being there. . . . The form of Kenneth King's piece was his absence. . . . He sent regrets from Hong Kong. . . ." And so on. I was very happy about this "review." I followed it up with "A Likely Story," jabbing lightly and sardonically at the Harkness ballet. I announced my intention: "I'll be a crude customer. The *Times* will say something respectable." I said what I really wanted: "in my lifetime to see one of them stop dead in his elegant tracks and scream bloody murder." I said where I really wanted to be: "in Piccadilly Circus." I compared things: the graffiti in the ladies' room was more interesting than some story about a Prince and a Courtesan and a slave called Sebastian. I said something precociously feminist: "The boys do amazing things, first one, then the other. After you, Alphonse. They're good. And cavalier, too. So polite with the lady. 'Wait till I get you home, dolly.' " Finally, I threatened them: "Argh, they'll pay for this. I'll submit a petition for Ray Johnson to give the world its next *Firebird*." I loved it. I was very pleased with myself, especially over the use of the word "Argh." I felt I was on to something. A new criticism could have an Argh-ness about it. I could channel my depression into Argh.

But, alas, my pleasure was short-lived. That very week when "A Likely Story" appeared, a sort of Argh manifesto, my new competitor's serious dance criticism was splashed down all over the page in front of me. Cover headlines that week happened to read WHAT'S NEW IN AMERICA (about the Maharishi Mahesh Yogi), and NOTES ON A CONFRONTATION (about a Pentagon march). "Oh, to be in England," I had dropped in, closing my Argh.

I called up David instantly to find out if this was the end of my critical career. He assured me it was not. Or, rather, he conveyed the hopeful thought that this new entry should release me to write about "everything else"—in which I had already demonstrated an interest. I was not convinced. I had no franchise for giving up criticism. I had no good idea what "everything else" could be. I had never written anything but a review, regardless of some kinkiness or promising departures from the subject. My new creative Argh was nipped in the bud. I could never write clever, sarcastic criticism next to such supportive, serious-looking stuff. Besides, the paper was obviously trying to get rid of me. I was in a state that week. The energy of it propelled me right out of bed and up the walls. There was never any conversation between myself and the paper. I wondered what they wanted from me, if anything, and I suppose they wondered what I would do, if anything. The old Voice was never organized around normal principles of assignment. The paper thought nothing of printing reviews by different people of the same show or book in identical or successive issues, so I knew I could duplicate my competitor's subjects, provided it didn't happen too regularly and that I could find something distinctive to say that was neither serious (no chance of that) nor simply nihilistic, the vein I had just opened up. But I worried needlessly. My competitor's interests ran basically to real old-fashioned dancing, both the ballet and the moderns. The territory I had carved out—Judson, nondance, the Happenings, Intermedia, Fluxus, Dada, Zen, etc.—remained essentially mine, if I wanted it. I did—at least for the time being. I just had to approach the work with less intent to kill.

I made some very curious compromises at this time. My main strategy was to surround the work I reviewed with nonsense, leaving the work itself intact, by description or neutral commentary, but playing it off against my rapidly developing appetite for the absurd. In this I had some striking help from the absurd work around town that I picked out to cover. My opening rejoinder to this new threat to my career was to write a piece about John Cage called "Poets and Kings," positing, though not advertently, our great American Overlord of the Absurd, establishing a kind of beachhead of operations, at the head of my "troops." Several years earlier I had done something similar, writing ecstatically about Cage's book *Silence*, but this time I had a different intent. I was no longer the critic outside the work, egging on the artists who best represented my subversive or rebellious interests; now I had moved myself right up against the work, threatening to consume or co-opt it by my own absurd writing. As the weeks went on (and I was now writing very consistently), I pushed the work, my review object, further and further out of the frame. By the summer of 1968 I was finally writing about "everything else," just as David had predicted I might. In April '68 I had saluted my Judson dance friends with three "farewell" pieces: "Paxton's People," "Rainer's Muscle," and "Hay's Group." My competitor could have them, I must have thought to myself, for I now had the world. John Cage, incidentally, was not the last to recognize my defection. Once my coup was complete and criticism had given way to "everything else" (as had been foretold, in a way, by my "voices" of '65 and my "visions" of '66), Cage let me know, whenever it was I happened to see him that year, that my work had ceased being very interesting—i.e., useful to him. The feeling became mutual; his work shortly no longer interested me, either. From his point of view, if he no longer had my support, I was not his

Left: The leather vest matched a miniskirt acquired in London, 1968. Pants, shades, drink, and tin-can jewelry was a basic late-sixties look. *Photo by Peter Hujar*.

Right: A later adaptation. The sleeker mod look was replaced by a secondhand derby, combat boots, old denims, military jacket . . .

Two Museum of Modern Art openings: (*above*) Jill with her friend and Ultra Violet, an Andy Warhol superstar. Jill's suit, cowboy hat, belt, and yo-yo are all from Houston, courtesy of John de Menil. (*Right*) Jill in a rented tuxedo and top hat. *Photos © 1968 Fred W. McDarrah.*

peer. As mentor, he had been distant and impersonal. My development was no special concern of his. Mentors and their "progeny" frequently become estranged, but estrangement had been built into this particular variety of the model. The relationship was a one-way affair; my attentions were never requited, except to reinforce my attentions. And my background had not really set me up for that. A man like Cage had plenty of lady admirers, who had no creative interests of their own or who subsumed them under his. Cage himself admired only male artists. At issue for me after '65 was a conflict between serving artists and becoming one. I dared not think of myself as an artist or as a writer per se. If my background made it difficult or impossible to sustain a supportive role, it had not been conducive to thinking in terms of one who might be supported, either. In this latter respect I was hardly different from women at large; the problem has always been how to become oneself without offending the view that one exists only for others. In order to approach a creative role, I had to subvert myself as well as my newspaper. The key to this subversion, I believe, was Apollinaire, my long-dead mentor.

One advantage of a dead mentor, for a girl at least, is that his price has gone to the grave with him. Another is that his unavailability makes it possible to imagine he has nothing to do with the important relationship of which he's a part. During this time I suppressed all thought of Apollinaire. I was extremely embarrassed, after I "came down," to realize I had told everybody Apollinaire was my father. Besides, I discovered he was too fat to be my father (that portrait of him in the derby had been misleading). I consigned him to the depths from whence he had come. There, evidently, he went right on with his "work," profoundly affecting the chapter of my life about to ensue. "Save me, doctor!" Apollinaire exclaimed on his deathbed. "I want to live! I still have so much to say." I would never become a poet, certainly, but the prose I would write would look increasingly idiosyncratic. If I couldn't be a poet, I could distort my prose and perhaps invoke that infamous question of Gertrude Stein's:

"What is poetry and if you know what poetry is what is prose?"
But I took it very slowly. I was sane and sober and only one or
two years old. The territory was uncharted. I took baby steps
toward freedom (from criticism), always reaching back to claim
the property I was leaving behind. From November '67 through
May '68, writing every week, I alternated between serious and
absurdist treatment of subjects, reverting to the old earnestness
in handling work by Judson choreographers, including the
younger Meredith Monk, and the new talent Twyla Tharp, yet
wherever possible disrupting the subject with jokes, "found" sentences or quotes, non sequiturs, silly asides, autobiographical
bits, anecdotes—elements I could wield most effectively or easily in the context of "absurd" subjects. James Byars came to the
rescue, visiting me on the Bowery and barraging me with out-
landish information which I jotted down excitedly, then used to
surround a description of an event of his at the CBS plaza in
which a heavy-duty weather balloon launched by an expert from
the Weather Bureau at JFK Airport was supposed to carry a
mile of gold thread up to the sky and hopefully off to England
(the thread got stuck on a building, decorating some trees on
Fifty-third Street; a second balloon exploded on the street), and
a projected event in which Byars would put his head in a hole
at one end of a piece of pink silk twelve by one hundred feet and
act as a "consciousness ornament" to somebody with his head in
a hole at the other end, echoing everything he said and did. He
babbled enthusiastically about this "dress," and I wrote it all
down. "He'll try seducing other people into the holes to be addi-
tional ornaments. 'What is a dress?' 'How do you negotiate a
door in a one-hundred-foot dress?' 'How do you sit down?'
'What does plural clothing mean?' 'Why shouldn't a man and
a woman wear the same dress?' 'What is a group?' 'It's a pleasure to see pink in midwinter.' 'Pink is such an abused color in
the U.S.' 'We could dress up the whole city in an hour.' " Byars
made great copy, I thought. This particular piece I called "On a
White Camel, Investigating Everything." "My mission," Byars
had said, "is to investigate everything."

Byars had already been helpful two months earlier when I wrote something called "Canceled." Elaine Sturtevant had revived a performance of Satie's *Relâche* (1924); the title means "no performance." As in '24, a prospective audience found the theatre shut tight. I loved the event, especially as it provided the opportunity to meet Duchamp, who arrived in a taxi with his wife just when I was leaving. We had a few words (he kept his taxi waiting). I told him there was no performance. He confirmed having appeared nude in the original production (in '24, the week following the performance's cancellation, a production did take place). For "Canceled" I included notice of another Byars event: a five-hundred-foot paper man laid out on Fifty-third Street between Fifth and Sixth Avenues, its head at the Museum of Modern Art, its crotch at the Craft Museum, its feet at the CBS Building. Byars had engaged the city sanitation department to move in with flusher trucks, destroying the paper in ten minutes with twenty thousand gallons of water. The half-mile of dissolvable paper had been furnished by Gilreth International Company—a recent biochemical discovery. Byars said it was "spy paper . . . a sterile edible material" and that "spies could now eat their information." Byars was an inexhaustible fountain of Zen trivia, momentous whimsy. Some of his statements and questions resonated with my own cosmologies of '65 and '66. I put him forward as an intelligent and deranged spirit of the time.

I found another one in Kenneth King, whom I asked to visit me to explain his identity in a solo concert he gave at Judson Church. The program note said the performer was one Sergei Alexandrovitch, a young Russian dancer from Leningrad. To me, he was obviously King. When King came to visit, I asked him who the figure really was. He said it was Pablo. Who was Pablo? I wanted to know. He was one of King's men, King replied. I asked him where he, King, was during the performance. He was out, he said. And where was Sergei, the identified performer? He was out too, it was actually Pablo doing the performing. Later, on the telephone, he told me it was Sergei and confessed that he did look quite a bit like him. I asked him where Sergei was now. In Leningrad resting, he said. "He's just a dancer. He carries airline bags and eats cottage cheese. He's tall, thin, nice, hardly ever talks. He calls on a blue plastic phone." "Yours or his?" I asked. "Excuse me," he said, "I'm eating a baloney sandwich." And I concluded that King was in Hong Kong (possibly talking to Zora Zash, the man or woman who had discovered Sergei) and that I'd really been talking to Pablo. I vowed to ask Sergei where Kenneth was when Sergei returned from Leningrad. I called the piece "Where's Kenneth?" This hugely satisfied a longing for my own suppressed alter-identities. Both King and Byars seemed to be safely realizing the kinds of fantasies that had caused my downfall.

I then retreated hastily to write a reasonably conventional piece about how various choreographers had been using films and photos. Next I surged ahead again into uncharted areas, this time taking on José Limón, whom I knew my competitor would also review—trying to claim priority, I believe, by establishing my personal history with the man. It was my first assay into autobiography, reaching back into the fifties for material, revealing intimacies considered taboo for critics. I called the piece "Time Tunnel." The following week I retreated once again, writing "criticism" about Twyla Tharp. The next week I wrote something unprecedented, constructed of aphorisms, suspending normal syntax. The title was "Well-Hung"; my inspiration was Norman Brown's style in *Love's Body*. Collecting about ten artists in two short paragraphs, I deployed various sexual metaphors around a central one of "equipment."

I was quite hooked on Brown's book, using it almost like a Bible, quoting from it and adapting its style to my own subjects. If Laing's *The Politics of Experience* was thought to exalt and romanticize madness, Brown's *Love's Body* was an earlier, even grander elevation of that state. Before finding Laing, I had Brown. A justification for my experience motivated my writing more than any need to supersede criticism and become a writer —or perhaps they were the same thing. To establish credibility as a writer would be justification in itself. But that was not going to be enough. Backed up by Brown, later by Laing and others, I used the writing to push the superiority of madness.

Soon after "Well-Hung," a good chance presented itself. An Austrian artist, Hermann Nitsch, brought his Orgy-Mystery Theatre to Soho, a wild Dionysian/Christian bloodbath. Nitsch saturated carcasses of lamb, clumps of brains, entrails, and liver, draining big bottles of red liquid, blood perhaps, projecting images and ritual fragments of brutal sacrifice, etc. In my piece ("The Holy Hurricane," March '68) I called it "the eye of insanity, of the dissolution of boundary . . . a holy hurricane of blood . . . a holocaust of bodies . . . a catechism and a cataclysm . . . the baptism by fire . . . the resurrection and the life . . . a consummation devoutly to be wished . . . Inferno Purgatorio Paradiso." I equated "lunacy"—the "perception of disintegrating boundaries"—with this sort of artwork, which I upheld as "brilliant hemorrhage" or "insurrections of the flesh" or "theatre of gang bang" or "a world united by its garbage." I quoted Brown: "The solution to the problem of identity is, get lost."

A broadside like this can be seen in perspective. America was coming apart. That June Bobby Kennedy was shot. In our own world, Andy Warhol was shot and nearly killed, and the woman who shot him had written something called the SCUM (Society for Cutting Up Men) Manifesto. Antiwar forces had stepped up activities: the big peace march on the Pentagon (in which lots of people were clubbed, gassed, and arrested) took place that spring. (Among the arrested was Norman Mailer, who later marketed the event as *Armies of the Night*.) The infamous Be-In or Yip-In at Grand Central Station, eliciting scandalous cop behavior, occurred about the same time. The Haight-Ashbury drug and flower-child scene in San Francisco was peaking. The psychedelic movement in general was flourishing. Race riots were still vigorous. The violent underground of Weathermen had formed itself. The demonstrations at the Democratic convention in Chicago resulted in the Chicago Seven trials. Feminist forces were gathering rapidly. And the

Stonewall riots, initiating the gay or homosexual movement, were on the horizon. Revelry and disruption were everywhere rampant. Even had my newspaper not roused me, I doubt I would have stayed depressed too long in such a carnival atmosphere. By March and April I was beginning to enjoy at least my writing. World-shaking events such as the Chicago demonstrations and the Grand Central Yip-In astonished and puzzled me or just left me indifferent; reflections of these events in the art world delighted me. Connections between the two escaped me.

16

Persona

Something like the assassination of Bobby Kennedy I put in a class by itself. The Kennedy brothers were heroes in death for me, not in life. I had voted for Jack because he was so handsome and stylish; what he stood for or planned or promised to do and then actually did were very vague to me. Similarly, I was transfixed by Bobby, whom I watched hawkishly on television. Behind his campaign statements I detected a big sadness and resignation, a detachment thoroughly atypical of politicians. I felt he had already joined his brother, though I would not have said or thought so until after he was shot. I had begun to think that people like assassins were really agents of the assassinated. Or at the least that assassins reflected forces much larger than their own interests. Results seemed to bear that out. I was one of the stunned millions watching the replays on television over and over again: Bobby Kennedy lying unconscious on the hotel kitchen floor in Los Angeles, echoing that frame of his brother in '63 lurching forward and reaching for his head in the car in Dallas. The myth of the hero who dies violently, "before his time," was integral to the sixties. I had my own personal, however unconscious, stake in it. "Before their time" for me had to mean before I had the chance to know them. As father symbols, the Kennedys, like Apollinaire, had the kind of ending that fit with my mother's story. JFK was forty-six when he died, precisely the same age as my father when he died according to my mother's original story. Behind that was the actual death of her own father, Frederick Crowe, at forty-six. Bobby Kennedy, of course, was only forty-three. Behind the Kennedys was the example of my mother's paternal grandfather, Chauncey Crow, who died of a gunshot wound to the head. Behind Chauncey was his father, Almond, who died youngishly at fifty-seven. None of these connections were available to me in the sixties. They were simply contained somewhere in the maze of explosive and fantastic associations I had made when deranged. I could only mine them when I no longer needed my mother's original story, to which, through Apollinaire, I had regressed. I had transposed the earlier "truth" and applied it to other men (excepting Freud) well known for having died young or before their time. Such men are noted for coming back to life. The lives they lead after death can be ubiquitous and extraordinary. "Preserve my memory," Galois wrote on the eve of his death, "since fate has not given me life enough for my country to know my name." Any man as important as a father must have died at a time and in a way that made it impossible for us to meet. It was easier to deny the knowledge that such a man had grown old enough to meet me but never had. The sixties meant a regression to a bonnier time, when everything my mother had told me was true and there were no crippling contradictions. That was the essence of my experiences in '65 and '66. Then, though of course I went right on knowing the real truth, my mother's belated correction, I acted as if I did not.

This third stage of life—open rebellion—represented a traditional male solution. For males, it is usually a second stage of life, occurring between adolescence and manhood. My second stage was more typically female: prolonged subversiveness and self-destructiveness. For women generally there has traditionally been nothing else, except a good adaptation. Many women like myself rode in on the open rebellion of young men in the sixties. Most of them became attached to the civil rights and antiwar movements, the psychedelic or rock-concert celebrations. In the art world, women seemed to lag more behind the revolting young men of the Dada and Fluxus movements. But they only looked different because they weren't out on the streets waving banners and confronting cops or looking dangerous for making bombs in town-house basements. In both worlds, art and at large, women supported the interests of male youth. John Cage was a pretty old "male youth" (fifty-three in 1965), but like Timothy Leary in his way, and Mailer in his, and perhaps the Berrigan brothers and certainly the Kennedys in theirs, he was a *puer aeternus*, eternal boy, a kind of "mother's son" whose creative flowering is pitted against the settled and repressive bourgeois values of the father. Apollinaire was a quintessential sort of mother's son. Boys born without fathers have very special problems growing up. John Cage was not a fatherless son, but he was an only child with a very possessive mother. The "heroes" of Otto Rank's famous essay were all fatherless; some were orphans. A modern Western prototype of the mother's son was Arthur Rimbaud, whom I read deliriously at the age of twenty-seven. Roger Shattuck wrote: "With Rimbaud a new personage emerges: the 'child-man,' the grown-up who has refrained from putting off childish things." To the art of these child-men, Shattuck ascribed such qualities as obscurity, illogicality, ineptness, abruptness, humor, irony, dream or the fusion of conscious and unconscious into a continuum, a breakdown of the "barriers between sleeping and waking," between life and art ("turning the private life into a public performance"), between subject-object distinctions. Of Shattuck's quartet, the two writers, Jarry and Apollinaire, were the ones who died young. Satie, Cage's model, died at fifty-nine, eternally young at heart. I suspect Jack Kennedy grew up a lot during his term as President, but the image with which he left us was quite youthful. Images of youth and maturity in our society still tend to remain separate. Maturity in America has meant joining the corporation and dying in it. To grow up and to remain young at heart seem like mutually exclusive concepts. Certainly they seemed so in the sixties, though quite a few leaders of the youth movement were over forty. However, their deaths were crucial to the completion of their myths—the sacrifice of the hero to a larger cause. Though Cage, of course, didn't die, I killed him off by no longer needing him or needing his need of me. With my coronation of Apollinaire, evoking my mother's original story (a man who died too young to know me), I was free to become a mother's son, a boy whose need to kill off the father (an event that has already occurred) disguises his quest for paternal identity—the classic conflict of a time like the sixties. I was already, after all, a *garçon manqué*.

That March of '68, I found an opportunity to announce my new persona. The date was the 25th, the opening of the Dada-surrealist show at the Museum of Modern Art. Where some art-rebel types demonstrated outside the museum, others, like myself, challenged authority from within. If there was any real difference, it was that I had no idea that this was what I was doing. Costume, in my case, was everything. Highly attuned to the event as a showcase, I went out and rented a tuxedo and top hat for twenty-five dollars. I was exactly the age of Apollinaire when he died. My compromise was a garish pink tie decorated with large green polka dots. Fred McDarrah immortalized me in the outfit, holding a drink and talking to a "femme" in a regular black evening gown showing an expanse of bare back. My appearance felt like a debut. I hardly looked at the art, which was *my* art; I was much more interested in how I looked myself— standing around drinking, laughing, and basking in the spectacle I hoped or imagined I was creating. I was definitely born (again) that evening. I rose right up at the vernal equinox, a seasonal convulsion that had always meant Easter holiday to me, and new green leaves, never social/personal upheaval. Spring was exploding in America and New York that year. Just four days before this Dada opening, I had witnessed Charlotte Moorman at the "Destruction in Art" symposium use a violin to bash in the head of the man who had tried to stop her performance. By the time I appeared in a rented tuxedo at MOMA, my piece about this ("Over His Dead Body") had been printed. A week earlier, my Hermann Nitsch–inspired piece had appeared. On March 22 Steve Paxton presented an evening that I thought was sublime, in particular a "dance" called *Satisfyin'*

Lover for thirty-two people, who walked across the performing area (a gymnasium) one after the other in regular street clothes. The Yip-In at Grand Central happened the same night.

Around that time I became acquainted with two people who bridged the worlds of art and politics and who would mean a great deal to me in the months to come. One of them had organized the demonstration outside MOMA the night of the Dada-surrealist opening; the other lived down the street from me, at the big, sprawling intersection of Canal Street and the Bowery where the Manhattan Bridge lies.

17

Good Copy

Both had also been to Bellevue. Of the two, Ann Wilson, who lived down the street, had not gone crazy exactly but had tried to commit suicide by consuming quantities of pills. That was in late August '65, her stay at Bellevue preceding mine by several weeks. She moved into her loft on the Bowery and Canal January '67, about nine months after I had inhabited mine a little farther north. Her friend, Gene Swenson, a well-known art critic in the sixties, lost his mind several times between '67 and '69, the year he died in a car crash with his mother in Kansas. I wrote a peculiar sort of obit for him in the Voice in September '69. I had known him well for about a year. I knew Ann first; probably I saw her on the street one day, recognized her from a party or someplace, struck up a conversation, and ended up visiting her in her loft. That had to be one day during '67, when I was hiding out in bed most of the time. Here was another sixties casualty down the block, trying to piece together the shattered fragments of herself. My vision of Ann then was leaning intently over a drawing board making detailed drawings, as if her new life depended on it. I resisted seeing her as a friend for at least a year. We had altogether too many things in common. The women I had liked, as friends at least, approximated the ideal Vogue cover image. Ann came nowhere near it, and she wasn't old enough to be perceived as some kind of crazy wise lady like Agnes Martin. Agnes, incidentally, was to Ann much as she was to me—the only older lady in New York she esteemed, or for that matter knew. We both aspired to be Agnes someday.

Ann had come to New York about 1954 from Pittsburgh, where she had studied art at Carnegie Tech (now Carnegie Mellon), a class behind Andy Warhol. She said she had gotten off the Greyhound bus in Manhattan with a bunch of framed paintings and was met by Ray Johnson, who took her directly to America's leading gallery, the Janis. There Sidney Janis removed a Degas from a velvet platform, placed one of Ann's framed watercolors of the Pittsburgh mountains on it, and said he wasn't sure but he thought they were showing younger Americans at a place called Tenth Street. Ann thought he was such a nice man to look at her work. Ray joked by saying you might as well start at the top. Within two years she was living in a loft building on Coenties Slip also occupied by Agnes Martin and Ellsworth Kelly. Nearby were Lenore Tawney, Robert Indiana, Jack Youngerman, John Chamberlain, Jasper Johns, and Rauschenberg. Ann left the Slip in 1960 to marry Bill Wilson, college professor, critic, writer, and son of a well-known art-world character called May Wilson. By the time I met Ann she was quite a well-known art-world character herself. With Bill she had twin daughters and a son, losing her standing with the artists by becoming a mother. She then lost her standing as a mother by falling in love with Gene Swenson ("a romantic escape," she has described it, "from the harshness and domestic responsibility of marriage") and running away from home. With Gene her standing was precarious because Gene was mostly homosexual. Adrift between Gene and her marriage, homeless and without funds, barred from seeing her children except at her husband's house, stigmatized as a runaway mother, she tried suicide with a bottle of pills. Once stabilized on the Bowery, she was less threatening to Gene and could assimilate him as a close friend in a new, complex life.

Her life was ever complex. I had never known anyone like Ann. Her interests seemed to fly off in a hundred directions at once. She was truly omnivorous. She devoured people, books, ideas, landscape, art, religion, politics, everything, like a great hydraulic toothed shovel let loose in a world library archaeological deposit. And being socially reactive, completely inured to the niceties of exchange, the amenities of reciprocity, she unloaded her vast store of information much the way she had taken it all in. When Ann was "on," people found her pretty overwhelming. Her normal manner sounded like mine while crazy. But I got very hyper myself in the late sixties and could compete with Ann in outrageous bouts of mounting verbiage. Eventually our conversations consisted of nothing but mutual interruption, which I would try in vain to point out. We both seemed compelled to urge our enthusiasms on each other. I felt I had no choice but to imitate her defensively.

Yet there was a side to Ann that ever delighted me, once I got past my resistance to perceiving her as a friend. She had a really wicked sense of humor, a well-developed sense of the bitter irony of things, and when her shoulders hiked up and she crossed her arms and hugged her diaphragm and pulled in her chin and squirreled out her cheeks and flushed different blotchy colors of red and smiled maliciously and started this low, cackling gallows sort of laugh, you knew you were in for some high entertainment. In the best female-comic tradition, she could turn the worst things that had happened to her into hilarious travesties of herself. This was how she revealed her personal life. It was too awful to be serious, and burlesquing it raised the stigma from it. Whereas I daily huffed and complained, she took refuge in personal absurdity, which I would channel into my writing. By the end of '68, in fact, I was channeling Ann herself into my columns, quoting her most delectable remarks (e.g., "I'm thirty-eight years old and I don't own an ironing board"), robbing her in a way and thereby further exacerbating our competitiveness. For two people with as much in common as we had—outsider-type women and only children, close in age, who had grown up in the same America and loved books and ideas and art and experienced similar misfortunes in marriage and crashed into Bellevue—the lack of compassion between us was certainly outstanding; but we were both still unaffected by feminism, and the world we lived in remained marked by a driving need to keep up a pretense that all was well and to take what was not well off someplace to a shrink. The worst thing you might do was to show your vulnerabilities. At the height of our friendship we never had any kind of exchange that could pass for mutual sympathy—about the guilt of being condemned mothers, the guilt over our children, the anger at our ex-husbands or at being made to feel we were wrong, our rage at our parents and society and art-world compatriots who had damned us, etc., etc. Everything was channeled into humor and absurdity or sublimated in the great quest for new ideas and people and beautiful art and exciting books and crazy political or cultural events. The thing is, we really did believe we were wrong, and that was inadmissible. And wrong people usually make each other wrong. Compassion transcends any sense of wrongness or rightness. Women had to pass through righteousness before they could approach mutuality. But before righteousness, they had to realize they had been made to feel they were wrong. Of the two of us, Ann seemed more resolutely sublimated, but that was perhaps only because she hid her despair better.

A big difference between us was that Ann felt deprived of art because she had to teach. The problem of being an artist and making a living was a recurrent theme in our conversations. Ann's position was that she *had* to teach, and her parents and the doctor whom her parents paid to have her see all said the same. Art was a luxury or a hobby, not a profession. My position was that she should stop teaching and find a way to sell her art. I thought she should be a successful artist—or at the least be like me, impoverished but uncompromised, so that I wouldn't have to feel guilty about her teaching, and she wouldn't have to be angry about my freedom to write. During '68 and '69 I did quite well—paying twenty-five dollars a month rent (charging my Japanese artist the seventy-five balance), milking the city in welfare payments for what I believed they owed me in indemnity for brutal treatment in hospitals, and collecting forty dollars for each *Voice* column. I could live easily on fifteen hundred a year. Anything seemed possible to me. It was very frustrating that Ann saw things differently. Of course, had I realized she was baiting me, thus feeding our competitiveness, I might have ignored her complaints. It was her only complaint (that is, the only one not clothed in high romp or obscured completely in abstractions and religious yearnings), and my stock response to any complaint not my own was to look for an answer that would make it go away. This was usually a true waste of energy. A complaint as serious as Ann's about art and teaching was rooted in the deep belief that one was not possible without the other, or, deeper yet, that she had no right to the one, while the other was her moral obligation. She believed her parents and the doctor—and naturally hated them for it. Her antisocial behavior was embedded in this contradiction. Mine was too, in another edition of it; but by '68 I had canned my mother and was acting as if she had ceased to exist. Ann had sought creative autonomy in her marriage, painting ambitiously in the midst of babies; then, when her marriage collapsed, she reverted to the position of a woman alone who has to earn a living. Ann had married a man whose mother had become an artist living alone in New York—a counter to her father, whose wife found her outlet in golf tournaments at the country club, who also painted; thus Ann was very much her mother while married, afterwards turning into a version of her husband's mother. Married or not, though, and despite all her years among artists in New York, she still saw herself as a woman whose art was secondary to a man or to her "moral obligation." She could conveniently label the three stages of her life in New York to date. First she was an initiate, unmarried and ambitious, too young to get a good gallery. Next, as wife and mother, she (felt she) was unacceptable as a painter. Third, as "fallen woman," she felt too guilty to paint ambitiously, and would have been excluded everywhere anyway. At this stage, she energetically subsumed herself under Gene—who was a political radical by '67—becoming one of those women of the sixties who attached themselves to the open rebellion of male youth. I coasted in on the same rebellion, then arrogated a certain leadership or male position to myself. That was a serious difference between us. Ann was an only child whose golfing-and-painting mother was strongly aligned with her father. I could say the same, except that the father with whom my mother was so aligned, or about whom she was so possessive, had never put in an appearance to let me know that anything wasn't possible. Deep down, I didn't believe (in) the father that was society, to which I had tried dutifully, mindlessly, and unsuccessfully to conform. Or deep down I believed I myself was this father. Ann now had a classic rationale for her "failure" to be a painter: the system was corrupt, art was used for capital profit by museums and dealers, artists themselves traded their souls for profit, the art world in its "art for art's sake" values and social elegance was unresponsive to the problems of urban poverty and to the war—the platform of Gene Swenson in the one-man battle he waged against the art establishment from '67 through '69.

Ann and I saw Gene wholly differently. I wasn't in love with him, for a start. For Ann, Gene was the first man or person who had loved her in a tender way, and for what she was, not as an object. A man like that could be worth following to the ends of the earth. And she accepted that he loved her without the capacity for commitment. Gene was an active homosexual, and during this period he had a boyfriend called Harry. Ann too had a very young lover, called Jules. Sometime during '67 Gene cracked up and went to Bellevue. I believe that event radicalized him. Unlike myself, he found an immediate target for his rage. That year he conducted a prolonged one-man picket outside the Museum of Modern Art, made a revolutionary speech on the steps of the Leo Castelli gallery, was arrested for charging a police barricade at an antiwar demonstration, delivered an address in front of the courthouse in which he was to be tried (and later acquitted), and wrote something called "A Critic's Farewell Address," openly declaring his disaffection from the New York art world. At the beginning of '68 he staged a series of solo protest events in front of MOMA, which banned him from entering the place. Later he organized a big group demonstration against the Dada-surrealist show the night of the opening I so blithely crashed in a tuxedo. Gene found it "absurd and obscene for official recognition to defuse the revolutionary ideals that lay behind these movements." He took out small ads in the *Voice* reading, "MOMA is dead. Dada is dead. Celebrate! Mausoleum of Modern Art" or "Artists and poets! Do your thing! Join les Enfants du Parody in the Transformation! Tea and black tie optional" or "Dedicated to the lost but not forgotten spirit of Dada and surrealism. Their historical bodies are now embalmed and on view at MOMA." I couldn't relate to it. I was inside the museum, "doing my thing," but I thought of it in no way politically. Politics to me still meant a bunch of brutish people in Washington who ran something called a government which had nothing to do with me. I had been sympathetic to artists like Claes Oldenburg and Jim Dine who made funky work in great poverty downtown and said they hated the museums; but I observed that within no time they were showing in the best galleries uptown and soon seemed to have no objection to being shown in the museums.

Possibly I was more sympathetic to Gene than I realized and just had no interest in doing things his way. I didn't want to be locked out of the establishment; I wanted to take it by storm from within. That was my unconscious position. As the sixties rolled to a close, I turned into a fool or a dancing bear. Earlier in the decade, I had shown promise for such a role by making a drunken spectacle of myself at parties: hanging upside down from overhead pipes, ripping my dresses, falling into skylights and losing my heels, cutting myself up, dancing wildly and sprawling incontinently, wearing ambivalent clothes, offending the rich in their very own homes, etc., etc. By 1969 I was actually expected, even solicited, practically hired, to act outrageously within establishment bounds. By then these acts had become the soul and substance of my columns, and my newspaper was cheering me on. In the spring of '68 I was still hiding behind the forward example of other art-world zanies. I saw Gene much the way I had seen James Byars and Kenneth King:

an intelligent and deranged spirit of the times, a man who would make good copy. Late in April I wrote a column called "Pieces of Gene," in which I surrounded notice of his most recent exploit—a visit to the U.N. to "give himself up as an international citizen"—with such loosely associated non sequiturs as "The lavender angels return from one white house to another" and "But I ask you, how much arms can you smuggle in a canoe?" and "God is alive but he doesn't want to get involved." In the same column I covered an event by Robert Wilson, alias Byrd Hoffman, later the famous maker of interminable "operas," whom I hoped to add to my collection of interesting nuts. I exalted madness again by quoting Cage, who said he knew when someone he knew was going out of her mind "because she would begin to speak the truth." And Alan Watts, who "told me there's no place to go in this country if you're enduring an expansion of consciousness." Clearly Gene felt there was no place for him. I noted that he had been thrown out of the U.N. and banned from the Dada-surrealist show. "Pieces of Gene" was how I envisioned him on the sidewalks outside these establishments.

So who was Gene Swenson? A good friend of his, a painter called Basil King, said he was a man who had been sent out of Kansas to be a genius. That says practically everything. Gene's father was a man who pumped gas in a gas station, his mother a schoolteacher, very ambitious for her son—a D. H. Lawrence sort of mother. He went through Yale and arrived in New York in 1956, becoming an art critic and historian. He lived in the same tenement on Fourth Street for eleven years, got a master's degree at N.Y.U., wrote reviews for the same magazine I did (*Art News*), and contributed essays to other periodicals, in particular about the art and artists that came to be known as pop. I first remember seeing him at a pop art symposium at MOMA in 1963 (presided over by a panel including Cage, Rauschenberg, Duchamp, Richard Huelsenbeck, and Roger Shattuck), speaking from the audience in an agitated, defensively authoritative manner. The museum was perhaps already his bête noire. Gene was a champion of the avant-garde like myself, his territory a lot less circumscribed than mine, its stakes hardly his alone to claim. When I met him, I was struck by a blaring incongruity in his appearance. His clean-cut, attractive, blue-eyed, all-American, Ivy League, charcoal-suit look was belied by his intense gaze—on edge, expectant, uncool, mischievous, wild. He had an air of permanently shocked naiveté, or of "signaling through the flames" from behind his glasses, an extreme idealism contradicted by some personal knowledge of brutality, which in fact he openly disclosed, perhaps boasted of, in the form of his S&M interests. Gene was a guy who never really made it out of Kansas—his prestigious Eastern education had not prepared him for the world. He remained like a girl, untutored in the rules of the game. Plucked out of his class, plopped down in a fast, competitive city where art has always been an instrument of wealth and power, he found himself out of his depth. He hated to see that deals were made and things were not pure, that art was not an ideal pursuit in itself. Once he understood that art served capitalist ends and was not just a beautiful autonomous tradition, he conceived a program to make it serve other interests, revolutionary ones that characterized the sixties and his own unfolding life. He wanted power himself but opposed it at large; his real program seemed to be to set an example by self-destruction. He would go after the power, then undermine any base or foothold he managed to get. The axis of change for him in the sixties must have been a show he organized at the Modern in November '66 called "Art in the Mirror." A long essay he had intended to write for the exhibition was cut short by an attack of acute appendicitis.

The following spring he went mad, and the rest of his career, until August '69 when he died, was marked by increasing political radicalization and intermittent bouts of insanity. Besides the Modern (which, I feel certain, had courted and rejected him), his other special targets were Leo Castelli and Henry Geldzahler, who had been a schoolmate of Gene's at Yale. Geldzahler, golden boy of art, ensconced as curator at the

Met, represented everything Gene both wanted and hated. The Gene I knew was this madman, either flipped right out, creating bizarre scenes (throwing eggs out his sixth-floor window onto the tops of cop cars, driving chariots or rocket ships naked on the roof of his building), or politically suicidal, waging this war singlehandedly against the sort of establishment that would be the last to see any serious uprising on the part of its peons, the artists. But I saw Gene in quiescent moods also: withdrawn, fragile, transparent, recovering from one collision or another with the hospitals or the police. I had a welter of feelings about him, none of them very consciously connected with the aspects of my life that mirrored his. One day he visited me in my loft and scared me by his mediumistic intensity and his "mission" of listening to my radio, his ear right against the speaker, to pick up the "number signals" for his rocket-machine assignment or operation or whatever it was. When not on his earthly political missions, he was soaring away visiting other planets and settling galactical disputes. He was definitely trying to get away. Nobody else I ever heard of had a Pan Am reservation to the moon. One time when he was sane and sober Ann brought him over to my loft with a mobile of our planetary system, the kind you might hang over a child's crib. Ann and I thought that if we could help him re-create one of his trips by hanging up the mobile and stimulating his memory and associations, I could then translate it all in family terms. Luckily, nothing came of it, because Gene didn't want to play. He held forth on art and politics as usual, enthralling Ann and boring me. In my obit for Gene in September '69, I quoted a line of his next to one of mine—that I had always claimed (I was a real know-it-all) his "political ravings . . . were nothing more nor less than his father." (Gene's line was: "Special to the N.Y. *Times*: The President of the U.S., clad only in scanty tribal costume, announced the resignation of the American Government last night.") I never heard him say anything about his parents. The men in the art world never said such things. Why think about home, from which art and New York represented the great escape? But Gene was obviously thinking about home—his last "mission" was a car crash with his mother on a Kansan highway, an "accident at the crossroads." His father survived them, and an older brother who was a colonel in the Marines. Gene was thirty-five (the same age, incidentally, as poet Frank O'Hara when he died in 1961 in a car accident on Fire Island). Compared to Ann, I was barely affected by Gene's death. I had lost one of my crazies, but crazies were everywhere at the end of the sixties, and Gene (along with Ann) had been angry or jealous of me for my freedom to write irrelevant (i.e., unpolitical) things week after week in a paper that had become successful. The last time I saw him he was yelling at me, the substance of which I don't remember, behind a violently extended arm and forefinger. Possibly it was because I had advised him not to go to Kansas. I rarely minded my own business, and I assumed that whatever worked for me would work for anybody else. I had disavowed my mother, therefore Gene would do well to do likewise. Gene had been seeing a shrink who told him he should get a nine-to-five job, the same message Ann got from hers and that I had gotten from mine in '66 at St. Vincent's. The presumption underlying these "therapies" was that our lives in New York had led us astray, our parents had been right about us, and a regular job would demonstrate a certain remorse and the desire to reform and to recapture our parents' values. In '67 Ann wrote in her journal: "Gene was sick in bed with a cold, furious with his Dr. because he had expected Gene to accept a 9–5 job. That's such a problem of anger and despair for us. This business of our art not being commercial coin and hence our time our gifts not respected in this pragmatic society. . . ." After he died, she wrote, "I am carrying [his] books down six tenement flights of stairs under the unsparing scrutiny of the bare light bulb on each landing—the only author who corresponds in any way to this life of those I carry is Céline . . . the hopes of a life of art in endless garbage-strewn tenements. No wonder that Gene's life was bitter and maddened by dreams of unreal success." Though I could not know it then, Gene was an important addition to my small pantheon of male heroes: child-men, mother's sons, eternal boys, foundering on the constructs of their fathers, ever proving that society moves by dissent as well as conformity.

It was the extreme case that interested me, any whose preemptive death seemed to pose mysterious, exciting questions about power and individual consciousness or growth processes. Those who had the most to overcome might have the greatest drive to move society to accommodate them. The anthem of the blacks in the sixties was "We Shall Overcome." The hippies cried "Give Peace a Chance." Freud, quoting Virgil in the *Aeneid*, inscribed his *Interpretation of Dreams*: "If I cannot bend the Higher Powers, I will move the Infernal Regions." As warrior, Gene was too distraught. As model, I found him too close for comfort—at first too alive and familiar, then ignominiously dead and considered a wasted life. Such struggles as his come clearer only later. The "wasted life" of Galois—his brief, tormented battle against France—could at length be described in relief against his mathematical accomplishment: the *symbol* of recognition, the impalement of his ego on the State. Apollinaire didn't have to wait. As he lay on his deathbed in Paris, crowds outside on the streets were shouting, "Down with Guillaume! Down with Guillaume!" Guillaume, of course, was actually Kaiser Wilhelm II, for it was 1918 and the Armistice had just been signed. The end of the war coincided with the death of the poet. Many children with dead fathers and anxious, possessive mothers will have strong tendencies to fail grandly. Much history has been made by these sorts of male children—exiles whose urgent need to establish themselves in a host country causes them to become isolated by their genius, to sacrifice themselves in their offering to the host State, which expands to include their inventions. In the case of military genius, like Napoleon's, the Corsican exile, a literal expansion of territory is involved. For the English, William the Conqueror, illegitimate son of Normandy, is their most stunning example. These men will try to conquer the country that was hostile to their origins. In Napoleon's case, his father had fought under General Paoli, champion of Corsican inde-

Above: Artist Les Levine. *Photo © Les Levine. Left*: Art critic David Bourdon. *Photo © 1969 Peter Moore.*

Above: Artist Ann Wilson and art critic Gene Swenson. *Photo by Peter Hujar. Right*: Art critic and professor Gregory Battcock.

pendence, and Napoleon's mother had spent the last months of her pregnancy carrying the future emperor of France in the Corsican mountains as a refugee. Napoleon was baptized with the name of a cousin who died fighting the French. He was born in 1768, the year France successfully quelled Corsica's bid for independence. In Napoleon's own person, as head of the State that had defeated his country, this particular political struggle was in a sense resumed. His foremost act was to "take" France by proving to be her best general; further imperialist expansion was repetitive and superfluous, psychologically speaking, and clearly designed to ruin not only himself but the country he led. In the heroic model, the fatherless boy follows faithfully in his father's footsteps, imitating his death and expanding his frustrated interests, urged on to glory and/or disaster by an ambitious, omnipresent mother. His overthrow/achievement becomes the occasion for any new, more inclusive organization of territories, either real or imagined. William united Normandy and Britain with the Vikings who were his ancestors in Normandy. Apollinaire forged new concepts of poetry and painting and criticism. Apollo, after all, was the most masculine of deities. Galois had a name that resonated well with his fatherland.

So what did Gene Swenson, midwestern descendant of Scandinavian immigrants, do? We don't know, because his writings have not yet been popularly published. By reputation, they were daring and original. Some of them, we know, were flawed by rage.

During '69, this happened to my own writing. The control I had in '68—still hiding behind a critic's pose, selectively promoting madness through the example of others, tentatively, then more aggressively, projecting an experimental prose style, yet maintaining structure and detachment—gave way in '69 to autobiographical ravings reflecting a new failure of ego to withstand intimations of success and to survive without a personal life. As a mother's son, I had barely stumbled to first base. At the end of '69, I felt washed up and back at square one. My imitations of Apollinaire, if that was my unconscious design in the late sixties, collapsed around my identity as a girl. In the fall of '68, I met a girl whose (dead) father appeared to be a lot more powerful than my own. Through her, the nadir of my Apollinairean existence was both attained and dashed. But before that, I had consolidated my rebirth as a critic (of "everything else") through the patronage of two real, live old men, one of whom created the first bridge I had known between America and England. And this was what led to my meeting with the girl whose family easily had the wherewithal to put me in my place.

18

Birthday

Considering the amount of money on which I survived during the sixties, the small patronage of Walter Gutman, stockbroker, writer, dilettante painter, between '62 and '65, meant a great deal to me. Three grants from him totaling two thousand dollars equaled one third more than what I lived on for a year. Walter was nearly sixty when I met him. For a long while I thought he was sixty-five, making his age conform to that of my father's at death. My first "old man," the philosophy professor, was sixty-five when I met him, and so was my next "patron," whom I met in May of '68. But Walter, happily for my scheme, was sixty-five the same year, '68, when I pressed him into service for the next-to-last time. It was April 30—I wrote that I was "dejected" by a loft break-in and "the plunder of my TV and typewriter," and I speculated spending time barricading the windows, or buying myself a present, or staying in bed, when I spied a forgotten postcard "in a litter of old mail," announcing an intriguing-sounding event to take place that very evening. The announcement read: "On April 30, 1968, in Sheboygan, Wisconsin, the Once Group will begin the trial of Anne Opie Wehrer and unknown accomplices for crimes against humanity." I decided immediately to try to go and called up Walter on Wall Street to solicit plane fare. Spontaneity was everything. Walter was obliging; I reserved a 2 p.m. flight to Chicago and had forty-five minutes to make it by taxi to Wall Street to pick up my fare and get to La Guardia. At Chicago, I caught a "decrepit aircraft" to a place called Manitowoc, where a student met me and drove me to the Witt's End Motel in Sheboygan. There I found the Once Group, which then comprised seven people, including three couples—an Intermedia collective of academics and artists based at the University of Michigan in Ann Arbor.

Nothing could've been more sexist than this event they were doing in Sheboygan: the trial of Anne Opie Wehrer, a member of the collective, wife of another member, Joseph Wehrer, professor of architecture at the university—the exposure of her intimate history, her deficiencies as a wife, the impending breakdown of her marriage. But I saw only an exciting trial, theatrically innovative, outrageously true to life, a realization of my dream of art merging with biography, a projection of my direst victim fantasies. Central to my interest was the revelation of family secrets. I was ecstatic over the event. "Where does private end and public begin or vice versa?" I asked in my review. Mrs. Wehrer, mother of five, ex-debutante and beauty, amputee (her left leg), had agreed to sit on stage before a screen upon which were shown slides and films of her life, and respond to the sadistic commands and questions of her husband, filmmaker/artist George Manupelli, and composer Robert Ashley—her three-in-one "prosecutor." The actual import of the "trial" escaped me completely. I had no idea how real it really was; had I known, I would have ganged up on Mrs. Wehrer myself. At some level I did, just by going there and later exalting the event. The next time I saw her she was separated or divorced. From the trial, it was clear she had no business being married.

The following February the Once Group invited me to Ann Arbor to be a judge at their annual film festival, at which time I had some pre-emptive feminist vision—based on little more than the prurient, leering interest of the males in my female companion and/or our relationship. I then looked around me and noticed that the women there were in bad shape, never mind Anne Wehrer. That was perhaps the first glimmer of consciousness I had that could be called feminist, and I was forty years old. Nor did it stop me from turning myself into the subject of my own trial: a determined, relentless run-on exposure, week after many a week, of intimacies and failings and complaints and cruelties and confidences and boasts and betrayals and losses and outrages and flippancies that filled up the huge self-travesty that my column became. In April '68, returning from Sheboygan, refreshed and triumphant from my adventure, I must have felt ready for anything. I could go anywhere—cover polliwogs or mountains, Ping-Pong in China, white camels in the Fernando Po, assassinations in South America, investitures in Wales, croquet and backgammon, talking dolphins, old people at large, wise children at home, etc., etc. I didn't actually think any of these things, and I was still "officially" depressed. But only two weeks later I met the man who would push me over the dividing line between past and future.

Around May 7 David Bourdon called and got me out of bed by inviting me to judge the annual art show of Time, Inc. employees. (David was then an assistant arts editor at *Life*.) He said Robert Dash and Ivan Karp would be the other two judges and that a nice lunch would be served afterwards in the Empire Room at the top of the building. I remember an enormous oval table, waiters in white and red, shrimp and caviar, Bloody Marys galore. David remembers Ivan Karp picking out the winners of the show and my having practically nothing to say about it. I was, in any case, only interested in the social occasion. Afterwards, I weaved my way downtown, drunk and euphoric, a sunny, bright day in May, to buy an outfit for the upcoming Merce Cunningham concert, opening night, at the Brooklyn Academy of Music. Along Greenwich Avenue I collected a floppy felt hat, an orange crepe shirt (sleeves and shoulder line both several inches too long), a purple-and-yellow diagonally striped tie, a pair of tight gray-and-white twill wool pants that I planned to wear with stockings and heels. The day of the event, May 15, I called David and asked him to be my escort. He declined, so I called June, Charlotte's good friend, who said she would love to go. Then David called back, saying he didn't realize it was the "social event of the season" and that he would like to go after all. Later he called again to say there was "this rich man" he thought I should meet and that the two of them would pick us up on the Bowery in the man's limo. June came to my loft (attired in black velvet gown) to wait with me.

Our "rich man," John de Menil, was a trim little person, sixty-five, with baby skin and rosy cheeks and a mellifluous baritone voice. Also in the car were his communications and management consultant, Simone Swan, and a tall, dark Native American friend or lover of hers. Gowns or tuxedos were worn by all the ladies and gents. The limo deposited us at the Brooklyn Academy steps. A brief conversation ensued in the lobby over plans for after the concert. June wanted to go along with de Menil and his party for dinner at the Plaza. I wanted to stay for the bash in the lobby—champagne, a Venezuelan dinner, the Velvet Underground. De Menil, whoever he was, had no meaning for me. I had dressed for the occasion and planned to get smashed to the gills and do as much damage as I could. That turned out to be commandeering the band's mike during an intermission, cheered on by David Whitney, and belting out my favorite silly college songs, chiefly "Lloyd George Knows My Father," an inane ditty consisting of those words alone, repeated ad nauseam or delectamentum to the tune of "Onward, Christion Soldiers." A chance to sing "Lloyd George" in public, facilitated only by a stuporous amount of alcohol, always left me gratified and mortally embarrassed—a feeling I evidently craved. The evening was a great success so far as I was concerned. Following as it did my "debut" in a tuxedo at the Modern in March and my appearance as a judge at Time, Inc., I seemed to have re-entered society. The next day June called me up to tell me about her dinner at the Plaza with John de Menil and company. She was thrilled to have been entertained by the rich. I was glad she was thrilled, and I was pleased about my comeback as entertainer at large, party smasher, and queen of fools. The Cunningham concert barely caught my attention.

Nonetheless, I planned to write about his season, so I went back the next night to see the work. I wore what I might have thrown on to go across the street for a newspaper, detritus of boarding school days: blue windbreaker, navy-blue wool skirt to the kneetops (not very pressed or clean), tan knee socks and loafers or sneakers or saddle shoes. In the lobby before the concert began, John de Menil came up and shook my hand, smiled, and said, "I liked the way you were dressed last night better." I flipped back, "I liked the way you were dressed last night better too." The house was not nearly full. I sat in an empty row in the orchestra behind Edwin Denby and a friend, leaning forward whenever I could to talk to Edwin between their shoulders. During an intermission I glanced over to the end of my row and noticed de Menil sitting there on the aisle. He asked me if I wanted to have dinner after the concert. I said to myself, "Why not?", to him, that I would. So when the concert was over I climbed into the back of his limo with him and answered various questions he asked me about the dance. Someone had told him I was a dance critic, I guessed. The limo drove us to Manny Wolf's Steak House on Third Avenue. We were joined by his daughter Adelaide and a male friend of hers, who had been at the concert. Close to midnight I checked the time, and just at midnight I notified my host and his daughter and his daughter's friend that it happened to be my birthday. Adelaide promptly removed a piece of rye bread from the dinner basket, stuck three matches in it, and lit them up. John said we would have to repair to his house uptown for a glass of champagne. We got back into the limo. At his five-storey pad on Seventy-third Street he opened a big safe to show me some ancient figurines or statuettes. I was impressed. But what was it all about? And why was he being so nice? I'd been entertained by the rich, assuredly, but never on my own account, always for something or somebody else. Anyway, rich folks were our acceptable enemies, whose places and stations in life we deemed contemptible. Now I was being constrained to find one of them charming. Instead of being rude as usual, I tried holding my own, gamely quoting a little French poem I had written that I thought was clever (my host was very French, though he had no accent to show it), and letting them know I had an important dead English father. The conversation turned to Paris in the springtime. I said I had always planned to visit my birthplace in England. These people obviously led charmed lives, I thought, stepping out of New York town houses full of ancient statuettes into limousines and Paris in the springtime. That was a subliminal thought. I was way under, immune to envy or strivings. I had a cheap loft, a newspaper that printed whatever I wrote, a city that supported me for my record as a mental patient. I saw myself in that condition forever—not a bad outcome for a condemned person. This was a pleasant evening, a welcome gratuity. "Thanks very much," I said to de Menil, as we shook hands in the backseat of his limo outside my door on the Bowery at three in the morning. I liked the little guy, so cherubic and avuncular. I thought he was a gentleman. Little gentlemen were the most attractive kind of men to me. But when he called me up at 10 a.m., I again had to ask myself, "What does he want?" Certainly I had nothing to give him. What he wanted was to know if and when I would be home that day, in order to send something down with his chauffeur. I said I would be home all day. Around 2 p.m. his chauffeur knocked on my fat tin door and presented me with a white box and a white envelope. This was quite a pleasant surprise. (I generally felt ignored and sorry for myself on my birthday.)

I had no idea what a surprise it really was. The content of the white box, a rich French cake of some sort, was normal enough. But the content of the white envelope altered my life forever and ever. What I found was a round-trip, high-season, open-date ticket to London. The last time I had been so surprised was when I was twenty-one and in college and had opened the letter from my mother containing my father's obituary. My new surprise was a ticket to the place where he had lived and died. Eighteen years had elapsed between surprises. The confusion, bewilderment, and excitement that attended the first surprise were now reinvoked. The news my mother had sent me in 1951 of my father's death had brought him to life. That he had actually lived after all was not, I believe, the essential cause of his resurrection in my mind; rather, it was simply the revela-

Walter Gutman—stockbroker, writer, dilettante painter. *Photo © 1965 Fred W. McDarrah.*

Thomas Hayes Proctor, the philosophy professor at Wellesley. *Photo: Wellesley College Archives.*

John de Menil—chairman of the board, Schlumberger, Inc., art patron, entrepreneur. *Photo © 1984 A. de Menil.*

Opposite: (*above*) The New York University panel at Loeb Student Center, 1969, "Jill Johnston: The Disintegration of a Critic"—Charlotte Moorman, John de Menil, Jill Johnston, Ultra Violet, David Bourdon, Gregory Battcock, Andy Warhol, Bridget Polk, Lil Picard, Walter Gutman. *Photo © 1969 Peter Moore.*

Opposite: (*below*) Jill Johnston's surprise appearance at the panel, with John de Menil and Charlotte Moorman. *Photo © 1969 Peter Moore.*

tion of the truth. It was my mother who was the surprise. It was her manipulation of reality that roused me. All commandments were still my mother's. The buffer I later created in Apollinaire, a reality exclusively my own, was not a bad beginning, but it was a construct without social approval—another secret. For all social purposes, I had retracted him. He was an inner operative, a powerful figment of imagination (even when I denied him) but cut off from the outside much the way my father had been. I had had to do to him what my mother had done to my father.

The surprise that May 17, 1968, was the appearance of a father with a command of his own. My whole small world turned around again. Suppose your mother had always told you never to go to a certain place, and nobody had ever contradicted her. Then, suddenly, latish in life, a rival of sorts appears and smothers all your (her) objections (namely, the very existence you had contrived to make various things impossible) in a single magnanimous gesture. I had no choice but to go.

I called David as soon as I caught my breath, to tell him about it and how surprised and delighted I was—and also that I hoped never to hear from my donor again. For "permission" to return to the fatherland, I must have wanted to imagine that the dead had spoken. The dead, in any case, were preferable to the rich. I told David that I would send my donor a telegram and hoped that would be that. David tried to reassure me by saying that de Menil was so incredibly wealthy that what he'd given me was like a bite off a candy bar. I sent the telegram and imagined that was indeed that.

But that is never quite that in the realm of the living. About three weeks later (a decorous amount of time), I had a call from Simone Swan, inviting me to a dinner party for Francois Truffaut at de Menil's town house. My question "What does he want?" lingered on, yet it hardly prevented me from accepting this new offer of interest. Anyway, by then I had my reservation for London, for June 27, and I was free to imagine that a trip across the ocean would make me unreachable forever. When I was born, after all, ordinary people still tended to land quite definitively or permanently on one side or the other after making such a trip. And I was one of them. But the truth is that all this attention was starting to go to my head. Once again, established society had invited me to its premises on my own account. Once again I was well treated, at least by my host, and made to feel acceptable to those for whom I was supposed to have no use. It looked suspiciously as if I was about to be considered a candidate for that rare breed: the acceptable outsider. At the party were such renowned outsiders as Norman Mailer and Jasper Johns—as well as Truffaut himself. Renata Adler was there, but I think she was a *New Yorker* critic then. In deference to my host, who made sure to take me aside and express a friendly interest in my upcoming trip, I refrained from misbehaving. Seated at dinner, I was sorely tempted, for Mailer, at my left, pointedly, I thought, ignored me. Possibly that was because I had turned down his invitation to be a "lady reporter" in a film he had said he intended to make. More likely it had something to do with his question to Simone—"How can you take this girl seriously?"—which Simone reported to me years later. After dinner, I remember seeing Truffaut standing alone, his left elbow resting on the mantel above a fireplace, regarding the company with some ironic detachment. I hadn't really noticed him till then. The guest of honor looked lonely. I think this was my introduction to "society." The event was formal, my invitation was kosher, the service was elegant, the company was select, and my hosts were the richest people in America.

This was almost true. In 1983 Dominique de Menil, John's widow (he died in '73), was high up on the *Forbes* list of the four hundred richest Americans—estimated net worth, two hundred million. The de Menil fortune derived from Schlumberger, Ltd., the multinational oil-field service corporation. Dominique was a Schlumberger, daughter of one of the firm's co-founding Frenchmen. During the twenties, her father and his brother invented the instruments or tools that would be capable of establishing depths and locations of oil with great precision, thus transforming and modernizing the oil industry. In 1983 the company was reported to be operating in ninety-two countries on five continents and to have a staff of seventy-five thousand people. I had the impression in '68 that John, along with some other sons-in-law of the Schlumberger brothers, ran the outfit. That was off somewhat. When I met John, he was chairman of the board. In '70 he retired, having worked for Schlumberger since 1939. Before that, he had been a Paris banker. Long ago, he and Dominique had become collectors and patrons of the arts, and they had been building a kind of cultural empire in Houston, their home base. Their collection of surrealist art has been valued at over seventy-five million.

My Cinderella story with the de Menils lasted somewhat over a year. After the dinner party in June I could no longer view John as just a deus ex machina. The question "What did he want?" remained, and I could see nothing in the murky future that might warrant more contact, but there seemed nothing to fear, either. Anyway, the immediate future was consumed by my first trip abroad since the age of about twenty months. On June 27 I went to Kennedy Airport, accompanied by Walter Gutman and Charlotte, who helped send me off (like surrogate parents) with Bloody Marys and happy best wishes.

19

Tourist

My first impression of England satisfied that most romantic of longings: for both the shocking and the familiar. Falling in love, we feel we have already known the exciting new stranger. Everything was different, unrecognizable, yet mysteriously well known. The passport official, noticing my birthplace as the United Kingdom, said "Welcome home." Echoing my mother's meeting with my father on shipboard, I encountered a familiar object in the guise of a foreigner. In one sense, my "romance" was a lot shorter than hers; in another, much more protracted. This first trip sated my appetite for the new and shocking; on later trips I tended to fold up inside a friend's flat and go to sleep, as if to act out my mother's depression when she gave birth and found herself alone (in Finchley), without family or social connections. That feeling went on for a long time. My mother's injunction against visiting the place was converted into a kind of ordinance against exploring it. It was all right to be a tourist, not all right to be a detective. After a breathtaking tour of the monuments, the ruins, the landscape, I had no place to go. More monuments, more ruins, more landscapes, were not on my agenda. Since I was there, however, I did strike out, blindly and feebly to be sure, in the forbidden direction, soliciting an American I knew to make a wildcat call to a remote part of the kingdom in search of a family member—thoroughly vague enough to be unproductive. I also rummaged inconclusively through the London telephone directories for relevant names.

The one thing I did with confidence was to reclaim my own

original name. This made sense. Having lived in my mother's country with my father's name, I now obtained the evidence that in my father's country I had once lived, however briefly, with my mother's name. I found myself inside Somerset House, a rotunda with great spiraling tiers of books where birth records were then still kept. There I was in a large green volume as Jill Crowe. I filled out an application for the birth certificate, submitted it with two pounds, and returned several days later to pick it up. A man behind a barred window handed me the certificate. I was certain he smirked at me and that that was because of the blanks under numbers 4 and 6: Name and Surname of Father and Occupation of Father. My mother, of course, was prominently represented: "Olive Marjorie Crowe" writ twice and identified as living at 175 Brighton Road in Worthing, Sussex. I sensed that this business of the names was at the root of my problems. The part of me that had been left in England didn't correspond to England itself; the part of me that had grown up in America didn't correspond to America. My mother had deposited herself in England, it could be said, a name in a well-guarded vault, and brought back a piece of England to America, a name appended to the child (and to herself, the "widow"), erasing identities in both places. I was, in other words, neither a Crowe in America nor a Johnston in England. And the Crowe in England was well concealed, barely legal, as the birth certificate reveals; the Johnston in America was just as phony, however legally assumed.

This was only an exaggeration, gross enough to be sure, of any normal girl's relationship to her parents. Any girl belongs to her mother, by birth, gender, early tutelage, and role assignation; yet she has the name, the social identity, of the parent who stands for the stranger. In the "normal" scheme of things, the girl is required to identify with her mother (her role/gender assignment and all its established attributes) and grow up to relinquish one stranger's name (her father's) for another's—the symbol of a proper or successful emotional transference. The obliteration of the mother's name symbolizes the negative feelings a girl must cultivate for the mother in order to idealize men. This separation from herself is endemic to motherhood as we have known it. And it epitomizes the normal feminine woman. The way my mother deviated from the model was to dramatize the separation on the one hand (pre-empting my own understanding of it by establishing it at birth) and to minimize it on the other by positing her own name in safekeeping, as it were, in the foreign preserve. Reclaiming my mother's name in England was a significant symbolic act. It meant that my mother and father were together again in one place, the place where I happened to be born, and that my mother's identity had not been lost there. Had I arrived in England with the British passport my mother had obtained for me in America when I was eight, serving as proof of birth as well as "legitimacy" (since I had become a Johnston), the connections would no doubt have seemed more powerful and complete. But I was already well armed for this first synodic encounter with myself abroad. I had established a stranger of my own (Apollinaire), had received orders from another exciting stranger (de Menil), and had been cross-dressing to state a certain refusal to be taken for a girl who would be separated from her mother. I had approached the traditional position of a boy. Having placed my mother at the accustomed derogatory distance, gaining a principled independence from her, I was now supposed to arouse her erotic and idealized interest in me (whoever she might be), provided I looked the part.

My basic outfit in London was revealing enough. Discarding the femmy items I had been including in New York (floppy hats, heels) and somewhat ambivalent features like the oversized soft crepe shirt, I wore the more uncompromising ensemble of pants, comfortable shoes, regular man's shirt and tie. My long hair remained the symbol of ambivalence. Yet long hair was the mark of rebellious male youth then. On the streets my gender, or at least my intentions, were in question. I didn't like that. Apparently I opposed my own display. The part I wanted to resemble was supposed to be a secret. It was certainly a secret to me. I have no memory of deciding to dress up one way or another for any particular reason. There were plenty of unisex outfits and looks around, and I was just capitalizing on the trend. The Beatles were said to have a lot to do with this drift of things, and I'd been in London no more than two days when I found myself in the center of Beatledom: their very recording studio in St. John's Wood.

From my hotel room in Russell Square, not far from Bloomsbury and the British Museum, I telephoned Yoko Ono at something called Apple Corps. The Apple Corps people were altogether snotty on the phone, but they agreed to get a message to Yoko that I had called. The last time I had seen Yoko was with husband Tony Cox in New York at Sloppy Louie's the summer of '66. They had been about to embark for London on a freighter out of Montreal. So what was Apple Corps? I wondered. When Yoko returned my call, she suggested I appear the next day at some gallery for the opening of a show she said she was doing. I found a very startling scene there. The gallery room was crowded, there were white balloons all over the place, photographers in abundance, and Yoko posing up against a white wall in a white outfit next to a young man similarly in white with glasses and longish hair. "Who is that guy?" I asked a man next to me, knowing who it was even as the words left my mouth. The man looked at me in disbelief. I kept my next question to myself. Was this a "new life" Yoko was leading or just an artistic collaboration with a Beatle? But really the answer was fairly obvious. Yoko left her white wall to come over and greet me and invite me to a recording studio after this event in the gallery. She said someone or other would tell me where it was. I watched her and Lennon disappear in a white Rolls in a cloud of photographers. I saw James Fox exit in a convertible Porsche. I waited ten minutes and hailed a taxi for the address in St. John's Wood. There I found Yoko and the four Beatles, who were very charming to me for hours on end; I liked Paul in particular. I wondered what Yoko had done with Tony. Around midnight (I stayed till 3 or 4 a.m., when the recording session broke up) I followed Yoko upstairs to a small room where she said she intended to rest. She lay down with the back of one hand over her forehead and told me she was having quite a difficult time: miscarriages; the Beatles distrusted her; and Tony was off in France somewhere (she wasn't sure where) with her daughter. She offered me her empty flat on Baker Street, near Regents Park. I went along with everything—even going home in the early hours after the recording session with James Taylor, who drove through London like a maniac, told me how famous he was going to be (the Beatles were about to record him on their label), how he would handle fame differently than anybody else, how he was an opium addict, and how he admired Wilhelm Reich. That meant sex, I realized, but I was dressed like a boy and talked as abstractly as he did and he let me go to sleep on one side of his bed, which reeked of unwashed sheets and blankets and/or some other unknown decay. When we got up, he took me over to Apple Corps headquarters, where he plucked at his guitar and sang "Sweet Baby James" to Paul from scraps of paper containing fragments of lines lying on the floor at his feet. Later that day I moved into Yoko's empty flat on Baker Street, which consisted of several oversized rooms, colorfully shabby, barely furnished. From there I deployed my outfit where it might actually count.

The other American I knew in London was artist George Brecht, a man much admired by the Dada/Fluxus people in New York for his exquisitely assembled boxes and objects and his conceptual originality. I asked George if he could tell me where I might find a gay women's bar. He said he would ask his girl friend, but that he was affronted by my interest because he didn't believe in that sort of thing. Reluctantly, he gave me the information I wanted. There was a well-known bar called the Gateways (which had even been featured in *The Killing of Sister George*) on King's Road not far from Sloane Square. I had never been to such a bar and had never gone to bed with a female stranger. The three women I had known intimately were strange enough, but they had been properly introduced or ac-

knowledged in some common, puritan setting. I was about to
derail my programming completely. Towards women my stance
had been that of a traditional girl: sex meant love, which was
forever and ever. At the Gateways, or Gates as it's called, I
found sex without love, a condition for a night. After my marriage, that had been my experience with boys. In marriage I had
worked up something I could call love, desperate and dependent. Before marriage, I had suffered sex with a man (my old
professor) for another kind of love: extreme idealism. Anyway,
sex without love was a familiar equation with men. I was not
at all prepared to assume such a position with women. I may
have looked the part, but I didn't feel it or know what the part
could mean. I expected to reciprocate any erotic/idealized interest I happened to attract. But the bar scene was traditionally
butch-femme, in which at least one partner was supposed to
have the good sense to remain emotionally detached, notwithstanding the fact that it was everybody's hidden agenda to find a
one-and-only forever and ever. (In 1971 I saw a couple in California who had met at the Gates and had been together more
than a decade.)

I arrived early, after shopping along King's Road for new
pants, shirts, and ties, and found a girl called Maureen who
wanted me to meet a roommate she had called Sammy who
would be at the bar later, she said. The Gates is a basement
room, entered by ringing an upstairs buzzer and presenting credentials—a membership card or, as in my case, a passport—
and paying a pound. By ten o'clock, when the place closes on
a weekend evening, the room is jammed like a sardine can
with frantic-looking women trying to figure out whom they
wish to leave with for the night. I left with Maureen and
Sammy, but not before I had a couple of other invitations in my
pocket: telephone numbers pressed hurriedly and discreetly into
my hand. In all, during the one week I spent in London, I had
the shocking total of three sexual encounters with women, equal-
ing the number of women I had known intimately to date. But

most shocking of all was the nature of these encounters. With the first, Sammy, a seasoned "bar dyke" at the age of no more than twenty-three, I hardly fell in love over the sex, which was quite satisfactory, but I did expect to see her again to confirm some feeling that I thought *must* be inherent in an encounter like this. I had a habit that the new setting didn't support. Sammy looked as blankly at me as had the last man I had fallen into bed with. She did point out that I was an American, saying matter-of-factly, "You are going home soon, aren't you?" My next, a very attractive "femme" who had pressed her phone number into my hand at the bar, came over to the flat on Baker Street, where we had sex that I only remember as disastrous. The third made things all too clear: if I was going to dress like a boy in a foreign country, I'd better behave like one—cavalier and unpresupposing. Her name was Roxanne; I met her in a bar at the Tower of London, where I had gone with George Brecht to see friends of his from an art school in Leeds. We all got thoroughly "pissed," as they say in England to mean drunk. I left with Roxanne and a male art student from Leeds and suggested we go to Baker Street. Tony returned from France with Yoko's daughter that very evening. He wasn't pleased to find me there in "congress" with these strangers, one of them female. The next day I tracked down Roxanne someplace (she was an *Ivanhoe* beauty, a Renoir voluptuary), and she refused to recognize me. To add injury to insult, I drove out of London for the week I had planned to see the countryside with a massive vaginal infection, a variety that rages with itching so bad it makes you try to tear yourself apart for want of anything that will satisfy it. Early in the morning I got to a hospital in Salisbury, where a doctor gave me medicine and sedatives and told me to take it easy and rest in Salisbury for a day or so. As a result, I discovered the great Salisbury Cathedral, which turned me instantly into a cathedral nut. Having left London with nothing in mind to do except see Stonehenge and possibly Stratford-on-Avon, cathedral hunting set some direction for the trip. Conceivably I meant to atone for my recent sins. If so, the thought never crossed my mind. But I'm sure my inner processes were fast at work figuring out my next moves.

In Paris, where I spent my third and last week abroad, I went to bed with a boy, and an American at that. Nor was this for lack of an introduction that might lead me to my "proper" quarry. In London I had bought black gabardine culottes with a matching vest which was capable of supporting a well-hewn cleavage. Before leaving Paris I went shopping on the Champs-Elysées (my plan was to arrive home penniless) and bought a leather miniskirt with vest which I would wear with tall boots and a man's shirt and tie. I cried most of the way home.

Back in America, after several encounters with women that seemed like a continuation of my London odyssey, though highly unpremeditated (they just *happened* to me), I turned into a real girl once again by falling irrevocably in love.

Had I been a real boy as well (real boys fall in love too, after all), I should have been able to get married. Real boys don't throw themselves away without some promise of security. Once more I had succeeded in rousing the right kind of interest in myself; once more I was neither mature nor well placed (or at the least, sane) enough to create a marriage out of a romance. To compensate for being the wrong gender, I would surely have needed special qualities and securities or status that I didn't have. Even so, I had changed since the last time, '64–'65, when I felt convinced that my (ex-)friend should go on to marry a real boy. Now I was ready to put up a fight, at the end anyway, to try to lead my new friend and family to imagine her future could stop with me.

I had every reason to do my best. My new friend was a beautiful heiress of substantial character (despite her youth, at twenty) and no sexual inhibitions. Unlike my last friend, she (Polly was her name) let me know right away what she thought I had to offer. She was thrilled by my glamorous art-world life and told me that this was exactly what she wanted just then.

She'd been living in an apartment on Gramercy Park, taking classes at the Art Students League, seeing a shrink on Park Avenue once a week, and having an affair with somebody called Joan whom she'd met in Central Park with Joan's brother George. She was with Joan when I saw her outside Max's Kansas City. It was October '68. A black man I knew happened to be standing there with me, and he made the approach, pretending to be one of the Chambers Brothers. Polly separated from her friend Joan and stepped into a cab with me and the black man. As if this were London several months earlier, when I took Roxanne and the art student from Leeds to the flat on Baker Street, I let another man pimp for me, in a way, by enticing another female stranger to my place. In variance this time, I "paid" the man off by waiting till he finished screwing her, not getting involved in the threesome it was supposed to be, then found myself handsomely rewarded to discover that she was merely paying him off too. In the morning I woke up with my new forever and ever. I barely knew her name, but she was surely that most romantic of objects: a figure as strange and striking as she was familiar. With her long, abundant straight brown hair and gold-button navy blue blazer, she could have been my boarding school twin, left behind long ago and layered over with odd-looking adjustments to a complicated world. There was no apparent sophistication about her, no makeup, no ladies stuff, nothing overtly boyish either, nor any hassled-seeming ambivalences. Like myself, too, at that age, she had a "story." Her athletic grace and healthy bloom were modified by some disturbance, which made her quiet. She lacked the bouncing, naive enthusiasm due her age. As soon as we were up and dressed and drinking coffee, she told me about her dead father, how he'd put a bullet through his head in Connecticut when she was nine. She didn't really tell me; she more like chanted or intoned it—an interior record that ran constantly—sitting on a chair facing me but telling it to the world or the wall or herself once again, staring at the floor. The story magnetized me; my life in art intrigued her; the sex had been mutually strong; her navy blue blazer sealed my interest: Within the week she left her apartment on Gramercy Park and moved into my loft on the Bowery.

The next few months epitomized the glamorous life that I believe it was possible for somebody of the class I would call "the privileged poor" to lead in a city like New York. As a writer, I had become a kind of cult figure. As lover, it looked as if I had nabbed another one of America's most desirable princesses. As plaything of the rich, none at that moment could surpass me. This was my "rich year." My new friend, Polly, belonged to old American wealth; my benefactor, John de Menil, represented new American wealth, rooted in European class. I was "born again" as a mascot to the rich. I might have asked myself if this was the blueprint for the future I had dreamed up in '66 in my altered state. As '68 climaxed, it became apparent that it most definitely was not, though of course I can only say that after the fact and have no way of knowing what this particular "future" might have generated had it not been aborted. The difficulty was that I couldn't marry these families, which used me up and turned me loose the moment I looked problematic. I could blame it all on cigarettes, which I stopped smoking again that October (for the third and last time), causing elation and the subsequent familiar disorientation; but I believe I used cigarettes once more to help eject me from a life for which I knew I was unfitted.

For what, then, was I fitted? For being passed among the wealthy as a lover and a fool? For entertaining the art world with my perversions and adventures? For upsetting my mother in her distant quarters where friends informed her of my indiscretions? For joining the movement soon to be called antipsychiatry and railing against the mistreatment of innocents? For providing good copy and helping to make my newspaper successful? For becoming the kind of mother who sees her children as wise and independent beyond their years? All the above, to be sure, and more, but not for the one thing I wanted—to be adopted by a substantial family. Somehow I had to find or found my own. The one I had founded with a husband and two children had faltered and flopped at its very inception. There had been no model or experience behind it to make it work.

So I would say I was fitted essentially for one thing, and that was a quest. I was supposed to find something I knew nothing about. The quester naturally knows not for what she or he quests, nor even necessarily that questing is going on. The moment the quester can identify her object, the quest is over. This is expressed in the traditional Grail legend as that moment when Perceval or whoever enters the castle of the ailing old king and asks the proper question—e.g., "To whom is the Grail brought?" or "Who is served from the Grail?" The mystery generally always involves the quester's descent. My position in '68 was that of a girl who still regarded herself as an orphan. Orphanhood may be a divine condition (Jesus was called "the son of the widow"), but only if accepted, implying an advanced state of individuation. I had not accepted the original split from my mother, who was herself still possessed by anger. My drive was to be adopted by a better mother or by a mother disguised as father; nothing within me suggested making peace with my mother or finding my father—the two projects of utter contingency. It's difficult to say which was the more pressing problem: an absent father or an angry, possessive mother. The acceptance of an absent father was not possible without first having him; the acceptance of my mother, without first being able to do without her. And since to have him would have been to risk losing her, I chose to keep her in her unacceptable state, as well as to deprive myself of even entertaining the thought that he was locatable. To date in 1968 I had shown three solutions to my problem, each, of course, an evasion of the reality that confronted me. One was the momentary illusion of adoption, one the look of abandonment and helplessness when adoption failed, the last and most recent one a flight from reality altogether. Writing served a primary purpose of attracting those who might be moved to adopt me. Certainly the families that now gathered me up, one in the form of de Menil, the other in my new young lover, saw me first as a writer, secondarily as a person, which was a long shot. To see me as a person would have been to see rather far beyond what I was. Anyway, my three basic solutions to life—adoption, abandonment, flight—were about to occur in rapid order, in overlapping salvos, hitherto unrealized on such a magnificent scale.

20

Foil

Behind my new protection racket was a great fear of institutional psychiatry. While I hurled myself enthusiastically into the life of exciting intimacy and social splendor afforded courtesy of America's wealthiest and most powerful, I was frequently anxious about my security in the event of a mental break. I trusted no one yet sought advice everywhere. Having stopped smoking again that October, at the very moment my life began to look so colorful, I must have sensed I didn't have long to figure something out. My innermost wish was to be able to fly away with impunity. I had, apparently, no hope of establishing myself on earth, despite current appearances; therefore I longed to get back in my space bubble and stay there. If I could get my new friend into the bubble with me, and occasionally drop in on John de Menil in Houston, then make my weekly reports on paradise back to earth, printed in things called columns, I could be happy ever after. This, I believe, was my fourfold project in the last months of 1968. I had become convinced that the best place to be was crazy, if only I could find out how to stay clear of America's loony bins.

To that end, I looked to religion for ideas and support. For Christians, getting high meant going to heaven after death. The Easterners preached getting high in the here and now. That was what I wanted. I just wasn't willing to go to India and sit in a cave or at the feet of a yogi to learn how to do it—nor even to do something of that nature in America. I thought I knew how to do it myself anyway, and all I needed was to learn how to *handle* it. And the best chance I might have at that was to avoid those who would want to take over my controls.

I crept up to the Easterners by the usual route: our Western intermediaries. Cage's Suzuki (D.T., at Columbia) had never grabbed me; but I'd read some Alan Watts, and Richard Alpert, the man fired from Harvard with Leary for LSD experimentation, had returned that very fall from India calling himself Baba Ram Dass. With my friend I went to hear him speak at a church someplace uptown in Manhattan. There was a throng there, all spellbound. He was very high indeed, and telling everybody they could do it without acid or dope, as if to say, "Look, Ma—no hands!" I was so impressed I wrote a long article about him for the paper. I equated the effects of drugs with insanity (having already studied the "trip" reports in the psychedelic literature), in the sense that both were discontinuous highs, and upheld our new American guru as a guy who had learned how to stay up and never come down. I romanticized India, though I had no intention of going there. I was sure I would have better protection in the East, especially if I belonged to some temple set. I saw India swarming with crazy people in white who were considered divine. I was certain Christ had been crazy (forty days in the desert without food?) but that he was part of a manic depressive society, which got off only by feeding on its victims, whom they sent aloft in order to shoot down.

Through LaMonte Young, I met a tall, handsome Indian therapist in his late twenties called Shyam Bhatnagar, who was the first to tell me personally that my experiences of '65 and '66 were valuable and positive. I decided to try out his therapy, which consisted of lying prone on the floor, a tape recorder at my head playing Indian drones, letting Shyam run his fingers up and down my spine or blow on it and probe the "chakra centers" for their health or impairment, agreeing to do the exercises he advised (standing on the head, etc.) and eat what he ordered and breathe the way he said to and finally, I think, dress and talk as he prescribed. At last, I'm sure, living spaces and sex partners would have been designated. I even went to a couple of his group meditations, and once I felt myself drift into the Void.

But the great thing about Shyam was that he invited me to a dinner party where Alan Watts was to be guest of honor. The rest of the guests, including his wife, were practically hypnotized by Watts, so overcome were they at being in the presence of a "great man." Only the king of England or Winston Churchill could have commanded my attention that way. Nonetheless, I was far from immune to Watts's reputation and had even, after all, admired his writing, and I considered it a windfall in a way to have this opportunity to buttonhole him and ask him a couple of very important questions. So during the buffet-style dinner, before the guests gathered round to hear the "great man" hold forth (which he did on his knees, sitting on his heels), I cornered him on a couch and told him very briefly what had happened to me in '65 and '66, then asked him what he thought I should do if it happened again. This was a certain moment for me. Watts was a man of stature, and he assured me that I had undergone "consciousness-expanding" experiences that were invaluable—my own sentiments precisely. On the issue of what to do or where to go if it happened again, he was less reassuring. He said I should go and stay with Allen Ginsberg. Allen had once been kind to me when we both appeared in the same performance in '64, but my outstanding impression of him was as the man who had also invited me back to his tenement apartment on the Lower East Side after a party to sleep with his friend Peter Orlovsky while he stayed up all night on the phone in another room talking to Jack Kerouac on Long Island. Ginsberg? I had my doubts. (Eventually I did visit Ginsberg on his "farm" in upstate New York, though not for refuge; the time for that had already passed.) The only place I heard about in '68 that sounded feasible was Kingsley Hall in London, the site of Ronnie Laing's project, where it was said that he and a few colleagues had open house for people who wished to go through a psychotic experience. Their best-known customer became

Mary Barnes, who collaborated with Joe Berke, an American who went to London to work with Laing, on a book called *Two Accounts of a Journey Through Madness.*

But alas, my best protection turned out to be right next to me, the girl in the gold-button navy blue blazer. Sex was a bigger draw than religion; anyway, I thought that the kind of sex I was having represented the better part of religion: kundalini energy retained by the body, not astrally expelled, or the incarnation of spirit ("the union of humanity and divinity in the body") so fervently announced by N. O. Brown. Besides sex and religion, if that is what one has when love and carnality unite, I was acquiring new models of travel which could help to ground me in the event of a split. Sex, religion, and a legal means of travel were three things I didn't have back in August '65 and August '66. By August '65 my ex-friend and I had already transcended each other; the following year, as described, I was alone. Both years I had a decrepit vehicle which I had finally to abandon. My project in late '68, whether I knew it or not, was to enter heaven without leaving earth.

Earth was difficult, but it had recently surprised me with unsuspected favors. The rich people I knew, for instance, seemed eager to take me places in exciting vehicles—or to exciting places in vehicles that were at least new and reliable. My first trip abroad qualified for the latter description. My young lover provided similar experiences the moment she turned twenty-one that November and was summoned to Wall Street to receive her inheritance—a bundle of papers twelve inches high—and ordered a new VW squareback, dark blue, which she parked in a garage one block east of the Bowery. She now whisked me out of Manhattan on six-hour journeys to New Hampshire, then back through Boston, to show me her family holdings in those parts and to recline in them with me as if we were properly engaged. In Boston they had a mansion as big as the Gardner Museum, Rolls-Royces in the garage, maids and butlers galore, Monets and Manets, framed genealogies, canopied beds, etc. She had already introduced me to her mother (the week after we met, in fact), who was resting momentarily in a fairly lavish apartment across from the Americana Hotel. These people were always on the go, mostly hopping across the Atlantic to keep a foot in their various establishments on both sides of the ocean. My young friend's mother, I sensed, both liked me and wished I would go away. She was actually quite distressed and called her husband (Polly's stepfather) in Europe about it and went to consult a shrink as well. She then wisely retreated, having decided apparently to wait for her daughter to come to her senses. It seemed to me that she had more to worry about from the various men her daughter had known, most currently her daughter's Park Avenue, middle-aged, recently divorced, Gary Cooperishly handsome shrink, who pumped my friend for wanton information about me, invited her to bring me to meet him, then tried to elope with her the moment I walked into his apartment. That didn't seem like a way to act for a man who was supposed to be trying to help a girl deal with the violent death of her father. But he no doubt felt entitled to represent *himself* as the "violent father," who would be grateful to have his daughter forcibly rescued from homosexual perdition. In four years I had changed, or else this updated edition of "Europa and the Bull" was easier to identify, thus rousing my true sense of outrage. Anyway, my instant reaction set the tone for the affair (I was going to guard my object jealously this time) and, more far-reachingly, a basis for welding my anger to the lesbian/feminist revolution two years later. I had good reason to guard my object jealously if I suspected, as I must have, that she was capable of helping me do the one thing that obsessed me then: to go crazy and not be tagged, or ruined, for it. As I got higher and higher during November and December, I became more and more impressed by the assortment of vehicles and remote, comfortable places that seemed available to transport and house a body in the process of being abandoned by its mind. That was not really a conscious thought. Nor did I dwell that much on my impending predicament. Mainly I let myself feel swept along, enjoying the waves of sex, the winds of travel, the swells of attention that my writing, and also my life, seemed to provoke.

The writing and the life were now nearly one. Each week I packed my experiences, encounters, quotes, and unusual information into tightly wedged columns of two thousand five hundred words or so. The staple sentence was a "found object" (quotes from many sources) woven into a fabric of thumbnail adventures and reflections. Major themes were great people I knew, great places I went, great deeds I did, great sex I had, great insights I culled. In a typical column I dropped at least twenty-five names, mentioned innumerable places, told maybe ten stories, and glued everything together with flotsam of jokes, quotes, puns, neologisms, and pronouncements—all designed to convey the feeling that nothing was necessarily relevant to anything else, or that pieces, sentences, could be moved at will or at random from any one place to another, if not out of the frame altogether. Any column was perhaps like a jigsaw puzzle in its fragmented state. A picture may have been there, if anyone cared to find or construct it. Or lots of pictures were there, and the readers could make their own. Ironically, I was very attached to the exact form of the columns. One word dropped or out of place or misspelled made me wild. I suppose I imagined the "picture" might be lost if the fragments were not all there. The newspaper packaged the "puzzle" and had a responsibility to get all the pieces in the box, as it were. I wanted my readers to put me together. I had a lot of anxiety every week over what might happen to my copy once I handed it over. I was identical with the column; thus any flaw in it magically affected my person. Since I lacked personal coherence, the column carried tremendous weight for me as a shaped and completed entity, despite, or because of, its atomized reflection of my disjointedness. I didn't think of it this way; I took the exalted view that the style had been forged from the way the mind works at its best: when insane. It was a poor imitation, perhaps; but poor was infinitely better than anything representing the tedium of reason. The model was the loss or dissolution of an ego (personal coherence) uncertain to begin with of its identity and boundaries. The world so far as I was concerned was a vast amoeba. Social arrangements were arbitrary and artificial constructs, not to be respected or recognized or tolerated. A polemic of this kind inhered in the form and content of the columns, which at the same time, by their density and phalanx-like nature, if not just their existence, defied penetration or engulfment. I was, in other words, trying to assert myself alone and whole against a hostile world. The highly centripetal structure of the columns—objects depicted "out there," debris floating around and seeking a center but without a center to sufficiently magnetize them—demonstrated a certain determined resistance to the world or protection against it. Yet I needed the protection of the world from which I sought to protect myself. For that I counted completely on the attention the columns provoked.

The wages of fame were now momentarily mine. Fame, after all, had figured heavily in my experiences of '65 and '66, both as delusion and as projection of something I thought I needed. Fame functions as a shield, or decoy, luring attention away from person to product, from self to representation of self—a process that, as we know, can backfire and end up imprisoning people in these objects outside themselves (books, paintings, films, whatever, as well as ideas about themselves) if in the meantime they haven't developed a personal life. Fame also sets adoption procedures in motion. The powerful and the famous can serve each other admirably. Those who adopted me at that moment had their own protection rackets going. It was quite an unequal exchange, however. In the end, I placed a much higher value on the wealth and position of my friends than I did on my own offering. That was realistic. In relation to both families, I was essentially the female, the one adopted in marriage by the male, who brings her into his family by giving her his name. In no way did I think of myself as the man who by virtue of his fame has acquired the right to adopt someone himself. Yet initially this was precisely how my new young lover tried to perceive me. Her family rejected me; she was somewhat estranged from it herself, definitely involved in some postadolescent reaction to her mother; she articulated her interest in (being adopted by) my art-world family, and she moved in with me on the Bowery. A certain undercover power struggle ensued. *Her* family, which was after all a *real* family and clearly of great substance, looked much grander to me than mine. Our solution finally was to abscond with each other, renouncing both my (art) family and hers, which never put in an appearance, anyway, after the one fateful meeting with her mother. My hope, I believe, unbeknownst to myself, was to get both of us adopted by the de Menils in Houston.

In November Simone Swan called me again to invite me to Houston for some art shindig there. I hadn't seen John since his party for Truffaut in June. I had, however, seen a chateau of his in France when I was there in July and his niece Benedicte Pesle, who ran the Iolas Gallery in Paris, had taken me out to the countryside for a day and a night. People brought down to Houston—writers, dealers, critics, collectors, curators, artists, widows of artists, friends of art, etc.—were treated like precious art cargo. A limousine picked me up on the Bowery and transported me to a private section of La Guardia where one of the Schlumberger six-seater Lear jets awaited. The jet refueled in Nashville, landed in Houston, and taxied into a hangar where rented cars were lined up for the ride to motels or to the de Menil house on San Felipe Road. On one of these trips I met Teeny Duchamp, Marcel's widow, who became a friend of mine. On another I got to know Gregory Battcock, the art critic, professor, and poseur, who was murdered in 1980; in fact, Gregory was aboard this first trip I made in November. We weren't directly solicited to write anything about the events for which we were invited; the de Menil policy was to "put things in God's hands," as Simone Swan has described it, trusting that a random percentage of people brought down would be moved to write or do business or make waves or whatever. I understood I was to write something, but I was hardly willing or able to give them any solid, accrediting type of coverage; and it appeared right away that I could be put to better use, which would in any case provide copy of some sort. On our way to a party at the house of one Mrs. Weingarten, of the grocery chain–food empire, before the main occasion, a museum opening, Simone explicitly suggested I might want to find a way to misbehave.

I suppose Mrs. Weingarten and her ilk were detestable in general to the de Menils and associates. For all their wealth and position, the de Menils were outsiders in America, and Houston, in their own way. Over a couple of decades they had been battling with Houston's town fathers and mothers for control of the cultural life of that city. The old families were provincial and conservative; the de Menils were adventurous and imaginative and represented international modernist concerns, including the American avant-garde of the fifties and sixties. Their collection ranged from the more obligatory Picassos, Braques, Légers, Cézannes, Rodins, Matisses, Klees, Mirós, et al., to Magrittes (most extensive), Ernsts, de Chiricos, and Mondrians, up through Pollacks, de Koonings, Rothkos, and the up-to-date Johnses, Rauschenbergs, Tinguelys, Warhols, Oldenburgs, etc. For John and Dominique, art was a passion and a profession; for their counterparts in Houston, it was more like the usual civic duty and source of prestige. Struggles were first waged to get the existing art institutions to hang modernist art, then for control over the institutions themselves; and the de Menils finally created and/or bought their own: St. Thomas University, the Rice University Museum, the Media Center, the Rothko Chapel. It's been said that nearly every gift they gave they wanted to control, so they ended up collecting institutions along with everything else. On a large scale, they outraged propriety in Houston. Their house itself, designed by Philip Johnson in the late forties (it was Johnson's first house), was an affront to the tastes of the old oil and cotton magnates.

John and Dominique had become U.S. citizens in 1962. Like my father, they were late American invaders; unlike my father, they stayed to establish a dominion exceeding the business that brought them here. Outside of his business, I was my father's only dominion in the U.S. (unless there are more I don't know about), and as such (a girl, unrecognized even by him), I was an extreme type of the displaced foreigner, thus well suited as a foil for the displaced and mighty like the de Menils, whose position required they maintain a certain decorum themselves. It shouldn't be thought that I was cognizant of these dynamics at that time. I loved John; I was eager to please; I knew nothing of their imbroglios in Houston; I liked Simone. I just picked up on the role that seemed expected of me. That wasn't difficult, since I was already practiced as a fool and affronted people by my mere presence and appearance. John even contributed to my foolish wardrobe, sending me off with a blank check to a Western store called Stelzig's, where I equipped myself with a gleaming silver-and-gold-threaded white-and-powdery-blue pantsuit, a ten-gallon hat, and ochre-colored chamois cowboy chaps. To Mrs. Weingarten's party before the Museum opening I recall wearing the leather miniskirt with vest and high boots and tie that I'd bought in London, to which I added the usual silly floppy hat. The guests were predictably offended, but I had to get my hands into a gooey green artichoke dip before fulfilling my part. Simone and Gregory were delighted. A horrible woman whom I described in my column as "redheaded" with "auburn-eyed rage" bore down on me with "instant denunciations." I called her "a kind of vulgarized Scarlett O'Hara." Simone asked her if she was the housekeeper. Gregory told her he was writing a book about etiquette and didn't know what she was talking about. Before leaving, she demanded a few moments with me alone in a corner, where she asked me angrily where I had come from. Corpus Christi, I told her, adding that I had flown in especially for the party. In my column, I said I had thought of inviting her to my room at the end of the evening's festivities in case she wanted to know more.

It surprises me now to see how forward I was then about my sexuality—before Stonewall ('69) and before the movement

with which I became identified in the early seventies. To understand what I was doing, I have to think myself back into a
particular time when I felt driven to please people by acting
"bad" for them. For a couple of years I enjoyed full protection
for this dubious sort of responsibility. Counting the several years
I then joined my sexuality to a public cause, I enjoyed this so-
called protection even longer. My friends changed; the enemy
was redefined; the dynamic remained essentially the same. Only
when the *times* changed did I begin to perceive the possibility of
another kind of existence. Coincidentally, as the times were
changing, my mother was dying; and once again my personal
circumstances corresponded with events at large.

The keynote of the sixties was identity through confrontation, which was accomplished by having the world divided into
three parts: those who had to be confronted, those who needed
to confront but lacked the means or position to do it, and those
who were willing and able to mess themselves up for the group
that couldn't. These three parts can be identified in various
ways, my favorite being: father (and mother), father's son, and
mother's son. Broadly, the parental establishment has an invest-
ment in both types of offspring, the father's son to hold down the
business, the mother's son to invent something new. In conservative times, father's sons can look indistinguishable from their
parents, mother's sons like criminals and failures. In volatile
times, father's sons begin to come unstuck from their parents,
expressing repressed needs to rebel by handing over all kinds of
parental machinery for the purpose of disruption to their outcast
siblings, who then have the chance to look like heroes and vi-
sionaries. The de Menils in America were "father's sons," par
excellence. John has even been characterized (in the *Texas
Monthly*) as "a man of great compassion for the unfortunate
and great impatience for the failings of those around him," an
"ultraliberal corporate executive." As leaders, the Kennedys had
the same kind of reputation. Like the Kennedys, incidentally,
the de Menils extended themselves to blacks, helping blacks get
a political foothold in Houston. The Kennedys, it will be re-

membered, also befriended artists, the one group that as a whole could be characterized as mother's sons. The artist who begins to look like a corporate executive can be a very disconcerting sight. There may be nothing quite so conservative as a mother's son fully accepted by the Establishment. And there may be nothing quite so pathetic as a successful artist still posing as a mother's son. The finer distinctions were not apparent to me in the sixties, but it wasn't much trouble sorting out the messages indicating where I belonged. If a girl wasn't properly married (a mother's daughter), she was either a father's helper in some other capacity or a subspecies of mother's son. On her own, certainly, she could never be a father's son, not unless she was Christina Onassis or Katherine Graham, though this is changing, and I believe a new species is emerging that might be called the father's daughter—the kind of daughter who, like an eldest son, like the anomaly of a Margaret Mead, inherits directly from a father. In the sixties, as a subspecies of mother's son, I was completely dependent on the benevolence and repressed subversive interests of various father's sons, along with the peer encouragement of certain real (outcast) sons or mother's sons proper, such as Les Levine, David Bourdon, and, most recently, Gregory Battcock, who actually thought of me for a while as an innovator. These males often have the kind of foothold in the Establishment that can make them indistinguishable from their more conservative brothers. Gregory had two distinct lives: professor and critic on the one hand, gay writer for underground newspapers and extensive promiscuous secret sex seeker on the other. He was, after all, the only son of a father he said he hated. He could never have been taken for a "more conservative brother" (he was too eccentric and full of pranks and fun), but his tenure at a university and entrenched position at E. P. Dutton as anthologist in liaison with an established editor there gave him similar authorities. Unlike Gene Swenson, who was too far out even for the sixties, Gregory had that perfect balance between the outrageous and the conservative that gave those times their special flavor. He imitated my style in his columns for radical newspapers, and in 1971 he published my first book in his capacity as anthologist at Dutton.

But in January of '69 I heard from a man who could be described as an unequivocal sort of father's son, a more conservative type swept up in the revolutionary fervor of the sixties, active in the civil rights movement and eager to support those best equipped to express his own disappointment with society.

On January 3 or 4 I received a note from Danny Moses at Simon & Schuster, asking me if I wanted to write a book. (He asked Jerry Rubin and Bucky Fuller then too, he told me a lot later.) But by that time I was again winging it far away into the global stratosphere. I was delighted with the note, overcome really, and fully intended to follow up on it; but I was heavily engaged just then trying to pull off a disappearing act. The coincidence, I think, was not insignificant. There was nothing I seemed to want more than to get away from the things my actions had wrought. During November and December, messages about my new life had crystallized into a frightening shape. Though nothing precisely frightened me (I was simply excited and amused), I have to imagine that I found my position untenable. The mother's son, of whatever variety, is somebody balancing on a tightrope between two worlds: that from which we came and that toward which we're propelled. He (or she) is a very transitional figure, long gone from home but still unacceptable to society, thus admirably suited to act out a certain passage, or suspension in that passage, that is understood to be perilous. For many people the so-called midlife crisis expresses this condition, midlife meaning neither here nor there but somewhere in between. It looked as if I could be one of those people for whom a midlife crisis never ends. The end of such a crisis implies some settlement in regard to society, an acceptance or recognition of place in the established order. Many women never accept a settlement that degrades them. The messages I was getting in November–December '68 were completely contradictory, suggesting once again that I belonged neither one place nor another (I was far from home, or mother, and hardly adopted in any true sense by those who courted me), therefore I might as well fall off that difficult tightrope and float into the bubble that would take me away from it all. I didn't *think* any of that; I was just drifting along in that direction.

And I remember only a fraction of the things I heard or experienced that confused me. At a fancy party where I was trussed up in one of those Houston cowboy outfits, playing with a yo-yo that lit up when you flung it out of your hand, Jasper Johns told me I was "the talk of the town." The talk of the town? For whom? For the *whole* town? For how long? To what end? Also in Houston, disembarking from a plane with Andy Warhol and a couple of his friends (we'd been flown there for the premiere of Andy's movie *Lonesome Cowboys*), a photographer herded us together for a picture and Andy remarked that he was making me famous. I said, "Listen, Andy, I was born famous." Born famous? What did I mean? Who was I? Why did it matter? Where were we going? Who was it for? And so on. But this one wasn't difficult. If I'd taken my own quotes seriously, I could have "read" this message quite clearly. "Project ego destruction by overexposure," I dropped into my column right after that little anecdote. Much more disturbing was a black-tie dinner at the house of the president of the trustees of the Whitney Museum, where I was invited as a guest of John de Menil (who came with Simone) and insulted by host, hostess, and other guests. The host didn't like my "velour Garbo hat or my crushed velvet pants," I wrote, and "he tried to take my drink away from me when we were going in to dinner." He asked in general, "Who reads the *Village Voice* anyway?" He wanted to know how I could tell what the color of one of his rooms was with my shades on. And when I expressed curiosity about a Dubuffet hanging on a wall he asked me "if I was interested in the visual arts." After I wrote this stuff, I heard he wanted to sue me. This made me both gleeful and paranoid. Internal questions were: Why was I insulted? What did I do to them? What was their problem? Was it me? Where was my protection? What was the relationship between the three parties:

me, my host, and my sponsor (de Menil)? John and Simone made it very clear that our host and company were insensitive people and that I was perfectly wonderful, as usual. This judgment, I assume, was supposed to take care of those insults. *It did not occur to me that I was being set up.* Nor, I'm sure, did it occur to John and Simone.

Most disturbing of all, though, was another triangle—that critical and mainly invisible one consisting of me, my newspaper, and my mother. Sometime during that winter I had a conversation with my editor-in-chief, Dan Wolf, a man I didn't know at all and had rarely even seen. On the phone he asked me who had given me permission to write my autobiography. It was a rhetorical question. My "autobiography" was a fait accompli, popular around town, and commercially viable to the paper. The question was related somehow to a letter he'd received from my mother begging the paper not to print me anymore, claiming she would be happy to pay me what the paper did! Again, I was thrilled (I told Dan he should print it as a letter to the editor) and even more paranoid. I would not have dared ask myself the kinds of questions that might have illumined this most central issue of my life. But how did I probably construe the message? For a start: I had gotten to her. That was what pleased me. She felt threatened and wanted to stop me. That was very challenging, a signal I was on the right track. But could she stop me? *Should* she? Would the paper see through my shenanigans to my use of its space as a personal battlefield? Yes, probably—but what did it matter to them if I risked my neck by personalizing the war against the parental establishment to which they also were committed? In fact, as it turned out, the paper thrived on this sort of thing—the intimate exposé—as did John and Simone, and everybody else who had something to lose by expressing their anger at the status quo personally. One thing they had to lose was the machinery they owned or controlled to make available to people like myself for subversive purposes. My bosses at the *Voice* ultimately lost their own paper. And Danny Moses, who became my editor at Simon & Schuster, lost several jobs in the seventies in personal struggles with his own superiors. Possibly John de Menil lost his life to the various causes he championed. That I don't know, but he was only sixty-nine when he died, and he had been very healthy-looking at sixty-five. My loss of *them*, when they died or defected or got fired or sold out, was the protracted event of the seventies that culminated in the death of my mother in 1978, terminating one extended stage of my struggle as a type of mother's son. Characteristic of this stage was the kind of serious internal conflict that causes people to opt out of their situations altogether. That is, I was against the very people I needed and used because of their need and use of me, which left me personally unprotected. The oldest issue of my mother's need and use of me was constantly reinvoked.

The dissociation of fame from personal caring in the adult world updates this earliest of equations: Everybody (mother) is looking at me, nobody cares about me. Put differently: They think I'm wonderful (so cute, so smart, so talented, so sexy, etc.), but they don't see me as an individual, with emotions, moods, thoughts, dreams, experiences, etc. My mother often said I didn't like her, which expressed her alienation from her own subjectivity. She too felt used and unappreciated for herself (which she formulated as a lack of gratitude for her *use*) and likewise unable to know that this was the case. There was not much self to appreciate, since it had been so dormant or uncultivated. Our use of each other tends to pass for caring. I had given up on my mother and replaced her earliest attention (Mother is looking at me, I'm a wonderful object), which was never succeeded by any acknowledgment of developing selfhood, with its inflated social equivalent, fame. Confusing my use with my person on a grand scale, I would naturally revolt against my use and drag my person into the fray (the two being indistinguishable), treating the world exactly as if it were my mother. One way to go about proving that the people who use you don't really care about you is to make yourself look quite useless and *then* see what happens. My intermediary solution to this central problem of neglect—still short of knowing what I needed or was missing—was to leave the place where I found myself in such great demand, which had dramatized my (inner) need to an insupportable extent. "Leaving the place," meaning New York, was what I had tried to do in '65 and '66, but I had been stopped and arrested each time. Mind and place were somehow synonymous. Leaving my mind meant getting away, but my resources for travel had been much too limited. The big difference now, in late '68, was that I was intimate with someone who had an excellent vehicle and was able to go away with me.

21

Chase

It was January 8, incidentally my daughter's birthday; I was alone in my loft, and I had a dentist's appointment that afternoon. Polly had driven to New Hampshire three or four days earlier. She was only going to visit friends on her family's estate, she had said, but I would have felt abandoned had she been going to attend a dying mother or an exclusive business conference. Since October, when we had gotten together, we had been inseparable except for *my* brief departures (to Houston), which didn't count as far as I was concerned. The moment my friend exited the loft, I split asunder. There was a "plan," I believe, and we were just following its instructions. As a getaway plan, it conformed to one well-known strategy or another. If she left first, pretending she was only leaving to visit friends but without inviting me to go along or explaining that she needed to go by herself, thus rousing the specter of abandonment, I could then be lured to follow her by imagining that if I didn't, I would never see her again. The trick on my part was to pretend I had not been abandoned, otherwise I could scare her away. She was already away, and I had to pretend we were still together. (Whether we were or not, I'll never know.) I said good-bye at the door as cheerfully and affectionately as I had to my ex-friend three and a half years earlier when she left our loft on Liberty Street with a suitcase. On that occasion I had already broken from reality, but within twenty-four hours of that particular departure I had us both in a car together traveling out of Manhattan at great speed. This time I could identify my break with reality quite precisely. I had already been very high, beginning in October, gathering momentum during November and December, as if my "rocket" had been ascending all that time, waiting for the moment when booster (body) and capsule (head) separate, and the latter enters orbit. That moment was when she departed on January 3 or 4. As soon as I said good-bye so cheerfully at the door, I walked over to my gas heater on the floor, sat down on a chair next to it, and sobbed convulsively —for about two minutes. Then I rose and walked upstairs to see Les, feeling nothing whatever except very light and high, bubbly and evanescent, free and untethered. I was speaking in puns, laughing deliriously at the endless flow of jokes, amazed at the wellspring of associations. It was not like the writing I had been doing for the paper, which was a *calculated* flow of puns and jokes, a mere imitation of this present, most divine state.

I talked to my friend on the phone in New Hampshire. All seemed well. I had only to go about my business, not concerning myself with her distance or her return. But within twenty-four hours or so I was most definitely concerned, if not about her exactly, about my own "divine state"—which once again threatened to make me look unreal enough for quarantine. I got frantic on the street, hearing my name and stuff like that. I had to stay supercool. Had I expressed how I really felt, I would have been racing down the street screaming, arms flying like tattered sails in a storm. As it was, I did get into a couple of rages, in particular, I remember, against Les, whose habit it was to contradict people, or at least me. When sane, I would just slug it out with him. Now I was in no mood to be contradicted, which is to put it mildly. I required total and unequivocal agreement. Getting mad had not until now been any part of my experience of "madness," except under threat of incarceration in 1966. And now, I believe it was this same threat, unspoken but felt, that caused my rage, which was expressed as reaction to any lack of agreement, suggesting nullification of my reality. Later this seemed to me like a healthy development—not that it's healthy to dump rage on others, but that its occurrence can provide insight into our histories and motivations. The dilation of sub-jectivity in "madness" says something about the lack of it in a normal history. A reservoir of rage can build up from accepted denials of personal reality, a rage that can be released under novel conditions, in which, say, a newly developing self, sud-denly inflated, feels threatened with extinction. If the threat of incarceration provokes rage, the rage thus provoked may be the most usual excuse for incarceration. I knew I had to get out of town.

On January 8 I developed a plan around my dentist's ap-pointment in the afternoon. I called Polly in New Hampshire to tell her I would probably take a train north later in the day and would call her back to confirm time and place. I cashed a check and caught a taxi to my dentist's office on Fifty-seventh Street, where I had two "attacks": the prospect of the dentist seemed menacing to me, and the elevator looked like a moving tomb as I ascended to the seventh floor. I pretended I felt ill and couldn't possibly keep my appointment, and I called Polly right there from the office to say I was on my way to the train station and would call her back; I persuaded the dentist's assistant to ac-company me in the elevator down to street level. Thereafter, I didn't see a dentist for years and rarely went in an elevator. On Fifty-seventh Street I got a taxi to Penn Station and found out they had no trains to Boston, where Polly would have to pick me up. I took another taxi to Grand Central, where I had many tiny adventures, all very large to me—trying to buy a ticket, deter-mine the time of departure and the track number of the train, and find the train itself—before actually getting on board. Once seated, I was immensely relieved, especially as I sat down opposite a sweet Spanish couple whose name was Class (the name was tagged on the man's army uniform), with an infant swaddled in pink bunting. At Back Bay Station in Boston I stepped off the train into a great cloud of steam, which made me realize I had the wrong stop . . . the train was moving as I jumped back on it.

My friend was sitting in the waiting room at North Station

when I arrived—not scared or upset, only suspicious and aloof. It was a two-hour drive to Squam Lake (the lake where *On Golden Pond* was shot) in the middle of New Hampshire. My friend's mother's establishment there was a big, wonderful octagonal boathouse that hung way out over the water, with picture windows consuming each side of the octagon, a huge fireplace of floor-to-ceiling brick, and fully equipped with kitchen, etc. The snow and winter and the peace and quiet decreased the speed in my head and helped make me less paranoid. The way I put it in a column called "About the Ash Tree," printed January 23, "my head was a windstorm, my body a silent lake," and "my legs were stopping still as a rock that isn't falling anywhere." For about twelve hours, it's true, I was paralyzed from the waist down. Polly had made a tall sculpture of seven chairs piled high and perfectly balanced and extremely precarious looking. "That's how I felt in my escape from our great city to slow down my head which was knowing too much and to see what my body might do about [it]." I had heard that it takes about twenty-one days to die if you simply stop eating. I decided to live. "I tensed up my neck and upper back" and in that way gradually got some energy into my lower extremities. I thought I was on "the critical list, although a hospital wouldn't take me, because I wouldn't go to one, nor to one of them doctors." The project was to make "my head dumb and my body smarter." I drank a lot of liquid and slept awhile "to get my waking dreams back into my sleeping dreams." It seemed too bad to have to reclaim my ego in order to go on living. Ego for me still meant difference and uniqueness, not an instrument of mediation (between self and other or outside). I lived in the either/or world. Either I was unique and alone, reactive and autonomous, or I was undifferentiated completely. Reclaiming my ego meant going on asserting myself independently against a hostile world. The delusions of my previous two "experiences" were dangerously close. I recognized their nearness and prompted my friend to help me keep them at bay. I told her to stop me the moment I talked genealogy or world saving. Briefly I imagined both of us galloping on a white steed across the George Washington Bridge to save New York. We did plan to drive back into the city, but only to close up the loft and collect some belongings before leaving for a tour of America.

We spent seven days in the boathouse on Squam Lake. I told nobody where I was except Ann Wilson, who sent me some Stelazine tablets, which I planned to use at night if I couldn't sleep. Polly arranged to have an oversized Finn she knew, a boy of about twenty, ex-football player, living in Canada, meet us in Manhattan to join us for the cross-country junket as a kind of bodyguard. I was weak when we left the boathouse, apprehensive about returning to the city, confident I had this "trip" under control, exultant about outfoxing the medical psychiatric establishment, convinced I had done something as extraordinary as climbing Everest without benefit of guides or rescue teams. I stayed high and whizzy for several months, satisfied in the end that I had gone as far as I could go on my own and that only my personal circumstances brought me down. That was all I wanted to know. I gained no new knowledge otherwise on this particular occasion, except to expand my repertory of "special powers" while so intoxicated. Numbers and number systems became obsessional, and words and letters on the highways of America became the signs of the future.

Driving back to New York to prepare for this trip, we stopped in Franklin, New Hampshire, to see Dick Alpert, alias Ram Dass, who was meditating by himself in his father's farmhouse on Webster Lake, surrounded by beads and nuts and photos of his guru. "Cosmic casting," he said after we knocked, as he leaned over a banister up one flight. I was disappointed that he didn't perceive me as a fellow high traveler. I had just survived a cataclysmic chemical transformation, and he didn't see it. The exchange was all one way. He had the divine message; we were initiates knocking at the gates. A couple of years later I saw him again, when I was down and depressed, and he very kindly snuffed out my complaints (sort of swallowing them and extinguishing them somewhere deep inside himself—with a flame, I imagined, residing in a hollow of his gut) but otherwise displayed no sign of interest in saving me. I also approached Trungpa Rinpoche and the Swami Muktananda, and I never knew whether they rejected me or I them—but perhaps I felt as if I had at least given the Eastern folks the old college try. In the end, anyway, I started understanding my problems and going through them rather than ignoring them or trying to transcend them. I had girl friends and knew other women who defected from their families or feminism or relationships to get high with Muktananda or Rinpoche or the Maharishi, and I always thought they were fooling themselves if they imagined they could resolve family issues that way. Thankfully, my young friend of 1968–69 was not attracted to any little Indian men. Like myself, she was preoccupied with her dead father and found "spiritual" satisfaction in other fatherless daughters, with whom she might exchange legal blessings (her inheritance) for creative alliances (my inheritance). I was coming close to fulfilling my fourfold wish: crazed with impunity, the company of my friend, a paper in which to make weekly reports on paradise, and a real family that would adopt us. Only this last was still missing; and while I continue to hold out for my friend's family, I can't imagine why we were driving south to Florida with the intention to veer west toward Texas and stop in Houston if not to see whether John would not entertain both of us in the style to which I alone had been treated and whether he might not then be moved to see me more as a relative than as a functionary he liked a lot.

I had called ahead from Louisiana to let him know we were coming. We were three, so we had to stay in a motel rather than at his house. He took us out to dinner and was gracious and charming as usual, but not really as welcoming and hospitable— certainly not as intimate. He was entertaining us, after all, at my invitation. It wasn't supposed to work like this. I was at *his* beck and call, not the other way round. Besides, under the circumstances I was not exclusively his. Nor was there any reason I should have been, since I was not there for one of his art events. The art event was the medium between us; we had no other business together, though on my part at least I found him attractive enough to be a romantic object, had this been another life. For me, he was the art event. For him, I remained the functionary he liked a lot. But now I must have left him with some doubts. Leaving the restaurant where we had dinner, Polly took her Finnish friend in the VW squareback, while I drove away with John alone, using the opportunity to tell him I was romantically involved with the other girl in our party. I made kind of a big, unnecessary deal over it. I must have thought he wondered what I was doing and I wished to satisfy his unstated curiosity or confirm his suspicions. It was as though I were "coming out" to a father. If so, it had to be my pitch for adoption, misguided as that might have been. As it was, my young friend didn't interest him at all, and my "confession" could only have put me at a further disadvantage.

As we drove west toward El Paso, I hallucinated a heavy family connection, the typical defense against what I knew was not really there. At El Paso, we sent Polly's Finnish friend flying back to Canada, continuing by ourselves to Tucson and Los Angeles. We stayed in Holiday Inns everywhere. I jabbered constantly, running off associations sparked by license-plate numbers and highway signs, frequently seeing all things in paranoid sexual terms—namely, the real or imagined interest I saw that men had in my young friend. I wrote long, run-on pieces home to the paper, getting up every morning at six to write furiously in the motel dining rooms. I took a blue Stelazine pill sometimes to get to sleep, which had the strange side effect of making my right arm go numb over my head. Wherever we encountered people I knew, with the exception of Houston, it seemed as if we screeched off in a dust cloud, narrowly escaping some imminent, unidentifiable disaster. In Taos, New Mexico, we settled down for a week in a fine place called the Sagebrush Inn, two miles south of the town, with superb views of the Sangre de Cristo mountain range. From there I sent a lengthy epistle to the paper called "Pubis Est Veritas," in effect complaining mightily about the heterosexual world in which I lived.

I worked about twenty-five historical characters into the column, mainly D. H. Lawrence, whose retreat where he lived with Frieda was just five miles away from where we were staying and whose story "The Fox" was made into a movie I had seen in London the previous summer, and was the subject of a pseudonymous feature in the *New York Times* that I had just read in Taos. The "gay revolution" was looming (Stonewall was four months away). The movie had excited and upset me a lot; now, seeing this feature about it in the *Times*, I seized the moment to broadcast my sexual interests, not pulling any punches, to align myself with the dead (Gertrude, Alice, Oscar, Virginia, et al.), and to malign the dead who saw things differently— Lawrence in particular, because he had killed off a girl called Jill in "The Fox" in order to have her female lover end up with the male intruder. I saw way beyond *The Fox* (and most certainly *The Killing of Sister George*, and even *Lianna* some fifteen years later) to an unmade movie in which two women settled down somewhere lovely forever and ever. My favorite song was Judy Collins's "My Father Always Promised Us" ("that we would live in France"), no doubt with Gertrude and Alice ever in mind. *Entre Nous* (1984) finally could be said to project some accounting of the ending I envisioned—it was made by a woman, of course (Diane Kurys).

Writing home back in February–March '69, I never said what was really happening. In Taos my friend developed a backache, which we or I attributed to her hauling suitcases in and out of motel rooms. We never talked about what we were doing or where we might be going or what we meant to each other or anything like that. I was dancing on the head of a celestial pin; she was reserved, quiet, practical, and wonderfully sexy at the end of every day. I was very much in love and unaware of who it was I loved exactly. As we drove east to Ann Arbor, where we stayed with the Once Group, whose annual film festival I had agreed to judge, her back got worse and worse. On a mountain in Pittsburgh, in a rambling old house belonging to friends of Ann Wilson's, she stopped moving altogether. I think she had some kind of hysterical paralysis. I thought it was psychological, and I really knew there was a big conflict going on in her mind or submind over me and her family, but we never talked about it except in the vaguest terms. I urged her to get out of bed and move; I half-carried her from bed to bathroom; I reassured Ann's friends, Charlie and Mitch, we'd be leaving as soon as we could; and after three days or so I bundled her into the squareback and drove us to Manhattan. It was too bad. The end of the trip proved to be the end. Things happened very swiftly once we walked in the door on the Bowery.

The first thing I remember happening was my friend's mother calling from Spain. Next I remember my friend going to see a doctor. Next I remember returning to the loft from shopping or lunch or something and finding a note saying she was on her way to the airport and would be flying to Madrid by TWA. I wrote a piece called "Ergo Sum," printed on March 27, in which I said Polly's back was better, mine was a mess, and I was going to Houston to "look at the Machine Show . . . with a pillow at the lower vertebrae against an airplane seat." I pretended we were still together. At the end of the piece I reported a little story Deborah Hay had told me about a concert she did in February titled 911. She said that though nobody had written up her concert, the following day she had read a notice in the *Times* instructing people about the use of this number, 911, in the event of medical emergencies, and she was very happy about this notice.

I was very unhappy and desperate in Houston. My fantasy was in great disarray. Now I was still in orbit, and my fellow astronaut, if you will, had fallen out of the capsule. They never sent astronauts up alone after the first suborbital flights. It hardly seemed fair. I could feel my control slipping away from me. Gregory was in Houston and said he wanted to help me. Back in New York I was assailed with delusions, which I had kept successfully at bay for three months. A leading delusion was that my affair was not really over. More classically, I imagined once again that Apollinaire was my father. My columns were chockablock with names and places, dates and connections —the living and the dead, the past and the future, the immediate present, different languages, vernacular . . . as if to demonstrate two things: that I knew my history ("I'm so involved in the facts, you see. The names and the dates. I was interrogated once") and that living well was the best revenge. I threw this most recent Houston trip at the page as if it were a giant pie in the sky hanging up there exclusively for me. If my writing had served to seduce those who would adopt me, it now served to let the rest of the world know—at the very moment I was being abandoned—that I was indeed well adopted and protected and there was therefore no need to worry about me. Moreover, as noted, I was in charge of the facts. And though I was intransigently arrogant or omniscient (I knew the secrets of the universe, the real story behind each fact, large or small), I threw in enough disclaimers ("Once I asked why was I chosen and they said you weren't, you were deported, to a hospital") to make the wary less suspicious, should that have been necessary. So while I kept up this steady patter with one hand, straight-arming the world, blowing big smoke rings at it, with the other I made last-ditch stands to grasp what I was losing, took desperate steps to stay at large, and organized my retreat.

Around April 15, no more than three weeks after my friend flew to Spain to join her mother, I embarked for London on what was then called BOAC, wearing a "teddy boy" jacket I'd bought on St. Marks Place in a store called Limbo: a blazer striped in two kinds of blue, with a monogram—the man said it had been imported from Eton or Harrow. I was much higher than the altitude of the plane. I regaled the flight attendants with intimations of my immortality. At a small, pleasant establishment called Somerset House Hotel, near Regents Park, a manager or desk clerk (I had wired the reservation ahead) came out to the taxi, took my bags, calling me "Miss Johnston" (he might have added "I presume"), and ushered me to a room that he described as "the famous guest room," where I spent two days, mostly sick to my stomach, while waiting for an answer to my telegrams to Spain. The desk clerk or manager seemed to know exactly what I should do and, of course, "who I was." At his suggestion I went to the BOAC office in London and let them make a reservation for me to Spain, via the Rock of Gibraltar. I lay back on a couch many feet from the reservation desk and let them do the whole thing. It was a very roundabout way to get to my destination, a large town on the Mediterranean called Estepona, best approached from Málaga, which had a decent airport. But the Rock was the British way, and if one didn't know any better, that was the way one got sent. I definitely didn't want to know any better. As I walked into each step of their plans for me, beginning with a turboprop night flight (upon which, by the way, I hallucinated a tall, youngish Englishman traveling with wife and two children to be my brother—he had two passports, like myself) from London to the Rock, I was able to imagine I had nothing to do with the whole thing and that the Somerset House Hotel clerk or manager, the first "agent" of the trip, had received orders from higher-ups regarding my purpose and destination and proper conduct from one place to another, as if I were an ambassador on an important secret mission. The turboprop jet taxied slowly to the Rock, lit up in fluorescent pinks and oranges, like we were the Staten Island ferry bumping into the Statue of Liberty. In the airport a little man with thinning gray hair called out my name to collect me and take me to a hotel where I was to spend the night. In the morning another little man collected me to take me to a ferry to cross over to Algeciras, where I was conducted to a garage and offered a small car to drive up the coast to Estepona. I knew it was a dream. I had never been in Spain, never seen the Mediterranean, never driven a car on the continent, never chased anybody halfway round the world or farther than crosstown in New York City. I didn't even know if my friend was in Estepona. For all I knew, she was in London or Timbuktu. My plan was to drive around this ancient town looking for her mother. I had no number, no address. I had a terrible time there, driving through

labyrinths of narrow cobbled or dirt-rutted streets running between jumbles of whitewashed structures glittering in the sun,
decorated in Spanish cuneiform, seeking one American who
might give me a lead on my friend's mother. I found one finally
in a tobacco store, an older lady who knew exactly where my
friend's mother was: a pink-and-white motellike complex near
the water.

Once I was safely collapsed in her living room, she would
not tell me, of course, if her daughter was in Estepona or not.
After a while I cried; I was so weary and lost—not too crazy to
know that the trip was probably in vain. But the crying must
have helped, because shortly she rose to go and told me to wait.
I waited, it seemed, for as long as it had taken me to get there
from New York, and when she returned she told me to get in my
car and follow her. She took me to a hilltop overlooking the sea,
near a hacienda she had recently bought which she planned to
move into soon. We settled down in some tall grass; a mule
ambled by below us, led by a Spaniard in one of those pineapple
cone hats; the sea glistened blue and gold, stretching in hot-
looking, wavering bands to infinity beyond; her husband walked
into the "set," bearing a basket of wine bottles; and soon her
daughter joined us, sitting quietly, knees drawn up to her chest,
arms clasped around her shins, looking impassively out to sea. I
hardly recognized her. This was another life. I don't know how
long we were all there. I fell asleep for a while in the tall grass.
The wine, the sultry air, the long journey . . . I never asked for
her hand or mentioned the past or the future. I told her mother it
was a shame this wasn't Paris and I couldn't be Gertrude. I
remember Polly saying one thing only, and that was that I
should wait for her. Our previous life together, just recently
ended, broke through once, like a tiny sliver of light darting
through a shutter in a dark room, when we left her mother and
stepfather momentarily because I had to pee and she took me
into the hacienda, where she smiled at me mischievously as if to
say "Now we're alone, we can have sex." Soon she disappeared,
and as the sun was setting I followed her mother and stepfather

back to the motellike complex near the water to spend the night. I never found out where she went. Early in the morning her parents drove me in their black Jaguar up the coast to Málaga; they had booked me on a first-class flight to New York through Barcelona and Lisbon. I also had been "paid off": in my pocket was a check for fifteen hundred dollars. I waved good-bye to them from the airplane ramp; they smiled and waved back. I imagined I was one of their children; I was thinking how attractive my friend's mother was and wondering whether I had mistaken my romantic object (I was closer in age to her than to her daughter) and whether she had been curious about me as well. All the way from Barcelona to New York I thought I was on a presidential plane, being flown back to report on my "mission" to the higher-ups, whoever they were. On April 24, the piece I wrote about my trip (I called it "477 Years Later," meaning 477 years after 1492) was printed. The day before, I had signed two contracts: with Gregory for a book of selected columns to be published by Dutton, the other with Danny Moses for an "autobiography" to be published by Simon & Schuster.

22

Welcome Home

I was now "famous" and abandoned and orbital all at once. If this were one of the columns I was writing then, I might say, "It was a useless, silly life, and I have missed it every day since." More seriously, but also out of context, I might quote a line by Vanessa Bell on her early life: "How did we ever get out of it? It seems to me almost too ghastly and unnatural now ever to have existed." And go on with: "A sad end, but a beautiful finish." What impresses me in retrospect about that period (and every period, in fact) is the perfect structuring of it, the gathering-up of past themes, the inventive variations, the interweaving of them in novel combinations, the rhythmic skill, the element of surprise, the appeal of tradition, the sense of closure, and the suggestion of something entirely new. The new thing about being in orbit was that my flight plan was uninterrupted . . . also, that for a while I had a flying partner. The old thing about it was that some of the patterns I made were like jagged lightning zig-zag lines, motivated by great panic. Another old thing was the return of Apollinaire when my flying partner evaporated. One new way I had of handling the danger was to hire someone for a week to stay with me all the time, not telling her exactly what my problem was. Otherwise, I darted in and out of New York, visiting people on Long Island, in Stony Point, in Boston and Wellesley, in New Jersey, or joining up with strangers on the seashore, careful not to spend time with anyone I knew too well or at all, flying crash visits (intense and brief), preparing all the while to jettison my entire life in New York in order to land back in England as a newborn, not a thought in my head about where I might live when I finished traveling.

I had lived in New York for seventeen years. Seventeen was my birthday number; seventeen years was the age difference between my father and mother (he was the same number of years older than his wife in England); seventeen was the number of the floor at the Waldorf-Astoria where my mother lived for five years when I was small; seventeen was my age at the time of my father's last visit to America. That May 1969, I obsessed sevens, not seventeen particularly. On May 7 I wrote a piece (printed May 15) called "Come Seven," explaining that seven was my lucky childhood number and compiling various private statistics involving sevens (e.g., the speedometer on the VW squareback had read 7777 on February 22), a magical exercise clearly intended as a kind of loaded roll of the dice that would bring me what I wanted—most urgently my friend in Spain, whom I refused to consider a new ex, all indications to the contrary. I wove a recounting of fragments of our recent cross-country travels into speculations about Alice and Gertrude, concluding with a remark I had made to my friend's mother in Spain ("The reason they made it is . . . they got stashed away in that house in Paris before anybody could do anything about it . . .") and the story of a visit I had made to George Segal's place in New Jersey in order, apparently, just to harangue him over a plaster-cast sculpture he had made of me and my friend in late December (called *The Girl Friends*), which I claimed that he had altered, making us look less intimate than we really were— as if to blame George for our separation! At the end I bravely asserted that none of this mattered, because "the beautiful seventies" were at hand, and all would change for the better once we entered the decade with sevens in every year. It didn't occur to me then, but my mother was entering her seventies as well, and her age at death turned out to be seventy-seven. In 1983 I discovered that her namesake, a great-grandmother she never knew or knew about, also died at seventy-seven, in 1871. Nor did I count the number of years I had spent in New York or know about the other seventeens in my past. I did nothing whatever according to any plan; I acted purely on impulse. People who act thus unconsciously conform most rigidly to a plan—one laid out for them long in advance of their actions. The superb coincidences that can be found in their tales show how the "plan" coheres, behaving like guideposts or markers in an otherwise jumbled picture of events. More general coherent aspects—repetitions and variations on the themes endemic to the plan—can be described in relation to coincidences like a grid laid over a map of points, which can be read as a system of coordinates. According to my current reading of the coordinates that then existed, my plan called for a massive sort of relocation.

It's easy to say that what happened was what was called for; but if we don't view the past as a series of mistakes or lucky breaks, clouded with regrets or illumined by unexpected favors, we tend to see it fatefully, as that which could never have been otherwise, thus as that of which it is easy to say it happened because it was called for. The pleasure in it is the picture we leave behind which can be reconstructed. People who act more consciously may have the pleasure of watching themselves construct their plan or picture as they go along, stepping right into it, because they know that whatever they do has particular consequences, short or long range. But more conscious people also have a past when they were unaware of consequences and acted according to plans laid out in advance of them, suffering effects caused by others and not necessarily beneficial to them. Assuming responsibility for the past (defined as the unconscious) is one of the harder human tasks. And an inability to do it generates more past—i.e., we continue to make or let external agents be responsible for present events, in this way conforming rigidly to undetected plot lines. Time-wise, I had lived exclusively either in this premeditated past or the impulsive (unplanned) future. The present was either lost on me or experienced as a condition of loss. A major theme for everybody is loss and how we deal with it. The way I kept dealing with it was by relocation.

Leaving both place and mind had at last conjoined to set me free, while keeping me tethered to a column. The freedom to wander and keep running is not what I would describe as true freedom (often confused with freedom from responsibility); but to be able to change my scene and not be stopped by the law at that point was for me an important sort of freedom. Any loss of civil liberty in our society is a personal catastrophe not easily surmounted. While I strongly defined myself in opposition to things, I also needed that sense of self which comes from the support of some peer group, which had evaporated on both occasions when the law detained me. By "peer group" in this instance I mean audience, not particularly or necessarily a bunch of friends. And as long as I had an audience, adoption could not be far off. And adoption meant romance, not marriage, which had thus far eluded me, even in marriage. As the dim promise of marriage once more vaporized, I reverted to the position of a boy for whom sex and love are separate events. This was something new. (I mean, new in relation to my own sex.) But having learned it the previous year, prior to my latest romance, it was an obvious consolation, and a kind of revenge, no doubt, for my loss. Divorcing love from sex in relation to other women was invaluable to my becoming less (emotionally) dependent on the sex that had dominated me. (Later, feminists would identify such behavior as "lesbian chauvinism," an obvious parallel to the way men are raised—a movement in which women momentarily turned each other into unpaid whores.)

Anyway, the freedom to wander and keep running could clearly be enhanced by the peculiar pleasures of sexual aggrandizement. A foretaste of what was to come on this score took shape one afternoon on the Bowery after my friend left for Spain, and before I pursued her there three weeks later, when a woman with an English accent who had phoned me and said she was from a British magazine called Queen and wished to interview me came to the loft and seduced me, or seduced me into seducing her (she had never had a woman before, she said), an event that I duly and gleefully reported in the paper. After returning from Spain I made sure to have more of this sort of thing by taking the initiative myself. Outstandingly, I found the young woman called Joan with whom my friend in Spain had been involved when we met. Joan was Greek and English; she looked somewhat like Joan Baez. With her brother George, she had met our friend one day in Central Park. George would later become the husband, for two years, of the girl we both loved—a rebound completely reminiscent of that of my former ex-friend back in '66, who after we separated lived for two years with the painter who had pursued her. By coincidence this fellow George was also a painter, though he was hardly famous and had not even shown. Moreover, he was living in a loft on the very same street as the painter my ex-friend had moved in with. During this May and early June I was intensely involved with Joan and George, sleeping with Joan or jabbering mythologically with George—a very tall, lean, nervous, violent type—trying to imagine the three of us as a team organized to rescue the girl we loved from her wicked mother and stepfather (wicked for the reason that they were harboring her from us). Sex with Joan was not only divorced of love but fairly unpleasant as well. Meetings with George were fraught with feelings of violence, which he once demonstrated only too clearly by picking up a large honey-colored boxer dog he had and dashing it to the floor a couple of times in a fit of rage over something—possibly me. This was the man who would marry my friend in Spain. In 1971 I saw George in New Paltz, New York, in a black velvet jacket torn under one arm, in a black Bentley, with another girl, coming out of a real estate office. Not much later I bumped into Joan (in Central Park!), who told me that our mutual friend had gotten together with the sister of her brother's wife!

In May–June of '69, still believing Polly was mine, thus keeping me high enough to jump from one point to another, motivated and energized enough to conquer all, I discharged three momentous events in preparation for putting America behind me and joining her, as I hoped, abroad. One was a visit to my first old man, the philosophy professor, now eighty-four, in

Wellesley. Another was a panel at New York University's Loeb Student Center called "The Disintegration of a Critic," all about myself, from which I intended to be absent. Last was the selling of my loft, the packing-up of all my things (and hers) and putting them in storage.

On the day of the panel, May 10 or 15 or so, I had sex with three different women, the third being Joan, before drunkenly deciding to crash my own show. I had provided David Bourdon, the moderator, with bank statements, letters, traffic tickets, memos, and the like, in case he wanted to use them. Other panel members were Andy Warhol, Charlotte Moorman, Gregory Battcock, John de Menil, Walter Gutman, Bridget Polk, and Ultra Violet. They were supposed to talk about me and/or my criticism or the lack of it. My idea was that it represented an official statement declaring the termination of my career as critic. Near the end of the event I reeled in to read the last piece I had written for the Voice, called "The Belles in the Towers," which my editor had cut in two without consulting me or even printing "To be continued" at the end of the first installment— the only time, by the way, that that ever happened to me. Tellingly, it had been cut at the word "panic." I picked it up from there (the last sentence was "I'm into a panic") and read the rest of the piece, which would be printed the following week, this being the very day the first part had come out, causing me considerable rage, propelling me right into the ready-made forum of the panel, where I could put myself back together, so to speak.

As fate would have it, "Belles in the Towers" was my very finest piece of that period; the usual density of information with which I packed my pieces here adhered neatly to the central image or theme of towers, woven into a story, dispersed in fragments, about a visit to a particular tower in Wellesley to which I had asked my old professor to take me. The tower was a kind of structural dream figure: an object to contemplate mathematically or philosophically, or to enter and climb, get lost, escape; from which to emerge, be born, or attain the top and be impaled or shot (like Gunga Din) or jump off into orbit. Sexual imagery made it clear that the tower represented my father and that my object was to get everything in there, notably the father who was my old philosophy professor, along with all *his* fathers—Plato, Socrates, Whitehead, Descartes, Hegel, Kant, et al.—and to build one big enough from which to fly back to England. By the middle of June I would be gone, my loft sold and my things in storage. Gathering up figures from the past like building blocks for my towers or stepping stones of a staircase winding "upward into a discovery of the unity in circles," I saw myself somehow hurtling from them into an unknown future abroad ("If you had a tower 22,000 miles high you could literally jump into orbit"), where I (a "belle") originated. My professor, Thomas Hayes Procter, was born in Liverpool on October 17 (seventeen again), 1885. He was one year younger than my father. I had met him when he was sixty-five, the same age as my father at death. Now, as a result of an editor's brutal decision to cut a piece in half, I was having the opportunity to drag all these fathers (philosophers, mathematicians, builders of towers, makers of belles, etc.) into a theatre where my other two old fathers —Walter Gutman and John de Menil—were sitting on stage for the express purpose of talking about me. These were my three old men in America. The first, my professor, had set me thinking and deflowered me; the second had made me part of his circle of beneficiaries, confidants, and party pals; the third had sent me back to the fatherland and restored me to society after my fall from it. This was surely a wonderful moment—in which I was absorbed at the time solely in reading the rest of my truncated column. "Gathering up figures from the past," etc., had not been my conscious intention, nor did it occur to me that that was what I had done after having done it. Every few years or so I tooled up to Wellesley to see my old professor, impulsively without exception, never announcing my visit, always wondering if he was still alive. This was the next-to-last time I saw him.

Though he was eighty-four (or because of it), he got it into his head that I would make myself available for some kind of sex. He had taken me over to that tower in the afternoon. I'd stolen a framed photograph hanging on the wall in the tower and raced back down to the street. Due to a sudden terror, I'd been unable to make it past a locked door, for which I had obtained the keys, to the topmost part of the tower to see the collection of bells. Back safely in the professor's car, "a view of the tower from across a river," I asked him to tell me his history. I had never asked him before. At his house I let him read a book called *Sappho's Daughters*, dime-store trash, that I had with me. He thought "it must be anatomically impossible to get two vaginas together." I think he thought two women together was an impossibility, period. The subject had never been discussed between us, except years earlier when I first met him and it was something to which I had confessed—providing, evidently, the excuse for his seduction, which had served the purpose of straightening me out for quite some time. Yet he had said back then that there was nothing wrong with my confessed interest. Now I had circled back to let him know I agreed with him. But clearly he didn't really believe it. As if he were twenty years younger, he tried once again to seduce me. I wanted to please him but was unable to transcend my revulsion at his age and/or my lack of feeling. In the morning, over boiled eggs and toast (made by his sister Hilda, who was seventy-three and had succeeded his wife, dead some years, as housekeeper), he paid me back by engaging me in a philosophical argument, at which, naturally, he was the master. It was clear to me that his pride was hurt. It made me wonder if philosophy was not simply a sophisticated instrument of revenge. When I was younger, it had seemed only like a tool for learning how to think. He had never argued with me then, possibly because I'd been available for sex. But sex was not what I ever wanted from this "father," either then or now. And I took my own revenge by writing this piece all about towers ("the pure tower must be a bell in the house of a dream"), incorporating both his history as an Englishman and bits of our philosophical argument, naturally weighting it on my side. The Platonic ideal was what I was after. "But listen," I wrote, quoting our argument, "if Descartes makes man a supernatural being by defining nature as a body of substance extended and moving and mind as the substance that thinks, where do you come off as a lover like Socrates whose chronicler [Plato] transformed all particulars into a unified system of being and thought?" He replied, "You can, of course . . . put things together by making mush out of them in a Waring blender." My next sentence read: "Forget it let's talk about sex." Then: "All we have to do is to make a certain number of equal piles. I tend to regard the structure as an amorphous mass out of which, say, two equal towers must be built." This was a motif in the piece: two equal towers. I had "twin towers . . . united by a garland of flowers arcing from spire to spire." These were clearly the "anatomically impossible . . . vaginas." Central to the piece was my refusal or inability to go to the top of the tower, a pinnacle of man's penetration in space. "I yell up the stairs an echo of a hollow man all headpiece jammed with straw the metal the clapper in my head I'm falling again . . . after all I'm awake I rush like crazy down the regular steps quite geometric. . . ." I was indeed terrified. I was ever on the run, but this was a striking instance of it. Yet my feelings never seemed to count.

Terror was a reaction to something, a result of not having felt the feelings from which I was running. I loved this old man, for instance, but sex and philosophy were its two modes of expression, and frustration over sex was converted into an abstract argument. The tower, the locked door, the keys, represented the dungeon or loony bin where people like myself got sent when their terror became internal and visible—running away from phantoms. Inside the tower were these bell(e)s, locked away for eternity. Inside me, apparently, were feelings locked away, if not for eternity, for long enough to have made me look either bats or sunk, or intelligently abstract. I was about to sink again, to become dumb and melancholic—and that was a good thing, because I was running out of illusions to support my flight, and the return to my body was essential to carry on alone. I predicted this return in the "Belles" piece by positing unities of mind and body in my "Cartesian" argument with the professor. I had been "gone" since January; now I intended to be gone with passport and international driver's license.

It would be my first trip abroad on my own—not having been sent by someone and not flying after someone. Now I was cut loose from my old men and had only myself to flee. I would certainly want to move as usual toward some good mother, that exterior figure who might temporarily manifest the caring feelings I had never internalized. The tower, dungeon, asylum, or elevator (moving tomb) from which I fled obviously represented the *punishing* mother, whose guilt and bad feelings both occupied and pursued me, and against whom I was as yet unable to take a stand, except by reaction and the discourse of ideas.

As my BOAC plane touched down in London, June 15 approximately, I landed with her. I was sitting at the back of the plane and had slept most of the way. As the passengers exited, I sat there looking out the window at the fog through my tears. Finally, as I was the last left on board, a flight attendant leaned over me and asked me if I was all right. I said no, I wasn't, so she asked me if I wanted to go to the medical center. I quickly put my face together, gathered my stuff, and left the empty plane. The customs people searched my bags. The passport official muttered "Welcome home," just as before. I had re-entered both mind and place, simultaneously as "we" drifted from sky to earth, born again as a little English girl, but this time far away from my American mother. At the large, modern hotel near Marble Arch where I had reserved a room, a bellboy asked me if I was a "head." I spent a week there, crying in the bathtub and reading *Oedipus Rex*. I went to visit Kingsley Hall, a heavy, depressing dark-brick structure in the Whitechapel area; broken windows stuffed with rags, a plaque saying Gandhi had once stayed there, and found a couple of tattered remnants of the mentally disturbed people whom Laing and associates had harbored for their experiment in tunneling through. I found George Brecht, who gave me an I Ching reading: number 36, "Darkening of the Light." I made my last attempt to find my friend, persuading a mediumistic lady who lived on the periphery of

London to locate her (in a family mansion on Eaton Square) and obtain the message that it was truly over. I wrote a piece home called "Loobie Loo," beginning: "This project of having a child by the mother and becoming the father of oneself seems a good enough reason to remain as situated or to travel somewhere according to the principle that any space at all may be a good space to hang your shirt or yourself." Courtesy of the mediumistic lady who lived on the periphery of London, I met a beautiful, long-blond-haired hippie called Patrick, aged eighteen, a son figure who had made the big trek to India and agreed to travel with me south through France. I bought a shiny old black Ford for a hundred and fifty dollars.

Paraphrasing *Oedipus Rex,* I finished my "letter" home: "For if in his quest for truth he has come to the final stage when the secret of his birth is to be disclosed, and he can think of nothing worse than a base origin .... or if this project of having a child by the mother and becoming the father of oneself . . . seems a good enough reason to remain as situated or to travel somewhere, I might go off with Loobie Loo and Teddy and Andy Pandy and I better not stay any longer than the cat considers me to be a guest."

Acknowledgments

I wish to thank Robert Cornfield, Robert Gottlieb, and Martha Kaplan for their continuing support for this project, the last for her patient editorial guidance as well as attention to the many details of production.

I'm grateful to Ingrid Nyeboe for her enduring interest and nurturing and objective reading of the work in progress.

I thank a number of friends from the sixties, some of whom appear in this book, and who generously shared their recollections with me: David Bourdon, Trisha Brown, John Cage, Thalia Christo, June Ekman, Edwin Fancher, Diane Fisher, Lee Fitzgerald (alias Wahundra), Simone Forti, Laura de Freitas, John Giorno, Walter Gutman, Alex Hay, Deborah Hay, Bill Katz, Les Levine, Steve Paxton, Yvonne Rainer, Robert Rauschenberg, George Segal, Helen Segal, Gerd Stern, Simone Swan, Robert Whitman, Ann Wilson (who also kindly let me read her journals from that era), Marilyn Wood, LaMonte Young, Marian Zazeela.

I also thank these friends, who have been a great help to me in their sustained expressions of interest and encouragement: my daughter Winifred Lanham, Candace Chaite, Lenora Champagne, Teeny Duchamp, Jamie Fowler, Lynn Fowler, Suzi Gablik, Sally Litchfield, Danny Moses, Lynn Scott, Maura Smithies, Richard Smithies, Gerald Sturman, Marianne Sturman, George Walsh, Stanley Weinstock, Warren Wynshaw.

In addition, I thank Merle Shore for her efforts in obtaining photographs in France of Apollinaire; Helen Winkler, who talked to me about the de Menils; and Dr. William Shevin, who kindly facilitated access to my medical records.

A NOTE ON THE TYPE

The text of this book is set in Electra, a typeface designed by W. A. Dwiggins for the Mergenthaler Linotype Company and first made available in 1935. Electra cannot be classified as either "modern" or "old style." It is not based on any historical model, and hence does not echo any particular period or style of type design. It avoids the extreme contrast between "thick" and "thin" elements that marks most modern faces, and is without eccentricities which catch the eye and interfere with reading. In general, Electra is a simple, readable typeface that attempts to give a feeling of fluidity, power, and speed.

Composed by Maryland Linotype, Inc.,
Baltimore, Maryland.
Printed and bound by Maple Press,
York, Pennsylvania.

Typography and binding design by Virginia Tan.